CH00676599

Praise for
Outrageous Reason: Madness and race in Britain

'This book is hugely ambitious, hugely provocative and brilliant. For Peter Barham, madness is no side issue; he is talking about White supremacy, patriarchy and capitalism. He tracks 'the long fuse of traumatised memory' from the Caribbean to south Asia, and from western Europe to central Africa. And here's the rub – these ideologies that drive people mad are themselves mad. We are all in the 'hold' of these forces – across the constructed imaginaries of race, class, gender, sexuality and disability. Moving 'mad psychology' to the centre of the historical analysis of imperialisms, Barham adds his voice to the chorus of calls for a completely new therapeutic environment. Black people will want to read this book because it is grounded in the Black experience, and White people will want to read it too. All mad lives matter.'
Colin Prescod, former Chair, Institute of Race Relations

'This is a welcome contribution to the discourse on "race" and madness. Barham unpacks how power, "race" and class – often overlooked in this discourse – intersect to maintain systems of racism that pervaded over the centuries. This book reminds us that systems of oppression affect us all and we should actively engage in dismantling them.'
Frank Keating, Professor of Social Work and Mental Health, Royal Holloway University of London

'A challenging, but ultimately rewarding, deep dive into the long history of racism in mental health services. *Outrageous Reason* takes us on a unique journey, exploring the way that black lives and mad lives are deeply entangled in the collective imagination of British society. Barham's analysis is brought to life through the stories of some key Black figures whose fates have helped shape the current landscape. Disturbing and enlightening.'
Hel Spandler, Professor of Mental Health, University of Central Lancashire and Managing Editor of *Asylum: The radical mental health magazine*

'At a time when the country is grappling with imperial nostalgia, fascism ideation and the impact of their consequent anti-blackness on the bodies and minds of people racialised as black, *Outrageous Reason* is a crucial undertaking. Not only to better understand their deadly intersections but also to imagine alternative forms of care.'

Guilaine Kinouani, radical psychologist and author of *White Minds*

'This is a powerful and impassioned analysis of the history of mental health and race, but not as a clinical problem, as has been customary in psychiatric discourse. Instead, the author situates race and mental health within the historical trajectory of the politics of reason and unreason. Peter Barham's book charts how psychiatric concepts and practice served to inferiorise and dehumanise racialised people and served to justify their oppression from the times of transatlantic slavery right up to our present-day context of institutional racism.'

Dr Errol Francis, Artistic Director and CEO of Culture&

'How could I not be truly impressed by this thought-provoking exploration of the intricate relationship between madness, race and the history of Western reason? For a psychotherapist who relishes in case study and conversations about race and identity politics, *Outrageous Reason* is a compelling and indispensable resource. Barham's in-depth analysis of how race and mental health have been historically intertwined resonates with my professional experience. His detailed unravelling of the complex interplay between racial liberalism and the practice of psychiatry is both enlightening and critical for understanding the challenges faced by marginalised communities today. *Outrageous Reason* sheds light on a topic that is often overlooked by white writers. If, like me, you consider yourself an advocate for social justice, I recommend this book as a must-read to increase your understanding of the complex dynamics of race, reason and mental health and also as a timely tool towards creating a more equitable and inclusive society.'

Rotimi Akinsete, psychotherapist, clinical supervisor and EDI consultant

OUTRAGEOUS REASON:

MADNESS AND RACE IN BRITAIN AND EMPIRE, 1780-2020

PETER BARHAM

*for Andrew,
much cherished friend,
warmest wishes
from
Peter.
25.11.2023*

PCCS
BOOKS

First published 2023

PCCS Books Ltd
Wyastone Business Park
Wyastone Leys
Monmouth NP25 3SR
UK
Tel +44 (0)1600 891 509
www.pccs-books.co.uk

Outrageous Reason: Madness and race in Britain and Empire, 1780–2020

British Library Cataloguing in Publication Data
A catalogue record for this book is available from the British Library.

ISBN   pbk – 978 1 915220 39 4
         epub – 978 1 915220 40 0

Cover design: Jason Anscomb.
Cover artwork: Denzil Forrester, 'All Hands on Deck', 2003.
Oil on linen, 153 x 183cm (60 1/4 x 72 1/8in). Copyright Denzil Forrester.
Courtesy the artist and Stephen Friedman Gallery, London and New York.

Printed in the UK by Severn, Gloucester.

'The politics of whiteness transcend the colour of anyone's skin. It is an occupying force in the mind. It is a political ideology that is concerned with maintaining power through domination and exclusion.'
Reni Eddo-Lodge (2017)

'… in our society when a Black person writes or speaks about race and racism their words are always regarded as political. Even today, after the murder of George Floyd and the great wave of protest, learning and acknowledgement that followed, there are still people who – with no sense of embarrassment – confidently assert that they just "don't see race", encouraging others to affect a similar myopia. To entertain that particular delusion, and to imagine oneself capable of that specific impossibility, is also to proclaim enormous privilege.'
David Olusoga (2021)

'I deeply distrust this tool I work with – language. It is a distrust rooted in certain historical events that are all of a piece with the events that took place on the *Zong*. The language in which those events took place promulgated the non-being of African peoples, and I distrust its order, which hides disorder; its logic hiding the illogic and its rationality, which is simultaneously irrational.'
M. NourbeSe Philip (2008)

'Finally, the twentieth century collars madness, and reduces it to a natural phenomenon bound up with the truth of the world. This positivist appropriation gave rise to… the scornful philanthropy which all psychiatry displays towards the madman.'
Michel Foucault (1961)

Contents

List of illustrations   *vii*

Acknowledgements   *xi*

Foreword by Dwight Turner   *xv*

Introduction   *1*

1   Credibility, madness and race   *9*

Part 1 – Jamaica, slavery and madness

Prologue   *26*

2   From *Zorg* to *Zong*: The *Zong* affair   *30*

3   A testimony from the female lunatic asylum: Henrietta Dawson   *45*
     and her distress

4   In the bowels of colonial modernity   *56*

5   The 'beneficent despotism' of racial liberalism   *64*

6   Revivalists, Rastafari and psychiatry   *76*

Part 2 – 'Poor whites'

Prologue   *90*

7   The mad poor as poor whites   *94*

8   Alice Rebecca Triggs: War, madness and migration   *103*

Part 3 – Pathologies of empire

Prologue   *122*

9   The strange career of R.R. Racey: Mad at his post or the   *125*
     madness of colonialism?

10   The Mir of Khairpur: Imperial doubts about his 'fitness' to   *138*
     rule

Part 4 – Holds that kill: Winston and Orville

    Prologue   *150*

11 Winston Rose: Humanity violated   *153*

12 Orville Blackwood: Humanity disavowed   *167*

Part 5 – After

    Prologue   *182*

13 Disturbing continuities   *184*

14 Burn the ship! Escape the hold!   *198*

    References   *215*

    Archives consulted   *233*

    Name index   *235*

    Subject index   *242*

List of illustrations

George Cruikshank, 'The New Union Club' (1819) © The Trustees of the British Museum — *36*

Julia Margaret Cameron, 'Sir Henry Taylor, from life' (albumen print, June 1865) © National Portrait Gallery — *68*

'Colonel Hobbs, Died mad', from a sheet titled 'Victims of the Jamaica Rebellion of 1865' (c. 1865), in *Photography Album Documenting the Morant Bay Rebellion in Jamaica,* courtesy of Special Collections, Princeton University Library — *74*

Revd Alexander Bedward — *78*

Leonard Percival Howell, 'The First Rasta' — *82*

James Johnston, *Jamaica: The New Riviera* (1903) © the Caribbean Photo Archive. — *91*

James Johnston, 'Domestics with yams, cocoanuts & c.' (1903), from *Jamaica: The New Riviera* © the Caribbean Photo Archive — *91*

Alice Rebecca Triggs (1885–1962) at Colney Hatch Lunatic Asylum in 1915, courtesy of London Metropolitan Archives: H12/CH/B/14/001-002 — *106*

Alice Rebecca Triggs (1885–1962) at Colney Hatch Lunatic Asylum in 1916, courtesy of London Metropolitan Archives: H12/CH/B/14/001-002 — *106*

Denzil Forrester MBE. First page of the draft of his MA dissertation on Winston Rose for the Royal College of Art, 1981 © and courtesy of Denzil Forrester MBE and the Cornubian Arts and Science Trust (www.c-a-s-t.org.uk) — *154*

Denzil Forrester MBE, 'Funeral of Winston Rose' (1981) © Denzil Forrester, courtesy of the artist and Stephen Friedman Gallery, London; photo © Mark Blower — *161*

Denzil Forrester MBE, 'Three Wicked Men' (1982) © and courtesy of the artist; photo © Tate Images — *161*

J.M.W.Turner, 'Slavers Throwing Overboard the Dead and Dying, Typhoon Coming On', commonly know as 'The Slave Ship' (1840); photograph © Museum of Fine Arts, Boston — *162*

Mrs Clara Buckley holding a photograph of her son, Orville Blackwood — *179*

Dedication

To the memory of Robert ('Bob') Maxwell Young
(1935–2019)

About the author

Peter Barham has been working, writing and engaging critically in the mental health field for more than 50 years. His work straddles clinical research, psychoanalysis, practical initiative, historical inquiry, mental health activism and film-making. He has PhDs in abnormal psychology from the University of Durham and in modern history from the University of Cambridge. He is a chartered psychologist and was elected a fellow of the British Psychological Society for his 'outstanding contribution to psychological approaches to the understanding of psychosis'. He is the founder of the Hamlet Trust, which pioneered grassroots mental health reform in Central and Eastern Europe, supported by George Soros' Open Society Institute. His books include *Forgotten Lunatics of the Great War* (2004) and *Closing the Asylum: The mental patient in modern society*, first published in 1992 and reissued in 2020 with a new prologue and a preface by Peter Campbell.

Acknowledgements

The journey to accomplish this book has been long and challenging, taking me in directions that I could not anticipate and forcing me to reconsider some of my most basic assumptions, and I am hugely grateful for the resources and opportunities, many of them fortuitous, that I have encountered and been able to draw upon along the way. The intellectual debts that I have accumulated, particularly among black scholars and activists whom I have never met, are enormous and I have tried to the best of my ability, though insufficiently I fear, to enumerate them in the text and in the bibliography.

At an early stage in the germination of this project, Mark Harrison gave me house space at what was then the Wellcome Unit for the History of Medicine at Oxford, and facilitated my association with the History Faculty. Numerous congenial and productive exchanges, about Jamaica especially, with Len Smith, who was then well advanced in the inquiries that resulted in his study, *Insanity, Race and Colonialism* (2014), have greatly assisted my thinking.

I give warm thanks to Thurstine Basset, the late Peter Campbell, Rhodri Hayward and Hel Spandler for their generous and insightful responses to an early version of this project and for encouraging me to take it to a next stage. I thank Claire Hilton, then Historian in Residence at the Royal College of Psychiatrists, for inviting me to contribute a paper, 'Speaking the Truth from Below: A patient in the Kingston Lunatic Asylum, Jamaica in 1859–60', to the symposium 'Learning from the Asylum Era: The patient's voice was loud and clear but did we hear it?' at the Royal College of Psychiatry's International Congress in 2021. Warm thanks also to my fellow contributors, Allan Beveridge and Diana Goslar, for their supportive comments.

It was a privilege to be invited by Hel Spandler, editor of *Asylum* magazine, at an early stage, to explore the intersections between Black Lives Matter and Mad Lives Matter, first in a book review on racism in American psychiatry, and then in a longer article, '"Eating at Joe's": The shared fate of Mad lives and Black lives' (Barham, 2020).

The opportunity to travel in Jamaica in 2017 taught me that the colonial history of Jamaica must be apprehended through an understanding of the dense and intricate topography of the island. Through my visit to his former home on the Hope Road in Kingston, especially, I became acutely aware of the colonial heritage of Robert Nesta Marley. Marley was born in 1945, when Jamaica was still a British colony, to a White Jamaican father – a philanderer and a plantation overseer who claimed to be a captain in the Royal Marines, in his early 60s – and Cedella Malcolm – a young Afro-Jamaican woman in her early 20s. Marley was neglected by his father, spurned by his white family, and ridiculed for being mixed race, provoking a defiance and indomitable staying power, discernible in songs such as 'Cornerstone', which celebrates how the stone that the builder rejects always becomes the head cornerstone.

I am grateful to the Institute of Jamaica and the National Museum Jamaica, especially for their excellent exhibition catalogues *Rastafari* (2013) and *Uprising: Morant Bay 1865 and its Afterlives* (2015); to the University Bookshop in Mona, Kingston, and also for the invaluable digital resources of *The Gleaner* newspaper.

During the period that this book was being hatched, I was closely associated with the Survivors History Group, which included Peter Campbell and David Kessel, both keen advocates and fine poets, who both sadly passed away in 2022, and was presided over by the galvanising spirit of historian and survivor Andrew Roberts. Andrew brought to each occasion a fierce, sometimes declamatory but always compassionate intelligence, continuously embracing connections – reflected in his marvellous website (http:// studymore.org.uk) – with individuals and causes that are mostly ignored by the complacent whiteness of the mainstream psychiatric survivors movement. One such is *Power Writers and the Struggle Against Slavery* (Gilbert, 2005), celebrating Black history and five African writers who came to the East End of London in the 18th century. Andrew has throughout been a powerful stimulus to me in thinking through this project.

This book was mostly written during the Covid pandemic, when, starved of direct contact, I discovered vital sustenance in the webinars organised by the ISPS UK (the International Society for Social and Psychological Approaches to Psychosis), such as 'Three Perspectives on Racism and Psychosis' (2021) and 'Dismantling the Master's House: Becoming anti-racist' (2020), with contributions from Suman Fernando, Jessica Pons and Sanah Ahsan, among others; the Liverpool Student Psychiatric Society (www.livpsych.wordpress. com), notably their 'Racism in Mental Health: How to be an anti-racist mental health researcher' series (2020–21), with thought-provoking interventions from, among others, Colin King, Doreen Joseph, Alison Faulkner and Akriti Mehta; and the Division of Counselling Psychology of the British Psychological Society for their webinar on 'Black Psychology and African Spirituality: The origins of therapeutic practice', in January 2021, with notable contributions by, among others, Willelmina ('Wil') Joseph-Loewenthal (born in Dominica) on 'Listening with Both Ears', and Malcolm Phillips (born in St Kitts) speaking about '"Sakhu": Illuminating the human spirit in mental health services'.

For access to a variety of records in their holdings, I am indebted to the British Library, the London Metropolitan Archives (LMA), the National Archives and the Wellcome Collection. My warm thanks to Stephanie Slight from the LMA for her assiduous efforts in tracking down the records of Alice Rebecca Triggs in the asylum and the Poor Law systems at a time when I was unable to search at LMA myself. For permission to reproduce images in their collections, I thank the British Museum, the Cornubian Arts and Science Trust, Tate Images, the National Portrait Gallery, the History of Photography Archive, the Museum of Fine Arts Boston, the Stephen Friedman Gallery, and the London Metropolitan Archives.

I am especially grateful to Denzil Forrester for his generosity in permitting me to reproduce images of some of his works and of his dissertation on Winston Rose, completed at the Royal College of Art, and also to quote from that dissertation. In an email to Denzil, I told him how, writing from a critical white position, I was exploring the racially charged historical terrain, dominated by the power house of whiteness, in which black lives and mad lives have been, and are still, entangled, and that the tone of book was inevitably quite angry. 'To your angry book!', he rejoined.

I have had numerous exchanges about this work and I fully acknowledge that not everyone will agree with the conclusions I have drawn, for which I assume complete responsibility. I am extremely fortunate to have had Catherine Jackson as a commissioning editor in embarking upon, and carrying through, this project and I am much indebted to her critical interventions in honing my arguments. Special thanks also to Tatjana Tairi, who fortuitously was at hand to provide vital technical assistance with the copy editing just when I most needed it. Last, I dedicate this book to the memory of Robert ('Bob') Maxwell Young, who sadly did not live to see it completed. He was himself a vital contributor to the extended conversations about the human sciences over several decades out of which this book has emerged, and would, I believe, have taken some pleasure in the result, though no doubt he would have disagreed wholeheartedly with parts of it.

Foreword

As an intersectional psychotherapist, I am fortunate to be influenced by a good number of Black activists, Black feminists and intersectionalists across the world, and to follow their work in its interesting guises. One thing common to us all is that our activism is designed to seek out and challenge the intersecting layers of oppression hidden within patriarchy, white supremacy and colonialism (née capitalism) – oppressions that have their own devastating impacts and also a massive influence on each other.

It was one of my favourite Black feminists, bell hooks, who wrote the simple, yet incredibly powerful and far-reaching phrase: 'Patriarchy is not about gender' (hooks, 2020). This statement, although apparently about patriarchy, has huge resonance for me in relation to race and racism. I would say, with hooks, 'Racism is not about colour.' These two statements open a door to a far deeper understanding of what racism actually is, how it works and how it might be dismantled. And this last element is especially important, as too many activists see race and racism as a binary between Black and white, often projecting their own issues about the oppressor or the oppressed on the other. It is about so much more than that.

When we broaden our thinking to recognise that racism is not about colour, we see that racism – systemic racism, institutional racism – is something that impacts on and influences all of us. We are all raised within systems of white supremacy, patriarchy and capitalism; these intersecting layers of oppression have forged who we are as individuals and collectively, and they also influence how we act on the other. They influence how we relate to immigrants crossing perilous seas on boats, the working classes claiming welfare support from the state, and those who have been diagnosed with a mental illness. And overall, racialised constructions in particular mould all of us, be we Black, brown or white, Asian or from an indigenous or other minority community.

Outrageous Reason addresses this toxic intersection of power, class and race, seen through the prism of Britain's colonial expansion and exploitation and its active pursuit of profit at the expense of the millions of enslaved people whose lives were destroyed within its clutches. It speaks to the way systems of racism have been used for centuries and over many generations to marginalise, incarcerate and control persons of difference, whether of class, culture, colour or social conformity, across the world. What makes it all the more powerful for me is that it delivers a strident call to our collective responsibility, irrespective of our racial designation, class or culture, in particular to learn about, challenge and dismantle the structures that have oppressed all those enmeshed within the psychiatric system – Black people, but also all the other exploited and marginalised groups who have found themselves imprisoned, drugged and crushed so that the imperialist industrial machinery can continue to roll forward.

And what *Outrageous Reason* also does so well is it highlights the importance of allyship. Something that activists often get wrong is they fail to recognise that the ally is as important, if not more so, in action to dismantle systems of intersectional oppression, as the activist fighting for their own cause. That Peter Barham has used his knowledge, expertise and wealth of inner and external resources to research and expose this incredibly difficult and far-reaching issue speaks loudly to me about this aspect of the ally's role. Barham's book raises into public awareness how science, social construction and capitalism have all come together to build and maintain the systems of racism that pervade within the psychiatric system, and demonstrates the pernicious power of psychiatry as a statutory agent of social control.

I myself have worked within mental health, so this book holds a personal resonance for me. In the early 2000s, I was employed by an organisation called Share In Maudsley Black Action (or SIMBA), based in south east London – a group of Black and brown mental health activists who were fighting to raise awareness of the systemic oppressions inflicted on people caught up within the psychiatric system. Their voices laid bare the excesses of the mental health system before the wider world – the layers of racialised, patriarchal and capitalist oppression and distress meted out to them from on high. Their performances, poetry and determined independence, the support they offered their community and the support they gave each other and many others outside of their membership spoke of the humanity that was within that group.

These were people who stepped up in the years following the Thatcher government's devastating neoliberal social reforms that invented 'care in the community' where no care or sense of collective humanity existed to look after those who were deemed to be mentally ill. Such people were abandoned to a poorly funded system that would gradually be stripped to the bone by successive governments, meaning that charities and self-help groups were often the ones who worked with and within the marginalised communities with mental health issues.

SIMBA was where I discovered, came to understand and then engaged with and started to challenge the systemic oppression, marginalisation and control of the Black community around mental health. And part of the reason it flourished, in addition to the sheer courage and determination of its core members, was that it worked with its allies – both activists and funders – who enabled its independence from the mental health system.

Outrageous Reason is an essential piece of reading. There is depth here, and breadth, and there is also great pain, all of which could have been excavated by a person of colour, but Peter Barham has brought to it the range and rage of an ally. So, when I say that racism is not about colour, and when I say that the fight against racist systems such as those embedded within the mental health arena are not just for those of colour to fight, that it needs allies from across the board to battle alongside us, I am saying that texts such as this will help us all dismantle those systems of oppression.

Dr Dwight Turner
Psychotherapist, Course Leader in Humanistic Counselling and Psychotherapy at the University of Brighton, and author of *Intersections of Privilege and Otherness in Counselling and Psychotherapy: Mockingbird* (2021) and *The Psychology of Supremacy: Imperium* (2023).

Introduction

This book is about the traumatic legacy of the entanglements of madness and race that were spawned by the founding narrative of Western reason. Scholars of the Black Atlantic have provocatively proposed that we must think reason in relation to race, to the abasement of blackness and the anti-black modernities inaugurated by the Middle Passage that cast the African as categorically mad. This was accompanied by the ascendancy of whiteness as a dominant power in the foundation of modern reason. For several centuries now, madness and blackness, mad lives and black lives, the psychiatric patient and the non-European, have been culturally and historically intertwined. Still today, outlooks on mental health and the emotional reflexes of practitioners participate and cohabit in a racialised terrain that pulsates, consciously and unconsciously, with assumptions about whiteness. Though frequently mythologised as the political philosophy of equal persons, liberalism has in actuality predominantly been a racial liberalism in which an egalitarian humanism has co-existed uneasily and tensely with a hierarchical racism (Mills, 2008; Mills, 1997/2022). This is the background against which the racial perturbations that still afflict the discourses, and the self-understanding, of the discipline of psychiatry, which came into its own in the slipstream of empire, must be interrogated (Fernando, 2017; Sashidharan, 2001). As I shall try to show in this book, the idea that we can discuss questions about mental health or madness without engaging with questions of race is faintly ridiculous, if not to say delusory.

As the historian Catherine Hall has described, the post-colonial project is about excavating and dismantling the deep assumption that only white people are fully human and their claim to be, in Victor Kiernan's classic phrase, 'the lords of human kind' (Hall, 2002, p.7; Kiernan, 1969/2015; McCulloch, 1995). In the movement to abolish slavery, outrage became re-moralised on behalf of the protesters, now attesting to a pathology of white power, a moral judgement on a racialised modernity, as the Afro-American scholar Barnor Hesse (2007) terms it. 'Outrage in the face of injustice or indeed of unbearable loss,' writes the political philosopher Judith Butler, 'has enormous political potential' (Butler, 2009, p.39). As I quickly discovered when embarking on the journey that led to this book, in which I try to shed light on the entanglement of mad lives and black lives in a historical terrain where white power has long prevailed, there was plenty to get outraged about. Indeed, throughout the period that concerns me, roughly from the end of the 18th century to the end of the 20th, expressions of outrage are so obviously present in the historical record that they leap out at you and grab your attention. They are there in what contemporaries are saying from multiple standpoints, giving vent to divergent paradigms of moral outrage, whether directed against or in defence of black bodies.

Most obviously, the mad themselves have been typecast as 'outrageous', in a vernacular period term used by asylum staff, but also by mad persons themselves, to signify mad, passionate, violent or disorderly behaviour (and one with a long history, as the Oxford English Dictionary verifies, citing, 'My Golden hair I rent and tear like one outrageous mad', from c.1678). It features as an integral element in a pathologising vocabulary applied by colonial authorities and by alienists in lunatic asylums to recalcitrant 'natives' or mental patients that, later in the 19th century, would segue into the diagnostic terminology of a fledgling psychological medicine. Mad persons did not always take these affronts lying down. While in prison in Jamaica in 1859, Ann Pratt, a mixed-race woman, was said to be 'outrageous, stripping herself naked', for which she was dispatched to the lunatic asylum. However, she soon turned her outrage back on her colonial keepers, publishing a pamphlet about the abuses she had suffered that would trigger a scandal and a public enquiry.

Within the anti-slavery movement, outrage was firmly co-opted in the cause of protest and resistance. The letters of Granville Sharp, the anti-slavery campaigner and a leading defender of black people in London, 'fairly rattle with outrage', remarks the historian of slavery James Walvin. We find 'angry words slashed across the page', along with heavy underscoring and the use of multiple exclamation marks ('the most obvious natural Right of Human Nature is at stake, viz the Right even to Life itself!!!') (Walvin, 2011, p.153; Faubert, 2018, p.86). Writes historian Adam Hochschild:

> The anti-slavery campaign in Britain in the late 18th century produced something never seen before. It was the first time a large number of people became outraged, and stayed outraged for many years, over someone else's rights. And most startling of all, the rights of people of another color, on another continent. (Hochschild, 2005, p.5)

In this book I endeavour to put questions to the history of mental health and psychiatry and to historical case materials in which whiteness and mental health form a moral compact. I use the lens of the agendas that have been set by critics of whiteness to explore the traumatic origins of psychiatry and the roots of contemporary scruples over the status of the mad in the convolutions of racism from the 17th century onwards, where an egalitarian humanism was constantly in tension with a hierarchical racism. Inevitably, this exploration will be faltering, edging forward across a racially charged historical terrain, uncovering in some places a disturbing 'complicity between rationality and the practice of racial terror' (Gilroy, 1993, p.39), and engaging with the fractured historical positions of subjects who were never considered to be fully human and whose historical experiences have frequently been abjected, silenced or expunged from the record, or exiled to hidden archives that even now are only tentatively and begrudgingly being brought to light. I shall be 'retrieving minor lives from oblivion' as a 'way of redressing the violence of history', to borrow from the Afro-American scholar Saidiya Hartman (2019, p.31).We shall journey from dark misdeeds on a slave ship in the Middle Passage in the late 18th century to assaults on female black bodies in an asylum in Jamaica in the mid-19th century; thence to declamations of the mentally ill as a stain on the purity of the national British stock, and finally to outrages committed on black mental patients in police custody and at Broadmoor special hospital at the end of the 20th century.

These are all individual bodies that we shall encounter, but grasped and gripped within, held onto and held down by the body of the state. The questions about humanity and the limits of the human that so much exercised and vexed Granville Sharp still reverberate two centuries later. It may sometimes seem that history of this sort belongs 'over there', or in some specialised enclave, and does not directly concern us 'over here'. But, as Stuart Hall (1932–2014), the Jamaican-born cultural theorist and radical intellectual, adroitly explains, this is actually 'the outside history that is inside the history of the English'. Or, to make this point more forcibly: 'There is no English history without this other history' (Hall, 1991/2018, cited in Goodfellow, 2020, p.47; see also Sanghera, 2021).

Throughout this journey I will be engaging with a history in which, by and large, neither mad lives nor black lives have mattered very much, and white lives have mattered a whole lot more. I am especially concerned to tease out the ways in which the questions of whether *black* lives matter or *mad* lives matter, and how they can be *made* to matter, are bound up with each other, and are still today much influenced by the sway of 'whiteness' (or ideological whiteness) over our understanding of mental health and much else besides. These questions are enmeshed with each other, for much is to be gained, I believe, by exploring the affinities between groups of people ('mad people', 'black people'), and between histories (Black history, Mad history) that have generally been treated quite separately, or ghettoised and eviscerated of their significance for mainstream historical narratives.[1]

In the pages that follow, I shall expose some of the affinities between the history of mental health and psychiatry and a colonial history that has turned whiteness into a racial ideology. In doing so, I shall excavate something of the rich and disturbing complexity of the colonial legacies with which mad lives and the field of mental health more generally in Britain are still entangled. 'Most British people,' the mixed-race writer Afua Hirsch commented recently, 'simply can't understand whiteness'.[2] The politics of whiteness transcends the colour of anyone's skin, remarks journalist Reni Eddo-Lodge, author of *Why I'm No Longer Talking to White People About Race*:

> It is an occupying force in the mind… a political ideology that is
> concerned with maintaining power through domination and exclusion
> (Eddo-Lodge, 2017, p.170)

Most white people 'have never had to think about what it means, in power terms, to be white' (Eddo-Lodge, 2017, p.170). 'We are immersed in Whiteness as fish are immersed in water and we breathe it in with every breath,' observes David S. Owen; it is more a condition than a colour, 'a deeply engrained way of being in the world', a structuring property of modern societies (Owen, 2007, p.214; Bonnett, 2000). 'How can I define White Privilege?' asks Eddo-Lodge; 'It's an absence of a lifetime of subtle marginalization and othering – exclusion from the narrative of being human' (2017, p.86).

This is the terrain etched by black writer and commentator Akala (aka. Kingslee Daley) in his fierce but convincing polemic *Natives: Race and class in the ruins of empire* (2018), where he confronts the lingering after-life in Britain of racial hierarchies and a dominant current of whiteness that tacitly link race to rationality and to the racialised subject positions of the 'mentally ill'. Both colonial and psychiatric ideologies have been defined by a will to certainty and a belief that racial and psychiatric identities are mostly self-evident. 'Colonial rule,' it is claimed, 'appealed to psychiatry's authoritative predisposition,' and in its 'preoccupation with social and moral order colonial psychiatry became a handmaiden of colonial hegemony' (Akyeampong et al., 2015, p.25). Yet, as it turns out, the constructions of social and psychiatric knowledge are

---

1. On colonialism and people with disabilities more broadly, see Cleall (2022).

2. Panel discussion, 'Africa Writes' festival, British Library, 30 June 2018, www.africawrites.org; see also Hirsch (2018).

mostly unstable and hard to define, 'tangled by multiple meanings' (Stoler, 1992, p.184). Anthropologist Ann Laura Stoler pertinently asks how we are to write the 'kind of history that retains the allusive, incomplete nature' of a form of knowledge at the core of which is, in actuality, incoherence rather than coherence. 'How do we represent that incoherence', asks Stoler, 'rather than write it over with a neater story we wish to tell?' (p.154).

Across the mutations and distortions of place and circumstance, two concepts, or themes, will recur throughout this journey. First is the idea of a 'hold' as a physical grasp, especially when applied by a person in authority, such as a police officer, to black people and frequently to black mental patients, in which the captive may be held down, or by the throat, and literally choked or suffocated to death. Second, 'hold' can describe a physical, ideological or, sometimes, figurative space, one of traumatic memory, in which persons, or the traces of persons such as records, are sheltered or stored, or, more commonly, held captive, as in 'held in the body of the state' (Dayan, 2002). Such spaces are to be found in prisons, mental hospitals and, archetypically, in the slave ships in which Africans were transported as human cargo, divested of their social identities and histories, and even of their names, across the Middle Passage from Africa to serve as chattel slaves in the Americas and West Indies. Here, a phrase like 'taken deep into a hold' signified minimally a profound uncertainty over the destiny of the person in question and a foreboding about the erasure of their historical memory and identity.

And third, and not unrelated to the first two, is the idea of 'living under occupation', whether it be fascist, colonial or capitalist, in which occupation is not merely a physical condition but also a state of mind, whether it takes the form of ideology, subjectification or psychic colonialism, as in Reni Eddo-Lodge's notion of whiteness as an occupying force in the mind, where in each case an 'insidious process constituted them as subjects and "occupied" them at the same time' (Eddo-Lodge, 2017, p.170; Robcis, 2016, p.212).

There is no point denying that the discipline of psychiatry will receive a battering in these pages. At the same time, it is not my purpose to present psychiatry as the villain of the piece so much as to insist that it must participate in the acknowledged shame of an era. It is not my purpose to add to the existing literature asking 'Are psychiatrists racist?', for it is not my experience, or my belief, that psychiatrists *are*, as a profession, racist (Lewis et al., 1990; Littlewood, 1993; Thomas & Sillen, 1972). It needs also to be said emphatically that I certainly do not claim any special expertise in whatever it is I should be expert on in embarking on a work such as this. This is a little disingenuous since manifestly I do have a background in mental health and in the history of psychiatry, and I have written quite extensively in these fields. All the same, where it really counts for present purposes, in thinking about the claims of whiteness on this whole field, I am not in the least writing from a 'knowing' position. Rather, I am trying to feel my way, challenging and exploring diverse forms of 'knowing' and drawing as much as I can on the exercise of the poet John Keats' (1817/1958) concept of 'negative capability' – that is, the ability to be in 'uncertainties, mysteries, doubts, without any irritable reaching after fact and reason'.

I have provided quite detailed references throughout the text but, for reasons of space, I have tried to keep the argument reasonably tight, so I am aware that there are many potential talking points along the way that have not been elaborated. In the same vein, the focus of this book is emphatically on Britain and its empire, and I have eschewed any comparisons with the United States. This is a great shame since, in point of fact, British and American realities are historically intertwined in almost everything that touches on the subject matter of this discussion, but it would have required a much longer book to do justice to this dimension. I will be talking mostly about 'black' and 'white' people, and their variations, and will capitalise as the context seems to require, especially when 'Black' and 'Mad', and 'Blackness' and 'Madness', are being used to refer to political categories of critique and resistance (Spandler & Poursanidou, 2019). There are, of course, a number of alternative locutions in circulation, but overall I favour terms with which, for the most part, the people to whom they apply identify. In quotes from other sources, I follow the original text.

The book is arranged as follows. Chapter 1 sketches the roots of contemporary dilemmas and conflicts in the legacies of the philosophical and scientific revolutions of the 17th and 18th centuries, which have unmistakably hastened an inflexible divide between the 'rational' and the 'irrational', engendering an enduring cultural condition in which the credibility of people judged to be mad is almost invariably put in question.

The body of the book is in five parts. Part 1 focuses on Jamaica in the era of slavery and its aftermath. In Chapter 2, we first explore the significance of the infamous episode when the crew of the *Zong*, a slave ship bound for Jamaica, cast a large number of the people who formed its cargo overboard, and then we examine Jamaica as a slave society. Against this background, in Chapter 3 we examine a crisis in Kingston Lunatic Asylum and hear the testimony of one of the female inmates. Following this, Chapter 4 examines the state of affairs at the asylum in more depth against the background both of what took place on the *Zong* and of what emancipation actually amounted to. The inmates of the asylum, it is proposed, were being punished both for the audacity of emancipation *and* for its 'failures'. We then, in Chapter 5, broaden the canvas to show how, in Jamaica, promises of emancipation soon gave way to the 'beneficent despotism' of racial liberalism, with freed slaves perceived through the lens of the management of lunacy. Finally, in Chapter 6, we consider the role of psychiatry in confronting challenges to the colonial symbolic order posed by Alexander Bedward, the leader of a Revival movement, and by the Rastafari leader Leonard Howell, and summarise the outlook in Jamaica at the turn of the 20th century.

In Part 2 the focus is on London in the late 19th century, where spectres of degeneration and hereditary taint resulted in a racialised moral economy, with the mad poor cast as 'poor whites' and a threat to the white race, producing a range of associated inquiries and culminating in the Mental Deficiency Act of 1913. The importance of domestic servitude for the labour market is also considered and in Chapter 8 we explore in some depth the life situation of Alice Triggs, a young woman making the transition from one form of servitude to another: from being a mental patient to becoming a residential domestic servant, and how, finally, she is detained for life as a moral imbecile in a mental institution for her failure to comply with male-dominated Edwardian norms for the white race.

In Part 3 the psychiatric spotlight is turned on the examination of the irrationalities of the imperial project itself, and the prologue reviews some of the ideas in play here. In Chapter 9, we examine the career of R.R. Racey, a colonial administrator in Uganda and present-day Malawi at the turn of the 20th century, who allegedly went mad at his post. His story is of exceptional interest, for the circumstances surrounding Racey's crisis, and the responses to it, can equally be understood as exposing vulnerabilities intrinsic to the colonial project itself. In Chapter 10, we look in detail at the case of the heir to a princely state in India, about whose competence to rule the British authorities had grave doubts, believing him unable to live up to the standards of the colonial norm of the 'manly Englishman'. However, their successive efforts to reach an authoritative opinion about him merely exposed fissures and conflicts in the façade of colonial psychiatric expertise.

Part 4 focuses on the vulnerability of the black body in post-war British society. The prologue discusses the tensions and conflicts between the claims of Afro-Caribbean migrants to belong and the racialised ideologies of Britishness with which they were confronted. Chapter 11 has as its focus the violation of the humanity of the Jamaican-born electrician Winston Rose, who had been experiencing severe mental health issues and who died at the hands of the police in 1981, and I draw on a thesis written by the artist Denzil Forrester MBE in the following year. In Chapter 12, I highlight the tensions visible at the former Broadmoor Criminal Lunatic Asylum, which opened in 1863 as an exclusively white institution and where, after the Second World War, the staff were ill-disposed towards the arrival of a generation of Afro-Caribbean migrants asserting their claims to be Black and British. We explore how the disavowal of Jamaican-born Orville Blackwood's humanity led to his tragic death in this institution in 1992, drawing on the report of the inquiry conducted by the criminologist and authority on forensic psychiatry Herschel Prins (1928–2016) and his team.

Part 5 focuses on the period after empire and ponders the question of how psychiatry, and mental health care more broadly, is now situated in relation to the racialised terrain in which it originated and which it cannot be said entirely to have vacated. In Chapter 13, I highlight some disturbing continuities between the *Zong* episode in the 1760s and a very recent case involving a Black deportee who died at the hands of security guards working on behalf of the British state. I contextualise what is at stake in this and related cases by examining how liberal racism operates in such a way as to value some social groups and disparage others, sometimes even as socially dead. As I explain, the intersection of blackness and mental illness not infrequently produces situations that are fraught and even life-threatening. I go on to examine more disturbing continuities in political struggles over the black body and psyche between Jamaica in the 19th century and Britain in the aftermath of empire. Drawing on research by the campaign group Inquest, I look more closely at the fight for justice for families where a member has died in state custody.

In the closing Chapter 14, I start by exploring a thought-provoking recent study titled *The Racial Code*, by Nicola Rollock (2022), that strives to show how racism is hard-wired into the fabric of a modern society like Britain. I review briefly the topical concept of 'intersectionality'. I then ask how British psychiatry sees itself now in relation to the racialised terrain in which it originated and still exists. The answer to this is, at best, equivocal, for there appears to be an unwillingness within the white British establishment to disturb its own complacency. Far more is to be learnt here from the experiences and reflections of two Black survivors, activists, advocates and teachers, Doreen Joseph and Colin King, who both speak back unabashedly to white psychiatry. Finally, I engage with the challenge of Afropessimism – an area of controversy that is identified especially with the outlook of the Afro-American scholar Frank Wilderson III in his book of that title (2020). This work, as I discuss, is both a philosophical *and* a mental health memoir, in the spirit of Frantz Fanon, recounted in part from, or around, a gurney in a psychiatric ward. Afropessimism is inevitably open to numerous interpretations but I distill from it an unflagging commitment to a revaluation of *pathology*, of all that the whole tradition of scientific naturalism in psychiatry reviles as abject or defective – a commitment that endorses and strengthens many of the questions and discoveries we have been making in the journey of this book and that beckons towards a new horizon and path of hope.

1

Credibility, madness and race

A n****r was being beaten near by. They said he had caused the fire in some way; be that as it may, he was screeching most horribly. 'What a row the brute makes!' said the indefatigable man with the moustaches, appearing near us. 'Serve him right. Transgression-punishment-bang! Pitiless, pitiless! That's the only way... I was just telling the manager!'
(*Heart of Darkness*, Joseph Conrad, 1899/2017)

Conrad's *Heart of Darkness*

Squatting on the deck of the *Nellie*, anchored on the Thames above Gravesend, Charlie Marlow recounts his memories to his small circle of listeners so as to make them 'understand the effect of it on me' – the traumatic change wrought in him by a voyage he undertook 'up that river', into the dark heart of Africa, to the place where 'I first met the poor chap'. *Heart of Darkness* was written in the winter of 1898–1899 by Joseph Conrad who, like Marlow, was an ex-seaman and an itinerant – a Polish writer, for whom English was his third language. Composed against a backdrop of revelations of abuses by European imperialists in their scrambles for Africa, a sample of which Conrad had witnessed for himself, *Heart of Darkness* has become an enduring reference point in debates about the legacies of colonialism and the continuing effects of empire, and for any historically informed reflection on madness, race and reason.

Fortuitously, its composition falls halfway in the span that concerns this book – between roughly the closing decades of the 18th century and the turn of the 21st. There are echoes in the text that hark back to what has gone on earlier in the saga of empire, and others that are more anticipatory and proleptic. The 'poor chap' to whom Charlie Marlow refers is the mysterious Kurtz, manager of an ivory trading station deep in the Congo, who before he dies entreats Marlow to 'take good care' of his writing. Marlow, as it turns out, will also 'have the care of his memory'. The Nigerian novelist and critic Chinua Achebe (1977) famously declared in a lecture in 1975 that Conrad's novel was racist and imperialist, igniting a vigorous debate that, after some years, shifted rather to a recognition of the contradictions in the text and a gathering consensus around the scholarly axiom 'that no element of *Heart of Darkness* stands untouched by troubled racial assumptions' (Seshagiri, 2010, p.42). This is also an apt statement of the racial perturbations that have afflicted and continue to afflict the discourses of psychiatry. Madness is everywhere on the horizon in the novel. 'Ever any madness in your family?' Marlow is asked by the trading company doctor before he sails for the Congo. Conrad himself described the novel rather laconically as 'an anecdote of a man who went mad in the centre of Africa', although the question of Kurtz's madness, if that is what it is, is ambiguous as to whether it is the pathology of an individual, a corporation, or even of the imperial enterprise itself writ large.

Marlow may seem disdainful of social systems, such as the gallows and the lunatic asylum, that repress difference, but at the same time he can appear offhand, or downright indifferent, in his treatment of the 'natives'. Rather than permit his deceased helmsman a proper burial, he unceremoniously heaves his body overboard. Yet, at the same time, he discomforts his listeners aboard the *Nellie* ('Try to be civil, Marlow') by exposing the hollowness of imperial assumptions about racial hierarchies, obliging them to confront the incoherence of all racial identities (Seshagiri, 2010, p.51). The text anticipates concerns that we will shortly encounter, such as a profound tension and ambivalence around questions of 'care', especially as regards what we might call mental health care, between colonisers and the colonised. *Heart of Darkness* continually poses questions about humanity, or the scope of the human, beyond the narrow, constricting, frequently vindictive vision of the colonial protagonists. As we shall see in other places in the imperial universe, 'sick cargoes', as they are commonly known, are frequently disposed of in the manner of Marlow's deceased helmsman, who at least was fortunate enough to have died before he was thrown overboard.

'N****rs' are routinely being beaten, in a manner that makes their treatment in the Congo seem relatively benign by comparison, across the gaps in space and time that separate Kingston Lunatic Asylum in Jamaica in the mid-19th century from Broadmoor special hospital, the former Broadmoor Criminal Lunatic Asylum, in rural Berkshire in England in the late 20th century. R.R. Racey, whom we shall encounter later, was a colonial official who served in the areas of central Africa now known as Uganda and Malawi in the closing years of the 19th and early years of the 20th centuries, at much the same time that Conrad was composing *Heart of Darkness*. Racey bears an uncanny resemblance in certain respects to Kurtz, both in himself and in the reactions he stirs up in others, and invites rather complementary questions: Did he actually go mad at his post? Can we distinguish between the pathology of an individual and the pathology of imperialism itself (Fabian, 2000; Thomson, 1999; Vaughan, 1993)?

Credibility in question

When it comes to questions about madness and reason, we can start by asking: What does it mean to be a mad person today and to lead a mad life? A prime contention in this book is that people with major psychiatric designations are still regarded, and are frequently brought to regard themselves, as people whose credibility has been put in question: their humanity compromised, their self-esteem shattered, sometimes irrevocably, and inclining to view themselves as inferior by the normative benchmark of mainstream psychiatry. With an experience of the psychiatric system reaching back to the late 1960s, veteran survivor, the late Peter Campbell, believed:

> A mental illness diagnosis leads to a complete loss of credibility. That is the stigma of so-called mental illness: not having credibility. Even today one is still at ground zero, or below ground zero, in a transaction with a mental health worker. (Personal communication, 2012; Campbell, 2022)

Health journalist Jeremy Laurance was struck by the deep discontent and shattered self-esteem of people who use mental health services when he researched for his book: 'Branded as a mental patient, he or she is no longer a credible witness, even about his or her own mind' (Laurance, 2003, p.72). Prominent social policy theorist Peter Beresford, who is also a mental health system survivor, pleads for a review of the philosophical base of mental health:

> The dominant 'mental illness' concept carries massive political and professional authority. We should not underestimate the power and credibility invested in it… [for] if we are seen to question the idea of 'mental illness', then that may just be taken as further evidence of our irrationality, leading to us being further discredited and excluded. (Beresford, 2002, pp.581–582; see also Spandler et al., 2015)

So much pivots on the assessment of credibility. As clinical psychologist David Pilgrim discerns:

> In modern times, to lose one's reason is a transgression that is difficult to recover from in the minds of others; hence the grave implications of the phrase 'has a history of mental illness'. (Pilgrim & Tomasini, 2012, p.635)

A professional philosopher hospitalised for psychotic depression and author of the recent study *Mental Patient: Psychiatric ethics from a patient's perspective*, Abigail Gosselin reflects (2022) on the 'huge fissure in my identity and experience' that resulted from her abrupt transition to mental patient status:

> To go from being a professional, grown woman in charge of many things to feeling like a lost and confused child victimized by psychosis and at the mercy of others was a seismic shift in how I experienced the world and how I understood myself. (Gosselin, 2022, p.1)

The routine default position in social life is to treat someone's testimony as true unless we have evidence that suggests otherwise, but in the context of someone with a mental health history the position may be reversed, on the assumption that the testimony of a mental health patient is most likely false unless there is compelling evidence to suggest otherwise. The person experiencing psychosis is thus positioned as needing to prove the accuracy of their testimony in order to acquire credibility. The result is that people with a mental health history are lumbered with an unjust credibility deficit, based on their social identity, or what philosopher Miranda Fricker calls an identity-prejudicial credibility deficit (Fricker, 2006, 2007; Gosselin, 2022, pp.146–148). Credibility and power are co-constitutive. Due to their mental illness and to the way they are situated as sick people in need of treatment, mental patients have diminished power and credibility. As Gosselin explains, experiencing a lack of epistemic power, as mental patients commonly do, diminishes a person's credibility; having diminished credibility, as mental patients also do, reduces a person's power because it decreases opportunities to participate in epistemic activities meaningfully (2022, p.149). Gosselin recounts how, on the ward one day, a nursing student struck up a conversation with her and inquired about her life outside the hospital. When she told the student that she was a professor at Regis University, she could tell immediately that the student was uncertain whether to believe her or not. Although she was grateful to the student for being brave enough to 'strike up a conversation with a mental patient… the experience of her initial scepticism was surreal'. Used to being in a position where she had credibility and authority and students and colleagues alike treated her with respect, now she found herself in a position where her credibility was in question (2022, p.136).

In 1887, in a letter addressed to the superintendent of the Royal Edinburgh Asylum, Thomas Clouston (1840–1915), John Home, an inmate, gave vent to his resentment at forever having to forfeit his credibility: 'You ask me to behave reasonably. How can you expect me [to] if you do not treat me with respect or reason?' (Barfoot & Beveridge, 1990, p.635). Likewise, a century later, Peter

Campbell makes a poignant and angry statement from within an experience of life that has continually been devalued and discredited:

> The feeling that the diagnosed mentally ill don't know what they are talking about limits the scope of our lives… If I am to be confined to a category of persons whose experience is devalued, status diminished, and rational evidence dismissed, simply because at a certain time, or times, I lost contact with the consensus view of reality agreed on by my peers, then it is scarcely possible to expect that my control over my life will ever be more than severely circumscribed… My experience is shared and is relevant. It is not an interesting cul-de-sac. Tut-tutting and sympathetic frowns from those who are paid to intervene in my affairs merely confirms my powerlessness. They accept me as an individual pathology; they deny me as a cogent element of a social reality. (Campbell, 1989, pp.12–13)

In a recent critique of what we may think of as the conventional outlook on madness, philosopher Justin Garson lights on just this patronising tendency to isolate the diagnosed person as an 'interesting cul-de-sac'. The very terminology of 'mental illness' or 'mental disorder' is shunned by many critics and survivors, he comments, precisely because it strips madness of any semblance of 'positive being', reducing it instead to deficit or lack, and placing it on a 'shelf as a kind of medical curio, along with a two-headed fetus or oversized tumor'. The mad are not a curiosity, he insists; 'madness is not always a disease to be cured but a force of disruption to be reckoned with' (Garson, 2022a, p.12). His words echo those of Peter Campbell.

In a 2016 article on 'philosophy and madness', the Dutch philosopher and writer Wouter Kusters draws on his own experience of psychosis to attempt to save 'madness from the oblivion of medical archives and the isolating discourse of medical illness' and 'bring it back to the communal world of life, meaning and philosophy' (2016, p.130). In a spirited review of Kusters' later book, *A Philosophy of Madness* (2020), Justin Garson (2022b) commends it as heralding an entirely new way of 'doing' the philosophy of psychiatry that recoils against the norms of a culture shaped by the 18th century Enlightenment, though with roots in an earlier period. In this culture, he argues, a loss of reason constitutes a transgression that in the 'official' mind is difficult, if not impossible, to row back from. There is a relentless insistence on philosophising about madness from the standpoint of sanity, with the result that madness is reduced – and again there is an echo of Peter Campbell here – 'to an interesting phenomenon that one is supposed to describe, study, classify and perhaps even "treat"' (Garson, 2022b; see also Rose, 2018; Spandler et al., 2015).

'In our age,' remarks Kusters, 'madness is mostly referred to as a zone of illness and suffering' in which 'those who wear the signs of overt madness are… perceived as specters of utter meaninglessness and senseless deviancy' (Kusters, 2016, p.130). The obsession with occupying a standpoint in sanity or non-madness had already been remarked upon by Michel Foucault in *Histoire de la Folie* in his excoriation of the illusions of positivism in aspiring to a knowledge of madness.

> The knowledge of madness supposes in the person who holds it an ability to distance the self from it, and to remain aloof from its perils and charms, a certain manner of not being mad. (Foucault, 1961/2006, p.460)

This consciousness of 'not being mad', Foucault goes on to claim, was 'at the heart of the positivist experience of mental illness'. According to the historian Emmanel Akyeampong, Michel Foucault reminds us:

> how the positivism of the 19th century, which cloaked psychiatry in the discourse of science, obscured the reality of psychiatry's foundations at the end of the 18th century in family and authority, law, and social and moral order. (Akyeampong et al., 2015, pp.24–25)

As the distinguished anthropologist and critic Ann Laura Stoler acidly remarks:

> It is the elevation of a parochial, local, and culture-bound sense of reason to a universal standard against which critical colonial studies has been rightly aimed – against epistemological commitments that have partitioned the world into unequally deserving and differentially capable social kinds, plotted on a grid that divides those who are either committed to or capable of reason from those who are not. (Stoler, 2013, p.6)

Modernity and the limits of the human

'Credibility predicaments' (Shapin, 2010, p.20) are by no means peculiar to former mental patients and their like; they embrace equally the domain and role of science in the making of the fabric of modernity, and hence they embrace scientists themselves (for scientists, read also alienists or psychiatrists), as is illustrated by the marvellous subtitle to Shapin's 2010 study: *Never Pure: Historical studies of science as if it was produced by people with bodies, situated in time, space, culture, and society, and struggling for credibility and authority*. Shapin means to interrogate the changing shapes of credibility in the understanding of science as the outcome of contingent social and cultural practices. All truth or validity claims must win credibility but, he insists, there can be no such thing as a general theory of how credibility is achieved. Grounded in a study of the social world of gentleman-philosophers in 17th-century England, a world in which scientific practice is embedded in codes and conventions of genteel conduct, Shapin adumbrates a social history of truth where knowledge-making is shown to be a collective enterprise held together by bonds of trust. Certain kinds of people were known to be more trustworthy than others. Who those 'others' were – the distribution of credibility – roughly followed the contours of power in English society: one simply *knew* what sorts of people were credible (Shapin, 2010, p.62). 'What underwrote assent to knowledge-claims was the word of a gentleman' (Shapin, 2010, p.87). Sometimes, though, it was necessary to resort to a dexterous fudging of these lines. When the Royal Society experimented on the transfusion of animal blood into a human being in 1667, it was considered expedient to use a human subject. Arthur Coga was indigent and possibly mad but, because he was also a Cambridge graduate, he could nonetheless be considered capable of providing reliable testimony of how he felt on receipt of sheep's blood (Shapin 2010, p.62).[1]

And here we encounter the historical roots of modern liberal democracy, widely mythologised as the political philosophy of equal persons. Yet, in actuality, as the Jamaican political philosopher Charles W. Mills (1951–2021) argued for many years , liberalism has predominantly been a *racial* liberalism in which an egalitarian humanism has co-existed with a hierarchical racism where full personhood is restricted to white, male, middle- and upper-class Europeans, while women, the lower orders and non-whites generally are relegated to 'sub-person' status or even cast as 'savages' or 'barbarians' (Mills, 2008, 1997/2022; Lorimer, 2013). The two philosophers identified as central to the liberal tradition, John Locke and Immanuel Kant, both set racial restrictions on property rights, self-ownership and personhood. Locke invested in African slavery and helped to write the Carolina constitution of 1669 that gave masters absolute power over their slaves; Kant has been described as the most important liberal theorist of sub-personhood and disrespect. Argues political theorist David Theo Goldberg in his book *The Racial State*, 'race is integral to the emergence, development and transformations (conceptually, philosophically, materially) of the modern nation state' (2002, p.4). Though modernity may have uprooted old social hierarchies, it simultaneously seeded new hierarchies of race.

---

1. For more on hierarchies of credibility, see Stoler (1992). For further discussion of other ways in which credibility issues have been taken up in modern science and medicine, see, for example, Steve Epstein's (1996) exploration of how knowledge about AIDS emerged.

All the same, this was a gradual process. Before the late 1600s, historians have suggested, Europeans did not use the label 'black' to refer to any race of people; it was only after the racialisation of slavery, by the late 17th century, that white and black came to represent racial categories. Indeed, even in the 18th-century Atlantic colonies, racial identities were relatively fluid and did not necessarily convey a message about slave status. The historian of racial passing, Allyson Hobbs, describes how these colonies 'had yet to reach the conclusion that blackness signalled slavery and whiteness signalled freedom' (Hobbs, 2014, p.35). As historian David Waldstreicher explains:

> To be white was not necessarily to be free; to be black was not necessarily to be a slave; and to be a mulatto or racially mixed was not necessarily to be either of these. (Waldstreicher, 1999, pp.261–262)

By the 1820s, however, the fluid and cosmopolitan Atlantic world had started to cede to a harder and increasingly segregated racial order in which status and race were aligned and whiteness had come to signify an elite racial group, now more and more associated with rationality and orderliness. In her study *Race and the Education of Desire*, Ann Laura Stoler (1995) seeks to show how fundamentally bourgeois identity has been tied to notions of being 'European' and being 'white'. The ruling of colonies entailed colonising both bodies and minds, producing parallels between the management of sexuality and the management of colonies. Accordingly, Stoler proposes that we should see race and sexuality as ordering mechanisms that share their emergence with the bourgeois order of the early 19th century, 'that beginning of the modern age' (Stoler, 1995, pp.9–12; see also Foucault, 1966/1970, p.xxii). So, far from being aberrant offshoots, race, racisms and their representations are actually formative features of modernity, deeply embedded in bourgeois liberalism (Lorimer, 2013).

Madness and Western modernity

Madness possesses enormous significance for the modern Western outlook, for, as historian Roy Porter explains (2001, 2003a), in the pre-modern universe, before the Renaissance and the Scientific Revolution, the crucial divide in the key values of Christendom lay between the godly and the ungodly, and the distinction between the mad and the sane did not count for anything like as much as it does today. With the dawning of the 'Age of Reason', all of this was set to change, and the divide between the rational and the irrational, or between reason and unreason, now became pivotal. It is in the 18th century that we can start to plot the origins of the historical sway of whiteness (or what is sometimes called ideological Whiteness) over the cultural apparatus of what we now call mental health. And a critical dimension here is self-control, for historically it is, above all, self-control that white people of good class and ability were believed to possess and mad people and black people, apparently, to lack. In the wake of the Enlightenment, the encounter between Whiteness and non-Whiteness came to be framed in sternly rationalistic terms, in which Whiteness was conflated with rationality, orderliness and self-control, and non-Whiteness signified chaos, irrationality, violence and the breakdown of self-regulation.

Whiteness became a dominating power, normative and unexamined, undergirding the rationality of Eurocentric culture and thought and serving to push to the margins not only those defined as not-White but also those considered not-Able. Born to a Jamaican father and Welsh mother in post-war London, Hazel Carby was disconcerted to discover at school that she was frequently an object of consternation in the gaze of her classmates. She was tormented with the repeated question, 'Where are you from?', meaning 'Are you black or white?', to which, at that historical place and moment especially, there was no acceptable answer:

> The girl was being asked to provide a reason for her being which she
> did not have. It was sobering to realize that 'where' and 'from' did not
> reference geography but the fiction of race in British national heritage.
> (Carby, 2019, pp.12–13)

Writes Carby, when 'all the answers she could invent were rejected, she reluctantly acknowledged that she was being rebuffed for what she was'.

This is the terrain on which black people, disabled people and those designated mad were constructed and maintained, all the time by reference to a white, male, middle-class norm (Kincheloe, 1999). An ineluctable stigma now attached to mental disorder and loss of reason was made into a transgression that was difficult to overcome. The era of colonialism amplified these polarities, giving prominence to the shifting dispositions of racial whiteness, as the historian Bill Schwarz has framed them (2013), in determining moral and ideological categories. The West 'regarded Africa and Africans in the 19th and 20th centuries through lenses tinted by psychiatry and presumptions of African inferiority' (Akyeampong et al., 2015, p.2). The founding narrative of Western reason was thus accompanied by an abasement of blackness in which both 'the mentally ill' and non-Europeans were represented as closely linked forms of alterity, and subsequently frequently identified as manifestations of the same 'alien' phenomenon (Mbembe, 2017, pp. 85–86; Littlewood & Lipsedge, 2014, p.37).

Here we are permitted a glimpse of the 'descriptive statement', to borrow anthropologist Gregory Bateson's phrase, that was to become foundational to what it means to be human in modernity (Bateson, 1968). Mental disturbance has played a significant role in the liberal political tradition, and, in Locke's system of thought, the 'mad Man' (for it is invariably a 'he') is a composite, or fiction, who in his permanent confinement in Locke's theory – in which he is routinely chided and sometimes taunted for being 'unreasonable' – serves as a foil for the norm of the autonomous self-governing agent and as the paradigmatic example of a condition that excludes an individual from full membership in a rights-bearing citizenry. Far from being dispensable, the mad person is integral to Locke's system, which requires his services absolutely, for he is Reason's nemesis.

The origins of psychiatry in the 'alien' encounter

Especially as regards the moralisation of the mad as inferior, the categories and assumptions of classic psychiatry – what we may think of as psychiatric epistemology – have in their *origins* been permeated by the encounter, directly or at a remove, with non-European, or what have been classed as 'alien', populations. A person whose credibility is in question is only doubtfully part of history, or not an historical agent at all. The Italian philosopher Benedetto Croce (1866–1952) provocatively accented the separation made in European thought since the time of the Enlightenment between those humans who were considered to be part of 'history' and those who, belonging to the 'inferior reality' of nature, were 'men only zoologically', inserted in history only by negation, for 'they are to be dominated':

> They may be tamed and trained; when this proves impossible they may
> be allowed to live on at the fringes of civilization'. (Croce, 1949, p.246;
> translated and quoted by Portelli, 1991, p.293)

Here we can locate the origins and consolidation within the modern period – although it possesses more ancient roots – of the style of thinking that philosopher Justin Garson labels as *madness-as-dysfunction*. This way of thinking takes as axiomatic the idea that, by reference to an authoritative conception of how a person is supposed to feel, think and behave, mental disorders declare themselves through multiple forms of deficiency, defect or lack (Garson, 2022a, p.2). It maintains that, when someone is mad, it is because something has gone awry inside that person – something in the mind or brain is not working as it should. Typically, this outlook gives rise to what Abigail Gosselin (2022) identifies as inappropriate medicalisation:

[This] has the effect of obscuring the social and political conditions that lead to the condition or that cause the condition to be interpreted as pathological. The motives for such over-medicalization or inappropriate medicalization are typically capitalist, involving the creation of industries devoted to addressing these conditions as problems of the individual rather than as social problems. (Gosselin, 2022, p.59)

According to Garson, it was the philosopher Immanuel Kant (1724–1804) who, in his youthful *Essay on the Maladies of the Head* (1764/2011), gave the clearest expression of madness-as-dysfunction in the history of psychiatry. This identified defects that corresponded to different faculties of the mind (for instance, insanity (*Wahnwitz*) for a defect in reason) and stimulated what was shortly to evolve into a hegemonic outlook that has instilled itself into the fabric of modernity. It is now:

so entrenched in contemporary psychiatric thought that it can be hard to find one's way out of it… a mesh that girdles our thought so tightly that it has become nearly impossible to see it *as* a tradition, as a *Denkstil*, as one among other ways of observing and interacting with the mad. (Garson, 2022a, pp.2, 11)

This is unmistakeably the terrain in which contemporary struggles for credibility among mad people are profoundly, and indissolubly, entrenched – the aporia of the modern mental health predicament.

The enduring colonial legacy

Like the 'natives' of the colonies, the 'mentally ill' have been subject to what Partha Chatterjee has called 'a rule of colonial difference', grounded in a powerful, though largely unacknowledged, norm of whiteness predicated on an assumption of 'fitness' for self-control and self-government (Chatterjee, 1994). 'Whiteness' is, above all, a moral category through which, historically, some human lives have been racialised as non-white, or as less than white, and hence as inferior or unworthy. Subordinate groups like the 'mentally ill' who, regardless of their efforts, do not quite succeed in providing convincing evidence of their 'fitness' for self-government, may never achieve a state of equality with their superiors, who unremittingly perceive them as 'not quite right', or credible, and so constrain them to go on 'living the colonial difference'. The right to rule presupposed an integral divide between metropole and colony, with civilization and reason on one side and barbarism and irrationality on the other. But such a fanciful schema was not so easy to maintain, for how was the abundance of life that fell in between these poles, like mixed-race children, to be classified (Bland, 2021; Furedi, 2001; Olusoga, 2016, pp.504–509)? The ambivalence produced by these uncertainties has given an undoubted fillip to mixed-race activists, writers and artists with African, Afro-Caribbean and Asian origins, from Henrietta Dawson and Ann Pratt in the 1850s, whom we shall meet later, to Robert Nesta Marley, Afua Hirsch , Hazel Carby, David Olusoga, Akala and countless others in our own time, in puncturing the hegemony of the complacency and coldness of 'official' whiteness or of what black actor David Harewood (2021) calls the 'white space' (Parker & Song, 2001).

In one of his last essays before his untimely death, historian Roy Porter reflected on the inner connections and resonances between madness in the colonial periphery and at home:

> As is often the case, the empire can offer a mirror for what was going on in the metropolitan domains… How far were the mad poor and other disadvantaged groups in London, Paris or New York being treated as colonized people? (Porter, 2003b, p.18)

Though Porter did not mean to imply that the metropolitan domain was reducible, or wholly analogous, to the colonial domain, at the same time he draws attention to what the post-colonial scholar China Mills terms 'the continued coloniality of psychiatry' – the sense in which psychiatry in the homeland may be read 'as enacting or mobilising a colonial relation' (Mills, 2018, pp.204–212). In a witty and acerbic essay, Mills observes:

> Colonialism and psychiatry are deeply historically implicated, co-constituted, and mutually reinforcing… woven into both colonization and psychiatry are metaphors and analogies of madness and savagery. (2018, pp.207–208)

Colonial realities thus beam a light on issues and dimensions that may otherwise be marginalised or pass unnoticed. The trials of 'being mad' and of living the life of a mad person in the 21st century are still entangled, enmeshed and embedded in a field of economic, political, cultural and ideological forces with roots in the 19th century and colonial periods.

'Keeping them alienated'

Psychiatrist Suman Fernando has powerfully argued:

It may be that in searching for scientific answers using the 19th century paradigm of 'science', psychiatry has lost its way as a caring profession and become de-humanised and in some contexts, such as modern Western societies, it continues to be racist. (Fernando, 2012, p.117)

In the late 1940s, a French West Indian from the island of Martinique made it his mission to study the entanglements of just this field of forces and to stimulate forms of action that might address the grievances, and improve the circumstances, of those otherwise condemned 'to live on at the fringes of civilization'. His name was Frantz Fanon (1925–1961). Fanon was an impassioned young psychiatrist who, despite growing up believing himself to be French and as good-as-white, became radicalised through his reading and his war experience. Fanon pursued a psychiatric training and career, first in France, then Algeria, and finally, following his expulsion from Algeria, in Tunisia. In the brief but intense span of his life, he turned his professional experience of the alienated to revolutionary account by making out of it a revealing and disturbing window on the alienated condition of a colonial society.

In recent years, scholars have started to ask that we acknowledge the vitality of Fanon's psychiatric work as inseparable from his political work (Razanajao et al., 1996, p.522). Fanon was, first and foremost, a clinical psychiatrist who saw the question of freedom as central to his understanding of mental illness, and who later became drawn into making revolution as a means to change the fortunes of the 'mentally ill' or alienated. It is worth remarking that Fanon's original title for what became his classic study of the black psyche under colonialism, *Black Skin, White Masks* (1952/2017), was 'Essay for the Disalienation of the Black Man' (Robcis, 2021). The alienated predicaments of the mental patient and the colonised subject are distinct but closely imbricated. The 'mentally ill' were another form of the colonised, of what it is to be 'other', and to be treated relentlessly and remorselessly as inferior. With their tendency to inferiorise and deprecate the humanity of their constituents, psychiatric ideologies provided a ready model for colonial authorities to emulate (Gillett, 2015). In their commentary on Fanon, Camille Razanajao and colleagues write:

We come here to the heart of the matter in that an essential function of 'official scientific' psychiatric discourse has to do with the application of apparently philanthropic rationalizations to an extremely violent relationship of domination where the patient, being indigenous, is not better than a slave and the plaything of the men who dominate him, with their absolute power, and their repressive re-education 'therapies'. (Razanajao et al., 1996, p.514)

Fanon's experience with the mentally ill in mental hospitals instructed him on the oppressive dynamics of colonialism. His knowledge of institutional psychotherapy that he had acquired from Francois Tosquelles and his team at Saint-Alban in France had given him the tools to diagnose what Tosquelles called the 'concentrationist logic' of the asylum and, as Fanon would later claim, of the colonial situation:

> Because it is a systematized negation of the other, a frenzied
> determination to deny the other any attribute of humanity, [the colonial
> situation] forces the colonized to constantly ask the question: 'Who am I
> in reality?' (Fanon, 1961/2001, p.182)

Fanon distinguished between a colonised and a dominated people, suggesting that a dominated people may nonetheless retain their humanity, while colonised people are deprived of any sense of personal identity or worth. Though Fanon did not specify how the mentally ill should be classified exactly, we may be drawn to conclude that, overall, under Western psychiatry, in the era of the lunatic asylums especially, the predicament of the mentally ill more closely resembled the situation of colonised people in the extent of its invasion into, and control over, every aspect of their being.

The segregation and seclusion of England's lunatics within a universe of asylums by alienists, as psychiatrists were known in that period, who made it their business to keep the inmates 'alienated', coincided pretty much with the heyday of British imperialism. Like the rest of the empire, the asylum universe seemed to many to be an indissoluble part of the providential order of things, communicating a sense of self-confidence and monumental power that, in Michel Foucault's apt phrase, asserted 'the absolute right of non-madness over madness' (Foucault, 1994, p.48). Well into the 20th century, the mad were perceived as a kind of 'dark continent' – a stain on the purity of the national stock and a threat to the myth of British superiority over other races. The lunatic asylum was inscribed in a project where something racially was always at stake. The administration of a mental hospital and the management of a colony were part of the same process and derived from the same impulse to manage the irrational. The colony was, in a sense, always already a mental hospital under management, and hence the colonial authorities were frequently reluctant to commit dedicated resources for psychiatry overseas, because they believed they were doing the job already in managing an 'abnormal' society. The psychological medicine of the period spawned a condemnatory rhetoric masquerading as science that served to accentuate the differences of those 'alienated' or 'excluded' (Haller, 1971).

The 'mental patient' and the 'non-European' are distinct, but complementary, forms of alterity that throw light on each other. As Roland Littlewood and Maurice Lipsedge underscored in their classic text, *Aliens and Alienists*:

> Two types of 'outsiders' – the mentally ill and non-Europeans – have been referred to as aliens – people set aside by various theories as being basically different... The paths of the non-European and the mental patient continually cross and sometimes run together. The same theories are used to keep them alienated. We even find them described as manifestations of the same phenomenon. (Littlewood & Lipsedge, 2014, p.37)

The development and self-understanding of psychiatry, as I shall argue in this book, must be located against the background of racial liberalism, for which it has frequently been an earnest, if insufficiently acknowledged, apologist (Lorimer, 2013). Even today, psychiatry is largely oblivious of its own whiteness, basking complacently in the unacknowledged privileges of its scandalous origins, unwilling, or unable, to acknowledge that being white has meaning and that white perspectives on mental health are necessarily racially problematic.

Although scientific objects such as quarks may achieve the conditions of credibility to qualify as what Steven Shapin (1995) calls 'authorized objects', there are many others – notably those associated with the states of affairs that are the concerns of the human and social sciences – that never succeed in establishing themselves authoritatively and, instead, continue to exist as 'conversational objects', by their very nature unstable and continuously contested, limping along with a credibility deficit. Arguably, despite the ardent hopes of many of its most prominent practitioners, psychiatry demonstrates throughout its history that mental illness, considered as a scientific object, has never succeeded in transcending its status as a 'conversational object' – albeit one located in a conversation in which the power stakes have generally been loaded in favour of a set of predominantly white speakers, with the voices of patients generally, and more especially those of black patients, frequently dismissed, discredited or, in the words of medical anthropologist Allan Young, 'simply pushed to the margins of "reasoned" discourse' (Young, 1982; see also Berrios & Markova, 2015, 2017; Markova & Berrios, 2012).

PART 1

Jamaica, slavery and madness

Part 1 – Prologue

In his *Critique of Black Reason*, the Cameroonian philosopher and political theorist Achille Mbembe (2017) shows how, for several centuries, race has operated as a foundational category for modernity that is at once material and phantasmic. Black reason is, in a critical sense, the founding narrative of the Western consciousness of blackness in which the 'Black Man' is produced both as a racial subject and as a site of savage exteriority made available for moral disqualification. Sylvia Wynter, the redoubtable Cuban critic of colonial modernity, argues that, in the wake of the West's reinvention in the 17th century of what she calls its 'True Christian Self' in the radically revised terms of the 'Rational Self of Man', it was now the peoples of the expropriated New World territories, together with the enslaved peoples of Black Africa, who were to be found wanting and made over into the position of the irrational, 'racially inferior' or non-evolved, backward 'Others' (Wynter, 2003, p.266, original capitalisations; McKittrick, 2015).

For Black disability studies scholar Theri Alyce Pickens, in her monograph, *Black Madness: Mad blackness* (2019), the meanings of disability, race and gender are inseparable:

> To address Blackness/madness imperils the twin pillars of whiteness and sanity that uphold Western notions of intellectual enterprise. (Pickens, 2019, p.15)

Recognising that they are culturally and historically intertwined, Pickens highlights the potential in viewing them together, while remaining mindful of the dangers of analogy ('madness is *like* race') and the risk of conflation that attends it (2019, pp.2–3, 17, 25). In his landmark 'modest proposal' for white disability studies, the Black disabilities studies scholar (the late) Christopher Bell famously chided the discipline not for excluding people of colour but, quite the opposite, for treating them as if they were *white* people:

> as if there are no critical exigencies involved in being people of color
> that might necessitate these individuals understanding and negotiating
> disability in a different way from their white counterparts. (Bell, 2006,
> pp.275, 282; see also Bell, 2012)

In his stimulating and suggestive *How to Go Mad Without Losing Your Mind* (2021), La Marr Jurelle Bruce, reflecting on the depth of the wound that the Middle Passage inflicts on modernity, deploys the word *derange* to describe its action in throwing millions of Africans 'askew across continents, oceans, centuries and worlds' and also to 'signal how the Atlantic slave trade, and the anti-black modernity it inaugurated, framed black people as always already wild, subrational, pathological, mentally unsound, mad' (Bruce, 2021, p.4):

> The Euro-modern patriarch affirmed his Reason and freedom, in part by
> casting the black African as his ontological foil, his unReasonable and
> enslaved Other. (2021, p.5)

Bruce is also drawn to the convergence between the ship of fools, famously and controversially apostrophised by Michel Foucault in his *History of Madness* (1961/2006), and the slave ship in the imagination of early Euromodernity, arguing that both defy positivist history, 'the ship of fools because it was likely unreal; the slave ship because it is so devastatingly real that it confounds comprehension' (Bruce, 2021, p.3). Although these two types of ship were not the same, and Bruce does not mean to imply a simplistic analogy between them, nonetheless they intersect in the early modern imagination and were both 'imagined to haul inferior, unreasonable beings who were metaphysically adrift amid the rising tide of Reason' (2021, p.4). This is also epitomised by the enduring powerful hold on writers and artists of the atrocities committed on the slave ship *Zong*, which we will explore in the next chapter (Baucom, 2005, p.305).

The next five chapters all take colonial Jamaica as their primary focus. As historian Trevor Burnard has described, from the end of the War of the Austrian Succession in 1748 to the beginning of the American Revolution in 1776, Jamaica was the powerhouse of the British Empire and white Jamaicans were among its wealthiest subjects (Burnard, 2004, p.12). By 1750, Jamaica had been a slave society for at least three-quarters of a century and was one of the most complete such societies in history. Some 90% of its population were racially distinctive chattel slaves and the system of laws in place was based on the nearly total obedience of slaves to white authority (Burnard, 2004, p.244). In this brutal society, in which white superiority was predicated on the enduring and ineradicable inferiority of blackness, the English-born slave owner and polemic defender of slavery Edward Long (1734–1813), author of a highly controversial *History of Jamaica* (1774), mocked the excesses of white colonial life as 'rioting in goatish embraces', being strongly of opinion that black people must first be tamed before they could be treated as human. In what became known as Tacky's Revolt, in 1760–1761, a movement of enslaved West Africans in Jamaica (then called Coromantees) had already very nearly succeeded in throwing off the imperial yoke and creating an independent state in the Caribbean. This instilled a climate of fear among the white majority, so that whites became 'much afraid of the Negroes rising, they being very impudent' (cited in Burnard 2004, pp.12, 170; Brown, 2020). The shock of the revolt intensified pre-existing polarities, and by the closing decades of the 18th century Jamaica had become a caste society in which the social and political distance between white men and black people, whether slaves or free coloureds, became incontrovertible.

In the opening chapter of this section, I engage with a traumatic episode that is also very much part of this history – the *Zong* affair of 1781, when a large number of enslaved Africans on board a ship bound for Jamaica were thrown overboard by the crew, giving rise to a court case, and a fierce controversy, in which it was attempted to rationalise the mass killing of the Africans on the basis that they were regarded as 'cargo' in the law rather than as 'persons'. What is significant about this episode is not so much *that* it happened – very likely there had been similar occurrences that had never attracted any fuss – but that it occurred at a historical moment when there was already a gathering humanitarian sensibility and that it produced such a revulsion against the depravity of the slave trade and the brutalisation of slave existence.

Abolition did not, however, bring about anything like the degree of improvement in the life situations of former slaves that had been wished for or anticipated, and there was strong resistance from the planter class to any kind of meaningful change. A momentary flowering of common humanity soon gave way to an uncommonly divided humanity, cleaving between the deserving and the undeserving, the civilised and the unredeemable. During the period of abolition, the same questions were being asked about 'the mad' and 'the blacks' alike:

> Can [they] govern themselves? Are they human beings like all others?
> Can one find among them the same humanity or do they exhibit a radical
> difference, a form of 'being-apart'? (Mbembe, 2017, p.86)

In the three chapters that then follow, I focus especially on the goings on at the Kingston public lunatic asylum (KLA), which had become the site of a major scandal and public inquiry. I contextualise the crisis at the KLA against the background of the *Zong* tragedy and ensuing controversy and the tensions and failures of emancipation. I argue that the KLA is an institution that voyages under the sign of *Zong*, a vessel in which care has been all but expunged and eliminated.

I go on in Chapter 4 to ask about the meaning of what is at stake here, where question marks hang over the 'be-ing' and humanity of 'the mad' (Mbembe, 2017, p.86); where 'the bounded integrity of whiteness' (Hartman, 1997, p.123) is secured by the abjection of black others; how it is that the mad are the left-overs, the discards, from a singular 'human' that was created at their expense; how psychiatry and mental health care are enmeshed in the racialised fabric of modernity. Although abolition has been projected as a triumph of British justice and morality, in actuality British institutions were deeply implicated in, and even violently supportive of, colonial slavery, as a recent study of the West India Interest, which I explain, has shown (Taylor, 2020).

In Chapter 5, in a discussion of the 'beneficent despotism' of racial liberalism, to borrow Sir Henry Taylor's phrase from 1862 (Holt, 1992, p.285), I will show how race became the 'organizing grammar of an imperial order' (Stoler, 1995, p.27) and the mental health sciences came to reflect a Eurocentric framework of human understanding that was naturalised as common sense. Increasingly, the social relations of colonial reality were framed through the lens of moral treatment and the management of lunacy, producing an image of black people as a failed therapeutic cadre, and an official rhetoric in which the lunatic asylum and Jamaican society became increasingly indistinguishable. In Britain and the colonies, legislation was being enacted for prisons and numerous other categories of reformatories that, in their style of operation, habits and discipline, were uncannily like slave plantations.

In the final decades of the 19th through into the 20th century, the real challenges to symbolic colonial order in Jamaica came from the Revival movement in its numerous varieties, and later from Rastafarianism. I explore the threat to the colonial order and the role of psychiatry in discrediting what the authorities perceived to be threatening and unwarranted forms of spiritual behaviour posed by two ground-breaking and charismatic religious leaders, Alexander Bedward (1848–1930), founder and leader of the Bedwardites, and Leonard Howell (1898–1981), a foundational Rastafari leader. Both were harassed and persecuted by the colonial authorities and confined in mental hospitals over several decades.

2

From *Zorg* to *Zong:* the *Zong* affair

The *Zorg* (or *De Zorg* or the *Zorgue* – which, ironically, translates into English as 'care') was a Dutch slave ship captured as a prize of war by the British in 1781. Following this, an error was apparently made in the re-painting of the ship's name – an 'r' was transposed into an 'n', and the vessel became the *Zong*. It was purchased by a syndicate of merchants led by William Gregson from Liverpool, a city built on slavery and a dominant force in the slave trade (Walvin, 2011, p.12). Like much else associated with the subsequent history of the *Zong*, a mystery hangs over the change of name. Was it to be attributed to an inattentive signwriter or was it intentional? Relatively trivial in itself, the change of name, and the erasure of '*Zorg*' (or '*care*'), was to become a figure for what was to be played out in the subsequent history of the vessel, which was to achieve an infamous notoriety. The history, meaning and significance of the *Zong* affair has already attracted a prodigious historiography, and here I only have space to highlight some of the critical issues that specially pertain to this discussion (Armstrong, 2005, 2007; Baucom, 2005; Burnard, 2019; Faubert, 2018; Hochschild, 2005; Rupprecht, 2007; Sharpe, 2016; Walvin, 2011; Webster, 2007).

Bound for Jamaica with a cargo of 470 slaves, with Captain Luke Collingwood at its helm, the *Zong* left the African coast on 18th August 1781 on the Middle Passage – the second leg of the 'triangular' voyage that took slave ships from England to Africa, from Africa to the Americas, and from the Americas back to England (Walvin, 2011, p.70). Collingwood was in actuality a ship's surgeon, and had never served as master of a slave ship before. Due to a number of setbacks and a major navigational error, the journey was taking far longer than expected. With water running short, the order was given for 132 African slaves (some accounts put it at 140, or 142, or 142 and an infant) to be thrown overboard, tied in pairs, in three batches or 'packages', on separate days. The order may have been given by Collingwood himself, although he had been sick for most of the journey and may have been demented and not even in command at the time. It was certainly given with the agreement of the rest of the crew. Nominally, the object was to preserve water for the survivors, even though, as it emerged later, rain had fallen for several days after the first batch of slaves had been cast into the deep, making the water shortage less critical or convincing as a motive. The crew were apparently fearful that, if they did not resort to such a drastic measure, many of the Africans would become 'seized with Madness for want of water', sparking an insurrection that would have overwhelmed the small crew (cited in Burnard, 2019). Robert Stubbs, a passenger, who may also have taken over as master of the vessel for a time, later described how from his cabin he heard the 'shrieks' of women and children being thrown into the deep 'singly through the cabin windows' (Burnard, 2019). J.M.W. Turner's haunting and controversial masterpiece, 'Slavers Throwing Overboard the Dead and Dying' (1840), commonly known as 'The Slave Ship' (Walvin, 2011, pp.1–11) and quite possibly inspired by the *Zong* affair, depicts black body parts and beseeching hands weltering on the waves, and succeeds in conveying, as no other painting has achieved, the sheer, unassailable inhumanity both of this happening and of the white slave trade as a whole (see p.162).

In a letter to the Admiralty, the redoubtable abolitionist Granville Sharp (1735–1813), who was to become closely involved in harrying the authorities and in publicising the whole affair, set out the most probable reason why the crew of the *Zong* murdered the Africans:

> A great number of the remaining Slaves on the day last mentioned were sick of some disorder or disorders and likely to die or not live long… the Dead and dying Slaves would have been a dead loss to the Owners… unless some pretence, or expedient, had been found to throw the loss upon the Insurers… as in the case of Jetsam or Jetson, i.e. a plea of Necessity to cast overboard some part of a Cargo to save the rest. (Cited in Faubert, 2018)

Sharp puts it in a nutshell: the status of the African captives was that simply of cargo, the value of which must be protected for purely commercial reasons. The plan was to collect insurance on the drowned Africans, who alive would have fetched a poor price, if any, on the slave market in Jamaica because they were likely all sick. The *Zong's* owners, the Gregson syndicate, could collect insurance for the Africans who had been killed out of 'Necessity' –the legal term that justified their decision to 'jettison' them – but not for those who died simply of disease. The shocking truth, as Lord Chief Justice Mansfield acknowledged, was that insurance law defined slaves as commodities and not as human beings. The 'case of the slaves', he famously remarked, 'was the same as if horses had been thrown overboard... The Question was whether there was an Absolute Necessity for throwing them overboard to save the rest, the Jury were of opinion there was' (Faubert, 2018, p.40).

Despite the enormity of what took place on the *Zong*, no criminal prosecution ever issued from it. The effrontery of the episode, which left contemporaries seething with outrage, lay above all in the complicity that it revealed between the savagery and inhumanity of the system of slavery on the one hand and the British legal system on the other. Granville Sharp had been visited in March 1783 by Olaudah Equiano, a freed slave who had been working as a house servant in London, who regaled him with an account of 'one hundred and thirty Negroes being thrown alive into the sea from on board an English slave ship'. In the court, Mr John Lee, the Solicitor General, representing the owners of the *Zong*, maintained that 'the case was the same as if the assets had been thrown overboard', and that a master could drown his slaves without any 'surmise of impropriety', implicitly referencing the condition of chattel slavery that, by legally categorising slaves as chattels and thus as private property owned by the slaver, denied their humanity (Hochschild, 2005, p.81). Sharp recorded in his journal that, at one point during the hearing, Lee 'violently exclaimed to the Judges, that a person was in the Court (at the same time turning round and looking at me) who intended to bring on a criminal prosecution for murder against the parties concerned'. But, retorted Lee, such a course 'would be madness', since 'the Blacks were property' (p.81) – an engagingly perverse but revealing definition of madness, in which the irrational affront apparently consists in the attempt to claim the humanity of the slaves. What was being insured was not the 'life' of a slave as such, but his or her status as cargo – essentially, as goods in transit.

Yet, as this and related cases brought out, matters were not so clear cut: slaves considered as human cargoes in transit on the seas occupied a problematic and liminal position in maritime law, somewhere between personhood and property. As legal historian Jane Webster has argued:

> it is not difficult to understand the difficulties that human 'cargoes' posed for insurers. Most categories of maritime cargo were inanimate. Slaves – however the law theoretically regarded them – were not only animate, they had agency. When slaves used their agency at sea – for example, in acts of insurrection or suicide – insurance law struggled to know how to respond. (Webster, 2007, p.296; see also Armstrong, 2005, p.170)

Cultural historian Tim Armstrong describes how the unstable status of the insured slave, deriving from the admixture of personhood and property that was intrinsic to slavery, became absorbed into, and contributed to, 'the evolving conception of risk, compensation, and the commoditization of human relations implicit within modernity' (Armstrong, 2005, p.168). Disputes over the insurance of slave ships 'forced to the surface the issue of the humanity and agency of slaves. Every time counsel mentioned murder in the *Zong* case... personhood was implied in court, undermining the legal status of slaves as cargo'. Granville Sharp clearly understood the huge importance of the *Zong* case in this regard, and 'it is for this reason too that the *Zong* continues to exert such a powerful influence on the modern imagination ' (Webster, 2007, p.297).

'I have become convinced,' writes the eminent historian of slavery James Walvin, 'that the story of the *Zong* is too central (and too instructive) to be left simply as a marginal story, tangential to other historical narratives' (Walvin, 2011, p.10). Africans consistently challenged and rejected their status as human cargo and as commodities, and hence 'their translation into fungible items for which monetary compensation could be found', leading the captains of slave ships to anticipate 'outrage and rebellion' from their captives, as historian Anita Rupprecht has explained, and to extract from traders and underwriters a begrudging recognition of slave humanity, bound to violence, and to the violation of the law of commodity exchange, though it inescapably was (Rupprecht, 2007, p.21–22).

After the *Zong* docked at Black River in south western Jamaica, the crew may actually have tried to conceal the ship's identity, or reverted to the ship's original name, calling it now the *Zorg* or *Zorgue*. Certainly an article in the Jamaican *Cornwall Chronicle* on 5 January 1782, describing the precarious state of the ship upon landing, referred to it as the *Zorgue*. Moreover, very soon after it reached Jamaica, the name of the ship was formally changed to the homely '*Richard*' (Faubert, 2018, p.15). What happened to the African survivors of the *Zong* voyage after the vessel docked at Black River? After all, the events of the *Zong* were an episode not just in British but above all in Jamaican history (Burnard, 2019, 2020, pp.9, 16). As James Walvin remarks, these are the people about whom we know least:

> Today, their descendants must surely be scattered among the people of modern Jamaica... What happened to their memories of that voyage? At what point did old Jamaican slaves stop reciting the nightmare stories of their crossing on the *Zong*, and when did the folk memory fade? Or were those stories too traumatic to repeat, remaining bottled up and hidden away within the *Zong's* survivors? (Walvin, 2011, p.210)

The enormity of what had taken place on the *Zong* could not, however, remain concealed for very long, and although initially the case was not widely reported and had little immediate impact on public consciousness, before long it had acquired a status as 'a pivotal moment in the development of a humanitarian sensibility' and 'the cause celèbre that galvanised the anti-slavery movement from being a minor campaign by a set of marginal figures infected by evangelical enthusiasm to becoming the most significant moral campaign in British history' (Burnard, 2020, p.192). The *Zong* killings, Granville Sharp believed, offered 'proof of the extreme depravity which the Slave Trade introduces amongst those that become inured to it' (Walvin, 2011, p.159). It was an event 'unparalled in the memory of man', one of 'so black and complicated a nature', averred the prominent abolitionist Thomas Clarkson (1760–1846) (Clarkson, 1788, p.99).

From the late 1780s onwards, outrage over the *Zong*, and over the slave trade more widely, became the order of the day. It spawned the emergence of a new form of popular politics (Walvin, 2011, p.182). 'That a mass murder was committed because of a water shortage defied credibility – and outraged humanity,' comments James Walvin (2011, p.146). Turner's painting 'fairly bristles with outrage: about slave ships and about killings on those ships' (p.204). Today, the *Zong* case 'has become an enduring symbol of the terror associated with the Middle Passage' (Rupprecht, 2007, p.330). The subsequent and continued witnessing of the *Zong* atrocities by writers and artists points to 'an order of historical time' that does not so much pass as 'accumulate' (Baucom, 2005, p.305).

M. NourbeSe Philip, poet, writer and lawyer, born in Tobago, has excavated the legal text of *Gregson v. Gilbert* from 1783, the only extant public document relating to the massacre of these African slaves, to retell the story that does not bear telling. In *Zong!* (Philip, 2008) – a series of compositions with accompanying commentary, in equal parts song, moan, shout, oath, ululation, curse and chant – Philip restructures the legal document in such a way as to reveal the irrational at the heart of reason. She writes:

> I deeply distrust this tool I work with – language. It is a distrust rooted
> in certain historical events that are all of a piece with the events that
> took place on the *Zong*. The language in which those events took place
> promulgated the non-being of African peoples, and I distrust its order,
> which hides disorder; its logic hiding the illogic and its rationality, which
> is simultaneously irrational. (Philip, 2008, p.197)

In erasing and forgetting the 'be-ing' and humanity of the Africans on board the *Zong*, the text of *Gregson v. Gilbert* has become a representation of the fugal state of amnesia that serves as a mechanism for erasure and alienation. In fragmenting and morcellating this text, consigning it to the ocean where, bobbing upon the waves, these slivers of language, shattered words and body parts may perhaps once again become companionate, combine, and regenerate meanings, through a not-telling that is the only kind of telling, Philip succeeds in turning the original into a fugal palimpsest through which its amnesia may, in part, be healed (2008, p.204). 'The ratio at the heart of *Zong!*... is simply the story of be-ing which cannot, but must, be told,' she writes (p.200). For instance:

```
        den the capta        in a man o
    f girth of har        sh mien and vo      ice eve
        n with the s          he ne
    groes i s        aw him r        ub his s
        ex aga        inst her i see      ek no g
```

Which delivers something like: 'Then the captain a man of girth of harsh mien and voice even with the she negroes i saw him rub his sex against her' (p.146). And a few lines on: '... i cannot bear this tale told bare of all truth ruth you are my most my can this story is not mine to tell it i must it was only'. As the black studies scholar Christina Sharpe aptly puts it:

> Philip aspirates these submerged lives and brings them back into the text from which they were ejected. (Sharpe, 2016, p.71)

Racism in late 18th and early 19th century Britain

As James Walvin acknowledges, by the mid-1790s the enthusiasm and optimism that had initially greeted the campaign for abolition between 1787 and 1792 had begun to flag, worn down by a growing current of reactionary alarms and warnings about dangers and rising unrest in Britain and in Europe, and also in the slave colonies (Walvin, 2011, p.196). Historian Ryan Hanley (2016) charts how, after about 1830, sympathy for the emancipation movement among British radicals was put under considerable strain. In considerable part, this was due to the manifest racism of leading radicals such as John Cartwright, William Cobbett and Richard Carlile, whose ideas were deeply significant in the formation of British working identity. John Cartwright, for instance, believed that the abolitionists had not taken adequate account of the situation of the poor English labourer. In his *Weekly Political Register* in August 1821, Cobbett wrote:

Certainly the Negroes are of a different sort from the Whites. An almost complete absence of the reasoning faculties, a sort of dog-like grin, and a ya-ya-ya laugh… I am… not presumptuous enough to take upon me to assert that the Blacks are not the superior beings; but I deny all equality. They are a different race; and for Whites to mix with them is not a bit less odious than the mixing with those creatures which, unjustly apparently, we call beasts. (Cobbett, 1821, p.147, cited in Hanley, 2016, p.118)

Hanley contends that, in expounding an ever-narrower nationalism, radicals like these were questioning the very humanity of enslaved and free Africans (p.123).

Over the course of the 1820s, the black slave was increasingly represented to working-class radicals as being essentially different from and inferior to them, conveying an image of a lesser racial antitype and contributing to a current of feeling that by the 1840s was to strengthen into a determined plebeian opposition to abolition (Hanley, 2016, p.104). There was plentiful evidence of a 'pairing between Englishness and whiteness' in the popular imagination and, overall, writes Hanley, 'it can fairly be concluded that the English working class understood itself as the white working class right from its inception' (p. 123). The menace of black freedom and the naivety of white abolitionists was perhaps satirised most savagely in the print by the British caricaturist and book illustrator George Cruikshank (1792–1878), celebrated as the modern Hogarth during his lifetime, entitled 'The New Union Club' (1819) (below). As art critic Marcus Wood has described, the print illustrates

George Cruikshank, 'The New Union Club' (1819) © The Trustees of the British Museum

and enacts, spurred on by the 'intensity of George Cruickshank's anti-black fantasies', virtually every stock negative assumption about black people, and overall 'constitutes both an apotheosis of black chaos and a vision of a hell for white people: it is a last judgement for abolition' (Wood, 2000, pp.165–172). We shall re-connect with some of these issues and currents of feeling in Britain again later, but for the moment let us return to Jamaica.

Jamaica as a slave society

> Jamaica was not a refined place. It was a raw frontier society marked by aggressively entrepreneurial planter elites. It had extremely exploitative social relations characterized by remarkable levels of violence against enslaved people. That violence included sexual rapacity by white men against black women on a grand scale. It resulted in a social system that was fluid, chaotic, destructive, and, for most of the enslaved population, full of trauma. (Burnard, 2020, p.8)

It is difficult to exaggerate the pivotal significance of Jamaica in the British imperial scheme of things on the eve of the American Revolution in the late 18th century. Unquestionably, it was the jewel in the British imperial crown, and the white residents of the colony were by all accounts the richest group of people in the British Empire (Burnard, 2020). However, all this was set to change over the next decades with the abolition of slavery, the upheavals and widely proclaimed failures of emancipation and the Morant Bay rebellion in 1865. By this time, the lustre of Jamaica's earlier reputation had long faded, and it was now seen by many as a hopeless case. Fast forward to the early 20th century and it had become a rather marginal colony (Burnard, 2020), and what is true of Jamaica holds for the Caribbean as a whole. As the cultural historian of the Caribbean Mimi Sheller succinctly puts it, the Caribbean 'has been spatially and temporally eviscerated from the imaginary geographies of "Western modernity"'. The imagined community of the West, she continues:

> has no space for the islands that were its origin, the horizon of its self-perception and the source of its wealth… Despite its indisputable narrative position at the origin of the plot of Western modernity, history has been edited and the Caribbean left on the cutting room floor. (Sheller, 2003, p.1)

The whole subject of madness, and of what would later become known as psychiatry, is intimately and inextricably entangled in this history, dominated as it is by trauma and violence. In his acclaimed textbook on Caribbean mental health, the Jamaican psychiatrist Frederick Hickling advances the argument that the seizure and development of the Caribbean by European powers over the period 1500–1800 is the expression of a European psychosis 'based on a complex collective delusion which deems all people in the world with white skins superior to all others with non-white skins', and which has 'gripped an entire racial group'. European colonisation has 'invented psychiatry as a handmaiden for oppression and control of its delusional system', and for negating the values, culture and social history of the colonised, underpinned by a psychology and philosophy 'propounded by the most prominent, qualified and educated intellectuals and academics of European society', which:

> asserted that the Black and coloured peoples of the world were inferior, were scarcely higher than the domesticated animals, and that their enslavement and backwardness resulted from this inferiority. (Hickling & Gibson, 2005, pp.75–76, 91–93).

Hickling's views are sometimes controversial, and some may dissent from the emphasis that he brings to them. But, without question he specifies an agenda with which any discussion of the entanglement of madness and race in modernity, and of the history of Britain with the history of Jamaica as a slave society and its enduring consequences, must engage.

Trevor Burnard, the historian of slavery, avers that any consideration of the huge economic power and political influence of colonial Jamaica has to reckon with the enormity of the collective traumatic experience out of which it was forged. The literature on slavery in 19th century America evinces a recognition that slavery produced what historian Nell Irvin Painter has defined as a form of 'soul murder' in which enslaved people suffered psychological trauma that had long-term consequences (cited in Burnard, 2020, p.99). Burnard points out that the happiness and prosperity of the plantocracy of white Jamaicans was predicated on the miserable lives endured by more than 200,000 enslaved men, women and children in a highly rationalised and efficient but peculiarly vicious and all-encompassing slave system, which embraced symbolic as well as real instruments of violence in order to manufacture tropical products for the delectation of the population in metropolitan Britain (Burnard, 2020, p.99).

Declares historian Vincent Brown, Jamaica was 'a society in which domination, dissent and the threat of incredible violence plagued every interaction' (Brown, 2003, p.46). Was slavery in Jamaica in the period of the American Revolution the worst kind of slavery experienced in colonial British America, asks Burnard? It is certainly at the far edge of exploitation, he believes, and while other slave societies emulated it, they probably did not surpass it in the brutality of their slave management systems (Burnard, 2020, p.98). Historians distinguish between societies with slaves, in which slaves comprise a minority of the population, and slave societies, in which the slave population forms a majority, of which Jamaica is a prima facie example. By the middle of the 18th century, Jamaica had been a slave society for at least three-quarters of a century, with more than 90% of the population made up of racially distinctive chattel slaves, in nearly total obedience to the authority of the white minority. It may thus be considered one of the most complete slave societies in history (Burnard, 2004, p.244; 2015).

African slavery was not simply one of many forms of demarcation between superiors and subordinates in a world marked by complex hierarchies; it was actually the foundation on which social order rested (Burnard, 2004, p.97). Lisa Lowe, the interdisciplinary scholar whose work is concerned with the analysis of race, capitalism and colonialism, has shown that what is at stake here, among other considerations, is the pronounced asymmetry of the colonial division of humanity. 'Race and social difference,' she suggests, 'are produced by educing a singular "human" from the "other humanities" that are its condition of possibility' (Lowe, 2015a, pp.94–95). By privileging particular subjects and societies as rational, civilised and human and treating others as labouring, replaceable or disposable, 'the liberal affirmation of the human is linked to the forcible forgetting of other forms of life, labour and resource necessary for the creation of liberal humanity'. The history of modernity is, in one sense, a 'history of liberal forms monopolizing the meaning of freedom for the human and denying it to others placed at a distance from the human', she concludes (Lowe, 2015a, p.94–95).

The idea of 'race'

A confrontation with the idea of 'race', claims sociologist Robert Miles, 'is a confrontation with the history and legacy of a central strand of Western thought' (Miles, 1988). Miles has repeatedly critiqued the sociology of 'race relations' and the way in which it uses the idea of 'race' as an analytical concept, concluding: 'There are no "races" and therefore no "race relations"; there is only:

> a belief that there are such things, a belief which is used by some social groups to construct an Other (and therefore the Self) in thought as a prelude to exclusion and domination, and by other social groups to define Self (and to construct an Other) as a means of resisting that exclusion. Hence, if it is used at all, the idea of 'race' should be used only to refer descriptively to such uses of the idea of 'race'. (Miles, 2000, p.135)

Miles draws on the work of the French sociologist Colette Guillaumin (1995), who exposes the ideological character of 'naturalness' as it is applied to race to insinuate that certain kinds of social relationships are natural and therefore inevitable. Social relations described as 'racial' are:

> represented as somatically determined and therefore outside social and historical determination. Consequently, the idea of 'race' is transformed into an active subject, a biological reality which determines historical processes. This amounts to a process of reification, as a result of which that which should be explained becomes an explanation of social relations. (Miles, 2000, pp.136–137)

The idea of 'race', Miles concludes, is *essentially* ideological.

The slave regime as 'modern'

The slave regime may have been brutal but it was that very brutality that, in part, made it modern, turning the slave into the ideal exemplar of the modern industrial worker. Writes Burnard:

> To call an agricultural system based on chattel slave labour 'modern' is to employ a problematic and anachronistic term but there is no better way to describe the agro-industrial system perfected in the booming years between 1760 and 1788 in Jamaica than to say it was remarkably modern, especially in its careful if callous management of human resources. (Burnard, 2020, p.11)

From the start, claims the Trinidadian historian C.L.R. James, the slave population 'lived a life that was in essence a modern life' (cited in Burnard, 2020, p.19). Sustained by the exercise of physical violence, Jamaica became the site of a gigantic industrial experiment that was ahead of its time in creating the conditions in which humans were transformed into anonymous units of labour and everything, and everybody, was commoditised (Burnard, 2020, p.19). Planters did little to make the material conditions of slavery any lighter, and the scientific methods of slave management adopted in the 18th century to increase the plantations' efficiency made the lot of the slave still more onerous. As a result, 'slaves were highly stressed, prone to disease, and likely to die' (Burnard, 2020, p.11).

Different accounts have been proposed of how slavery is enmeshed in the fabric of modernity. Reviving a claim first advanced by Eric Williams, a historian who later became prime minister of Trinidad and Tobago, in his classic book *Capitalism and Slavery* (1944), the proponents of the New History of Capitalism movement aver that slavery has played the central role in creating modern capitalism and is its 'beating heart' (Burnard, 2020, p.217). In a complementary analysis, historian Sven Beckert, in *Empire of Cotton*, claims that slavery was the emblematic institution of 'war capitalism'. The 'true importance of Caribbean planters', Beckert argues, was not the cotton or sugar that they grew, 'but the institutional innovation that the Caribbean experiment produced', which involved 'the recreation of the countryside through bodily coercion, something only possible under war capitalism' (Beckert, 2014, p.92; Burnard, 2020, p.224).

So anguished were they by the social isolation inflicted on them, their diminished status, the separation from their ancestral lands and connections, and the harshness of the labour regimes, that many 'new negros' succumbed to depression, and sought self-destruction, either by hanging or by cutting their own throats. In a world in which the dead were considered to be an active social presence, slave masters sought to strike back, assert their right to rule and disable the constant threat of dispossession by committing spectacular punishments on the bodies of the enslaved dead, using terror to inflame the spiritual imaginations of the enslaved and deter them from self-destruction (Brown, 2003). It is also possible that electric shocks were administered to the Obeah men in Tacky's Revolt in 1760, and that the slave plantations thus witnessed the first use of electricity for the purposes of torture, lending support to the contention of Paul Gilroy in *The Black Atlantic* that slavery and terror were actually integral aspects of modernity, and not its opposite, as has commonly been supposed (Brown, 2003, pp.38, 52 n.86; Gilroy, 1993, pp.53–54).

After abolition

As historians have shown, overall abolition did not bring about anything like the degree of change in the life-situations of former slaves that had been wished for or anticipated. For instance, historian Henrice Altink (2001) has examined the dismal fortunes of apprenticed women in Jamaican workhouses in the aftermath of slavery. Here was emancipation at work. As Altink describes, before 1834 planters had regularly, and indiscriminately, resorted to the whip, solitary confinement, the stocks and a wide range of other physical punishments to prevent insubordination and extract labour. However, the 1833 Abolition Act forbade Jamaican planters to punish their former slaves. The hated Apprentice System, which had been instituted to manage the transition from slavery to free market conditions, supposedly to benefit former slaves by providing them with a measure of support and training, actually ensured that they remained snaffled in the disciplinary halters of the planters. This was certainly the case for women. As Altink (2001) describes, under this regime, female apprentices who had committed an offence were brought before a Special Magistrate who, unable to punish women by whipping and beating, commonly sentenced them to hard labour in the workhouse, sometimes for extensive periods, and frequently subjected them to the treadmill as a 'salutary form of punishment', combined with hard labour in the 'penal gang', overseen by warders recruited from the long-term convicts in the gaol that was frequently annexed to the workhouse. In exchange for sexual favours, a woman could sometimes receive a lighter workload or not have to work ('to dance') the Mill as often as the other women. But, Altink reports (2001), once in the workhouse, the apprenticed women frequently faced disciplinary practices resembling those that they would have been all-too painfully familiar with before 1834. The majority of these practices inevitably visited intense suffering on women's bodies, often leaving long-lasting marks and inflicting mental torments as well.

For several years there was strong resistance by planters on the workhouse committees, in the Jamaican House of Assembly and in the juries on the island, to the concerted attempts by the Governor, and the British Secretary of State in London, to end female flogging, which was only achieved through an Act-in-Aid issued by the British Parliament in March 1838. In the immediate aftermath of abolition, the imperial government had set strict limits on what the Jamaican House of Assembly could do, and in the archive there is a list of acts that were disallowed during this period. At the Colonial Office in London, the official who had primary responsibility for managing the turbulent transition from Jamaica as an entrenched slave society into the era of abolition and emancipation was the colourful and idiosyncratic Sir Henry Taylor (1800–1886). Much more than a colonial civil servant, he was also a man of letters, a poet and dramatist, liberal in his sympathies up to a point, but also deeply and indefatigably a man of his period in upholding the valour and necessity, especially after 1865, of benevolent white paternal, not to say despotic, rule. In 1838, at the outset of emancipation, Taylor did not mince his words, lambasting the Jamaican Assembly as a highly irresponsible body, 'at all times inaccessible to any motives connected even with justice or humanity to the negroes, let alone their advancement in civilization and qualification for civil rights' (cited in Heuman, 2018, p.142). The official position was then being loudly proclaimed that 'henceforward, the Emancipated Class must be subjected to no penalties, restrains [sic], or disabilities which did not equally affect every other class of society'.

However, notwithstanding such liberal self-proclaiming about civil rights, equality and humanity, a realignment in the official position was achieved suspiciously quickly, with sympathies now tilting back towards the planters. In the minds of the Colonial Office, the continuing success of the plantations was essential to the survival of the colony, and they resisted all efforts to re-assess their economic strategy, doing very little to aid the freed people. In Jamaica, in the meantime, the planters had become increasingly petulant and resentful, voting in the House of Assembly to strike and to refuse to carry out their duties, insisting on the need for 'retrenchment' in state spending, refusing to pay bills and drastically cutting the amount to be spent (Paton, 2018, pp.128–129; Heuman, 2018).

The Kingston Lunatic Asylum

Commenting on the apathy that the planters and their political allies displayed towards the dismal conditions in the public hospital and, above all, in the lunatic asylum, the historian of psychiatry Leonard Smith remarks that 'less than twenty-five years after the ending of slavery, the Jamaican ruling elites had not yet concluded that all shared a common humanity' (Smith, 2014, p.73). Sadly, amidst the welter of post-abolition politics, it was the planters who were now making the running by dictating the terms of an uncommonly divided humanity. Official policy would soon follow. The 'welfare' services of the plantation system, such as they were, had all disappeared and been replaced by a racialised poor-relief system, reflecting in its structures and, most of all, in its attitudes, the British Poor Law system, treating black and brown post-Emancipation welfare supplicants as feckless and lazy and the authors of their own misfortunes (Jones, 2013).

The European elite in the colony was demonstrably unwilling to fund services for the majority Afro-Caribbean population. 'All too often in the sources,' writes historian of Jamaican public health Margaret Jones, 'European medical officers, local and colonial government officials and the social elites shifted responsibility for disease and hardship onto the sufferer' (2013). Beginning in the 1790s, the public hospital in Kingston received a number of insane patients but mounting pressures on space led to the establishment of a separate, but adjacent, lunatic asylum by around 1815. Conditions here declined quite rapidly, and most likely did so as the patient population was increasingly dominated by black and brown lunatic subjects (Smith, 2014, pp.39–40; Fryar, 2016, p.715).

By the mid-1830s, the Kingston Lunatic Asylum had become a problematic institution (Smith, 2014, p.40). In 1840, Dr Edward Bancroft, physician to the public hospital and the asylum, put the case to the Assembly that the asylum was not fit for purpose and that a new one should be erected. The Assembly responded by deciding that the hospital and asylum no longer required their own physician (Smith, 2014, p.51). The sanitary arrangements, with open tubs for excretions, were a health hazard and the drains and cesspools were all wholly inadequate. A considerable number of lunatics had died of bowel complaints and, more recently, a cholera outbreak in Jamaica had decimated the asylum population. Dr Lewis Quier Bowerbank (1814–1880), a Jamaican-born physician who for many years was an ardent campaigner for reform, recorded that the asylum suffered from acute overcrowding, leading to violence. All these problems, which had been known about and ignored for years, or dealt with in a very off-hand and desultory way, were to culminate in a major and much publicised scandal, centring on the gross maltreatment and abuse of patients and resulting in an exhaustive inquiry, instigated by the imperial government but conducted in Jamaica by the Public Hospital and Lunatic Asylum Commission, chaired by Judge Alan Ker, along with two members of the Legislative Council. This convened at the Kingston Court House on 14th May 1861 and considered evidence for three months, interviewing and receiving testimonies from numerous former inmates of the asylum.

The goings-on around the public hospital and the asylum, and the voluminous body of evidence that was collected, have already been the subject of quite extensive discussions by a number of historians (Fryar, 2016; Jones, 2008; Smith, 2014, Swartz, 2010). My purpose here is quite selective. I do not intend to rehearse all the details of the mounting disquiet and subsequent scandal over the conditions at the asylum. Instead, in the chapter that follows, I shall illustrate in some depth what happened there through the testimony of a mixed-race woman who was a former patient at the asylum.

3

A testimony from the female lunatic asylum: Henrietta Dawson and her distress

'I am a single woman. I was born in Spanish Town in the year 1825.' So begins the narrative of Henrietta Dawson,[1] a mixed-race woman who was admitted to the female Lunatic Asylum in Kingston, Jamaica, on two occasions between 1858 and 1860. All the medical staff in the asylum and the adjacent public hospital were white, as were some of the hospital officers. Mrs Ryan, the matron, whom we shall shortly encounter, was most probably white creole, and all the attendants and nurses were black or mixed race, as were all the inmates, variously referred to as lunatics and patients. However, this is emphatically not the story of a wrongful admission. Henrietta was emotionally deeply distressed and agitated, to the point that her friends and family and the local physicians were unable to manage her. The asylum was their only recourse, and Henrietta and her friends approached it in a spirit of hope.

Quite unbeknownst to them, however, the Kingston asylum was in the throes of a scandal. Allegations about the maltreatment of patients were soon to attract the attention of the colonial authorities in London, resulting in a major inquiry, held in Jamaica, where Henrietta and other patients were made to testify. This is the story of how a patient, finding herself in a situation wholly at variance with anything she could have anticipated, discovered in herself a resolve that enabled her to become a witness, not only to her own suffering, but also to that of her fellow inmates. In this period, the voices of ordinary mental patients scarcely figure in the historical record, least of all those of women of colour in colonial settings. Were it not for these exceptional circumstances, the emotional travails of Henrietta Dawson would have passed quite unremarked and we would never have known of her.

---

1. See under 'The National Archives (TNA)' in Archives Consulted for details of the sources I have drawn on here.

Henrietta's father was Mr James Dawson, an attorney at law, 'who, as long as he lived, supported me'. By implication, they did not share the same household. When she was three years old, she was sent away to school, to an establishment run by a Miss Bevan, where she remained until 1840. Her mother, sister and one of her brothers were among the first to be stricken by a scarlet fever epidemic in 1841, and after her mother's death she lived first with an uncle and then, when he left Spanish Town, with her aunt, supporting herself by doing needlework. In 1848, she took a situation as a governess to a lady with three children, but by the late 1850s she was living in the home of her friend Mrs John Grant, who kept a lodging house. One night in September 1858, learning of a great fire in the town in a house that had been struck by lightning, she went out to see it. Seeing the flames and the confusion, she felt very much alarmed: 'I felt very much excited; I could not sleep at all that night.' The next morning she was drawn back to the spot:

> I felt very strange, there was an indescribable feeling about me. I did my best to conceal it, but about two weeks after, Mrs Grant noticed that there was something wrong about me, and asked me if I would like to go to the country for a change.

After three days away, she found her unpleasant sensations increasing and returned home:

> I told Mrs Grant I was sick... but I had not the power to describe my feelings... I was low spirited and could not help crying. I kept my bed for weeks, and during this time Dr Philippo continued to visit and prescribe for me.

Two months after the fire, Mrs Grant and Henrietta's brother took her by carriage to the Public Hospital in Kingston, some 10 miles away, where Mrs Grant told Dr Scott, the medical attendant (as Henrietta describes him), that she did not know what the matter was, she had done all she could, but nothing appeared to make a difference. After a few minutes, a nurse, Mary Jones, came and took Henrietta down to the adjacent Asylum:

> I was desired to sit down on the bench in the yard, with the other people, which I did. The only food I received that day was a loaf of bread, which was given to me at dinner time. At bed time I was locked up in a cell with three others, Rosa Storks, Catalina, and another whose name I forget. We each had an iron bedstead with a canvas bottom to it, but no mattresses. All my clothes but my chemise were taken from me before

being locked up. Each of us had a pillow and a coarse sheet, both of which were marked in large letters PUBLIC HOSPITAL, with the letters F.L.A., meaning Female Lunatic Asylum, underneath. The next morning we were taken out of the cell and ordered to dress ourselves, and to sit down on the bench in the yard. At breakfast time, 9-o-clock, I got coffee and bread which I refused. Mrs Ryan insisted I should drink it, I would not as I did not want it, I do not like coffee. As soon as the people had finished their breakfast, they were ordered to bathe. When my time came, Mrs Ryan ordered Mary Jones to call the washerwomen to assist her and directed her to 'tank me well'. This they certainly did and they continued to do so for several mornings in succession.

'Tanking them well'

As Henrietta quickly learned, the administration of punishment in the institution centred on the 'tank', a cistern of brick and plaster about 7 foot long, 4 foot wide and 2½ foot deep, enclosed within a wooden screen, with a gutter leading to it by which it was filled, and at the bottom of it a plug, by which the water was let out.

In what follows I have, at points, interspersed Henrietta's own account of these procedures with others drawn from the collective account of a number of inmates in the report of the Commission of Inquiry.

Each morning the tank was filled with water, and as soon as the patients had swallowed their coffee and bread, the bathing and tanking commenced. Every inmate had to pass through the water, regardless of their health:

> The very feverish, nay the dying, are sometimes taken out of their bed
> and taken to the tank room. The usual average number of inmates may be
> from sixty to seventy – all must bathe each day in the same water.

As Henrietta discovered, the words 'bathing' and 'tanking' did not mean the same thing. Some of the patients were 'bathed', others were 'tanked':

> By bathing is understood the going into the tank or bath, one or more
> together, and then and there being allowed to wash one's self, or being
> washed, and even dipped by a nurse or attendant. By 'tanking' a very
> different thing is meant from bathing. When tanking is practised, it is
> intended as a punishment, and there is no doubt that it is a very severe
> and very cruel one – quite calculated to destroy life and, if it fails to do
> so directly, is sure, with other abuses and cruelties practised, to impair
> health – to aggravate existing disease of mind or body, or to induce

diseases endemic to the place, and which sap the strength and terminate usually in death.

Many may not have witnessed it themselves but few, if any, can say they have not heard of it, or that they have not seen the male and female labourers or assistants with their clothes wet, and who have not graphically described the part they acted. That when a person (a female) is to be tanked, a cry is raised 'Tank her! Tank her!' She is forthwith seized by nurses, labourers and fellow lunatics… She is then dragged or pulled along to the tank; she is stripped or not, as the case may be. This process of stripping is often effected in the open yard in the view of all. The cry of 'Tank! Tank!' strikes terror into the hearts of the Lunatics… in dragging the person over the brick yard, their persons are frequently shamefully exposed to the view of male labourers and others, and their bodies are often lacerated and contused.

To exacerbate the fear and apprehension in the minds of the inmates, the threat of tanking is often made the day before: 'You shall be well tanked tomorrow… I will see it done!'

When brought to the tank the person is seized, the hands and legs separated and extended, the head is taken hold of by one person, who, if there is any hair upon it, twists it round her hand. The person is then plunged under the water and kept submerged – two or three attendants having tucked up their clothes and got into the water, one sits or kneels upon the chest or back, another seizes the throat and grasps it, in order to make the sufferer swallow the water. This process is continued alternately, sinking and swaying the body up and down the bath, in doing so the person in charge of the head often strikes it against the sides of the bath till blood flows.

Thus the unfortunate is kept under till all resistance ceases, or till in some cases convulsions have occurred, or life itself has gone, according to the caprices of the matron, or sometimes of her assistants… I have repeatedly seen the matron, Mrs Ryan, standing by, crying out with apparent delight, 'Give it her well!' The punishment over, the poor creature is taken out, exhausted and barely sensible, and is thrown down on the bricks, her clothes forced upon her, and she is then carried and laid upon a bench where often she retches, and strains, until the nauseous draught of filthy water is ejected from her stomach.

Sunday was the great tanking day with Mrs Ryan, as on that day the water is most offensive from the use of soap… and usually presents a most horrible appearance – stinking, dirty, worked up into a many-coloured foam of soap suds and filth, feculent matter, urine, vomit, blood, menstrual fluid, and the secretions of sores and ulcers. That when the person is thought to be insensible, or is apparently dead, or convulsed, she is taken out, hauled over the rough edge of the tank and thrown down on the stone pavement: her clothes, if off, are then forced on her – if not, wet and dripping she is taken out, or if able to stand is pushed out to the bench or on the brick pavement of the piazza in the sun. That generally persons so tanked are made very sick and vomit. They often get bowel complaints after it. That in pulling females to the tank, nurses or attendants have been seen to grasp them by the hair of the head, as also of the genitals and thus drag them along. That from the horror the people have of the tank, they often fight as for their lives, great violence is used on both sides, kicks, blows, bites are given. That women tanked while 'unwell' have had their health seriously deranged and injured for months afterwards. That male labourers are at times called upon to carry naked females to the tank, and even to tank them. That on such occasions gross indecencies have been practised, and male labourers have made use of 'slang' to describe the accursed abuse, such as 'Bushy Park', a term well known to some, at least, of the hospital authorities and having allusion to the exposure of the female organs of generation.

'Every feeling of decency is outraged'

Besides the bathing and tanking, Henrietta Dawson continues:

The outrageous, or rather those who from any cause have provoked the anger of the matron or her assistants, have sometimes pails or tubs of water dashed upon them, their clothes being on or off as may be, or being held backwards with the face fixed upwards, the water is poured upon the face – this being repeated over and over again. When a person has been too weak to be tanked, or there has not been water sufficient for the purpose, or where the person has been very dirty from the effects of bowel complaint, I have frequently seen the attendants, and some of the lunatics, take the broom with which the yard is swept, and rub, and wipe, the bodies of other lunatics and their faces. I saw this done to Elsie James.

The water for drinking purposes is supplied in two pails, which are placed in the yard, with one old tin pan to drink out of, this serves all, sick and well. At night, those in the cells get water from the night nurse, and it is given to them by means of a tin vessel with a long spout, which is thrust through the iron railing of the window… There are no means whatever provided for washing, there is no place to wash one's hand and face, and if water was brought for any such purpose, it was put into one of the tubs used in the cells at night as a receptacle for filth. On asking for a little water to wash with, on being locked up at night, I have heard the request met on more than one occasion by indecent and disgusting remarks. Females at particular periods are not allowed to use the usual means, the consequence is that, besides what I have already mentioned as occurring in the cells, every feeling of decency is outraged during the day, the clothes of the unfortunate people being dirtied, and the very benches in the yard stained and bedaubed… If, on any occasion, the usual guard was used, and it was discovered, it was immediately taken away.

Becoming a witness

'I saw and heard much,' Henrietta says of her first stay in the asylum, 'but, in the state I was, I paid but little attention to it, I was wrapt up in myself, my own feelings engaged my attention.' For the whole time that she was there she refused her food, 'eating nothing but a little bread and water and that but seldom', and as consequence she became 'very weak and low'. Learning of her condition, Mrs Grant took her back home, but here, 'instead of improving, I felt I was getting worse. I felt more unhappy and more sad, I was quite sensible of doing out of the way things. I would destroy my clothes and try to escape from the house'. During these weeks also, she lost the power of speaking. On 2nd August, the physician came to see her, and after tearing her clothes in front of him, she heard him tell Mrs Grant that she should be removed again to the asylum.

Reaching the asylum the following day:

> as we went in we met Mrs Ryan on the step – she laughed and said, 'Ah! You are come in again! Nice lady, you are dressed to come to a madhouse as if you were going to a ballroom!', on which she struck me with her umbrella. On her doing so, unable to express my feelings in words, I took up my dress and tore it before her… From this day, my persecutions began at the hands of Mrs Ryan.

When Henrietta refused to eat her food at dinner time the following week, Mrs Ryan came up and kicked her. 'I turned round, and looked at her disdainfully (I could not speak), she exclaimed that I was insolent and called Alex [a male labourer] to bring a pail full of water.' Henrietta was then held down on the piazza while Mrs Ryan poured the water over her, and ordered her to go and take her dinner. This she did, only to throw it away. As her clothes were wet through, she took them off and sat down naked on the bench. Mrs Ryan ordered her to put them back on:

I would not, and she then said, 'In the morning you shall be well tanked for your insolence!' After some time, she gave me dry clothes which I put on. From this time, I felt my feelings wounded, and I watched Mrs Ryan and her proceedings, I took an interest in doing so.

This moment marked a definite change in Henrietta. From being wrapped up in her own feelings, not paying much attention to what was going on around her, she now became a determined observer and witness to the goings-on at the asylum. In November she recovered her speech:

I did this suddenly, when being greatly abused by Mrs Ryan, and, in a fit of passion and anger… I spoke out. Mrs Ryan said, 'Oh you have found your tongue today, eh! I will give it you well today for your rudeness!' She then took me to the tank. My clothes were taken off, and I was ordered to get into the water. I would not, and turning round to Mrs Ryan I said, 'Mrs Ryan let me ask you one question.' She said, 'What is that?' I said, 'Suppose anything hurt your feelings, Mrs Ryan, are you not at liberty to speak, to relieve your mind? If God almighty gives you power to speak, must you not speak?' She said 'Yes,' and then told me to put on my clothes, but that the next time I did anything saucy, she would give it to me well.

Dr Scott's visits

Dr Scott usually paid a visit each morning.

When the doctor was expected things were always put to rights. An injured or dirty person would be shut up , in a cell or the privy. As soon as the doctor entered, Mrs Ryan or a nurse would always be near him to prevent any person from speaking to him. If any one went to speak to the doctor, he often appeared to avoid conversing with them; he evidently did not like complaints. On any one complaining to him, he would immediately call out, 'Where was Mrs Ryan?' Generally, however, Mrs Ryan or a nurse would be always near him to prevent any person from speaking to him. She would be sure to interfere, and tell him the poor thing has her madness strong upon her, that she won't bathe herself. If the person has any marks of violence about her, this is always satisfactorily accounted for: she did it herself or struck herself accidentally as she resisted the nurse, or that another lunatic had done it. These statements are all backed by the other nurses and even some of the patients are put up to it – the whole thing is arranged beforehand. On Dr Scott, or any official, asking Mrs Ryan the cause of so and so being bruised or wounded, she will, in the most open and candid manner, call up Frances Bogle, or any other nurse, who will in an off-hand way tell the story of how it happened and all about it. Should the patient insist upon being heard, Mrs Ryan persuades the doctor that she is mad, and takes him away to another part of the yard and changes the subject of conversation. The doctor is not difficult to be convinced.

Those who died

At an earlier point, Henrietta mentions that her attention was particularly drawn to the circumstances of a woman of the name of Elizabeth Green:

> a stout black woman from Manchester, in central Jamaica, who was constantly kept locked up in a cell on the female side during the day, and at night was removed to the male side of the asylum, and was daily brought out of her cell to the tank by Alexander Fleming and male labourer John Hall, assisted by nurse Mary Jones. She was mostly naked, sometimes in carrying her they would throw a cloth over her, the same persons would tank her and hold her under the water.

She described how she heard Elizabeth Green tell Dr Scott that she had a 'pickney' (a child, in West Indian English) in her belly, and that Omnibus (Fleming's nickname) was the father. She used to ask for pieces of cloth, and would take anything she could get, to make into baby clothes and bibs. Dr Scott used to laugh and say she was dropsical.

> On the 26 November, while in the privy, she was confined of a girl child on the floor. After her confinement, she was taken and put into one of the cells, but the child died about four days after. The next day, she was taken to the sick room where she died, I think, on the 13th December, being thirteen days after her confinement.

This was not the only death witnessed by Henrietta:

> From 5th August 1859 to the day of my quitting the asylum in June 1860 I reckon that nineteen women died there and that two others were taken out in a dying state, and I declare that almost the whole of these cases were neglected at their commencement, and that the death of most of them was hastened, if not caused, by the treatment they received.

Henrietta then listed those she recollected to have died – 'I may in some cases be wrong as to the dates, or I may have omitted one or two cases, but I speak from memory' – among them Matilda Carey and Harriett Jarratt.

Matilda Carey, a black woman from Saint Thomas in the Vale, who was apparently in good health when she was brought in, was tanked one day by Frances Bogle, Antoinette Parola and Nancy Lloyd:

> They dragged her to the tank, they pulled and pushed her to the tank. I stood near and I heard a struggling in the water; and I heard Parola say, 'Lord! Lord! Lord! Let her blow!' Bogle said, 'Give the woman water!' I said out loud, intending it to be heard inside, 'The woman was sent here to be cured and not to be killed!' Antoinette Parola said a second time, 'Lord, let the woman blow, she will die!' A short time after, Parola came out; she saw me standing by, and I said to her: 'I hear all about it!' She said, 'Ah my child, I was frightened until I pissed myself!' When Mrs Carey came out, she was low and weak. Over and over again, I have said to Antoinette Parola that Mrs Carey would never go home after this last tanking.

Harriett Jarratt (sometimes called Gordon, more commonly Port Royal, or the Port Royal woman) came into the asylum as a patient in about March or April of 1860:

> She was a native of Sierra Leone – at least so I understand. When she came in, she appeared in good health. She was a black woman , but of a yellow complexion. She was good looking and clean skinned. She was troublesome, and she would not sit down on the bench, but would keep jumping up and about, saying she would go to Port Royal, and she was abusive to the nurses, or anyone who interfered with her… When she resisted they would beat her with broom sticks. I have seen them tank her till she was half dead… I have seen Mrs Ryan beat her with her fist, her umbrella, and a stave. I have seen her do so frequently, because she would not sit quiet and Harriett said: 'You beat me as if you were beating your old n****r!' This was about two or three weeks before her death.

Another day:

> when Jarratt was in the tank, I heard the splashing of the water and I heard Frances Bogle say, 'The old devil has fits'. As soon as the nurses came out, I went in and saw Harriett, who was then undressed, lying against the side of the tank; she seemed quite exhausted.
>
> Harriett was ill; she had bowel complaint and was very offensive; she remained in her cell up to a week before she died, when she was taken to

the sick room. The cell she was in at night had some ten or twelve persons in it. Two days before she was taken out of the cell, a rug and pillow were allowed her; before this, she was generally laid on the stone pavement or flags.

'That we may ascertain the real state of the lunatic'

Many persons were 'very cruelly treated both by Mrs Ryan and the nurses,' Henrietta reported, among them Ann Pratt, a woman from Lucea, who came in on 14 January 1860:

> Though there was nothing remarkable about her when she first came in, a few days after she became excited and violent. She cried and said she wanted to go home, that she was not mad. She slept in the same cell as myself and one night she was excited, she got on my bed and pulled my hair; for this she was taken over to the male side of the asylum, she remained there for several nights. On another occasion she was removed to a cell containing some ten or twelve persons, where she was badly treated by Bogle. She used to be tanked and beaten shamefully, and often made complaints to the doctors, and to Mr Hall and Mrs Ryan, but she was not listened to. From the treatment she received, I never thought she would live to get out of it. After she came out, she got a book published called, 'Seven Month in the Kingston Lunatic Asylum and What I saw There'. I have read this book and what Miss Pratt states is correct [Pratt, 1860; Fryar, 2018]. There are a number of others I might mention who were treated more like brutes than human beings but I am afraid of taking up too much time and space.

In November of that year, Henrietta reports: 'I felt a change come over me, I felt myself getting better. In December I told Dr Scott I was better and wished to go home and he said I was quite better and fit to go out.' However, it took several months to secure her discharge:

> The Sunday before I came out, Mrs Ryan was annoyed with me in consequence of something. I got very angry and behaved very rudely. She asked me if I was getting mad again. I said, 'yes, as long as I am in the madhouse, I will be a mad woman!' My friend came for me on Wednesday morning 27th June. No doctor examined me at all, as to my state, when I was going out, none saw me. I then thanked God and left the asylum. Such is a short and general statement of what I underwent, and saw others suffer, during my residence in the Lunatic Asylum.

Henrietta's lengthy statement before the inquiry in the Kingston Court House, in what Leonard Smith (2014) has characterised as a pivotal episode in the history of imperial psychiatric provision in the 19th century, must have absorbed the best part of a day. It is an index of her determination to share her experience and to serve as witness, since she feared that otherwise, as she put it, 'the real state of the Lunatic will never be ascertained. The truth of every word of it I am ready to swear to, and am prepared to prove' (Smith, 2014, p.72).

4

In the bowels of colonial modernity

The horrendous and scarcely imaginable state of affairs at the Kingston Lunatic Asylum is only intelligible against the background and events of the *Zong* case, its traumatic significance, the galvanising role it played in the movement for Abolition, and the subsequent reaction against it among the plantocracy in Jamaica. Scandals have, of course, occurred, quite routinely it sometimes appears, in lunatic asylums in other times and places, and I do not mean to diminish the moral significance of these other past happenings and disgraces. But the situation at Kingston Lunatic Asylum perhaps possesses something in excess of these that derives from the brutal history of what had taken place in Jamaica over the previous three centuries or so, combined with the repercussions of the profound and very specific tragedy of the *Zong* affair, impacting upon and becoming absorbed into Jamaican history and memory.[1]

The story of the *Zong*, it has been suggested, starting with Granville Sharp's records, has come to stand in place of the absence of first-hand accounts of the Middle Passage in abolitionist and anti-slavery narratives. As cultural historian Tim Armstrong notes:

> Sharp's records mark the beginning of a chain of memory which has secreted within it an unacknowledged freight; in which a single instance acts as the vehicle of a multiple horror. The ship is overloaded, as it were; it carries symbolic matter below the waterline in the form of legions of victims of slavery. (Armstrong, 2007, p.347)

---

1. For a copious and thought-provoking discussion of late 20th century mental hospital scandals over the care of older people in Britain, complementary in certain respects to the situation in 19th century Jamaica, see Hilton (2017).

This is helpful when thinking about Kingston Lunatic Asylum, which is a hugely over-determined site on which something is being acted out and performed. As Armstrong reminds us, 'any notion of history as trauma suggests that it visits us as "unfinished business".' In reprisal for the history of slave resistance and rebellion, and for the refusal of slaves to 'civilize' and comply, the inmates in the Kingston Asylum are being thrust back into the past, made to endure over and again the Middle Passage, and forced to experience the brutal life of a slave, from which they can either be redeemed by becoming 'rational, docile and productive' and attaining a status as fungible commodities in the market place, or be pushed under and treated as jettison. What does it stand for, this vessel, the *Zong*, in which the captives were stripped of all specificity, even including their names (Philip, 2008, p.194)?

The Kingston Lunatic Asylum re-enacts in its history, in its decline and degradation as a therapeutic institution, the transformation of the *Zorg* into the *Zong*. What starts, notionally, as a therapeutic environment, or an environment of care, has as a result of a multiplicity of influences been transformed into something else, to the point that one cannot say exactly what kind of institution it is, for it has been made 'strange' or uncanny. *Zong* represents an absence of care – or rather, it is the monster that is left after *Zorg* (care) has been abjected. In the same way that the sick Africans, or the 'sick cargo', were thrust overboard as worthless on the *Zong*, so in the Kingston Asylum the mental patients are treated as a 'sick cargo' in the business of life, punished for being sick and for being failed commodities.

There is an 'archive' of traumatic memory here that, for the most part, is not realisable and can only be gestured at. This is an awesome burden to carry. Hence it is not, for the most part, amenable to 'working-through' in a conventional sense and, more likely, will manifest in a disturbing and distressing, or haunted, present (Armstrong, 2007, p.355). The Kingston Asylum voyages under the sign of the *Zong*: here is an institution in which care has been all but expunged and eliminated. The story of the racialised origins, and passage, of psychiatry through modernity can, of course, be told in a number of ways, but the telling that can, perhaps, lay the most credible claim to historical truth is one that envisions psychiatry as a *Zong*-type vessel, with an uncertain, or equivocal, relation to *Zorg*, or care, that is forever haunted by residues and fragmented memories of passengers who have disappeared into the psychiatric equivalent of the slave hold – forever a *Zorg*-in-question, one might say.

The initiation of the mad subjects at the Kingston Lunatic asylum through the subjugation, spectacle and terror of 'tanking' is, in many respects, comparable with scenes of torture in the literature of slavery: notably the 'terrible spectacle' of the beating of his Aunt Hester that Frederick Douglass recounts in the first chapter of his 1845 *Narrative of the Life of Frederick Douglass,* which, as Saidiya Hartman discerns, 'establishes the centrality of violence to the making of the slave', identifying it as an 'original generative act equivalent to the statement "I was born"' (Hartman, 1997, p.3). The predicament of the mad subject at the Kingston Lunatic Asylum is, in this respect, on a par with that of the slave since, for both the enslaved and the mad subject, the 'passage through the blood-stained gate' is an inaugural moment that dramatises the origin of the subject and demonstrates that to be a slave, or a mental patient, under these circumstances, is to be under the brutal power and authority of another.

What was emancipation?

What did emancipation actually amount to? Achille Mbembe captures some of the doubts that were circulating around this time:

> Can Blacks govern themselves? Are they human beings like all others?
> Can one find among them the same humanity or do they exhibit a radical difference, a form of 'being-apart'? (Mbembe, 2017, p.86)

Following abolition, difference was relativised somewhat, but it continued to justify relationships of inequality and the colonial right to command. The roots of contemporary scruples over the credibility of mad people, and the status of the mad, are to be discovered here in this confrontation between reason and race. Confronted with racial sciences, which attempted to prove that black people were inferior, the African diaspora experienced the direct, and awful, application of 'rational' scientific inquiry when detached from ethics, as was the case with the *Zong,* where the presiding power elided the *Zorg,* or care.

As Paul Gilroy underscores, and as the state of affairs at the Kingston Lunatic Asylum makes all too evident, there is an 'obvious complicity, which both plantation slavery and colonial regimes revealed, between rationality and the practice of racial terror', leading the voices of the Black Atlantic (and other racially subordinated peoples) to ask whether 'excessive barbarity' has always been a condition of 'rational Western progress' (Gilroy, 1993, p.39). The brutal excesses of the slave plantation produced in their wake moral and political responses that tilted towards an idea of an innocent modernity 'purged of any traces of the people without history whose degraded lives might raise awkward questions about the limits of bourgeois humanism' (Gilroy, 1993, p.44).

In dismantling such conceits, Gilroy means to question the credibility of such a tidy or holistic conception of modernity, and to propose a reassessment of the relationship between modernity and slavery in which slavery becomes, in a sense, the premise of modernity. In doing so, he means to reconstruct the primal history of modernity from the slaves' point of view, and to undertake an 'archaeology of the icons of the blacks' that are signs of irrational disorder 'in a dualistic system that reproduces the dominance of bonded whiteness, masculinity and rationality', in which blacks inevitably enjoy a subordinate position (Gilroy, 1993, pp.45–46).

Ultimately, writes Saidiya Hartman, 'I am trying to grapple with the… non-event of emancipation, insinuated by the perpetuation of the plantation system and the re-figuration of subjection' (Hartman, 1997, p.116). At issue here are shifting and transformed relations of power in which subjection is not so much rejected, or abolished, as re-figured, resulting in:

> the re-subordination of the emancipated, the control and domination of the free black population, and the persistent production of blackness as abject, threatening, servile, dangerous, dependent, irrational and infectious. (Hartman, 1997, p.116)

The issue after emancipation was not simply about whether the blacks could be made to work but rather:

> whether they could be transformed into a rational, docile, and productive working class – that is, fully normalized in accordance with standards of productivity, sobriety, rationality, prudence, cleanliness, responsibility and so on. (p.127)

However, the nascent individualism of emancipation was in actuality a 'burdened individuality', for the burden of obligation was put on the blameworthy and isolated freed individual, who was at one and the same time emancipated and subordinated, self-possessed and indebted, equal and inferior, liberated and encumbered (Hartman, 1997, p.117). Moreover, any vestiges or indications of the enduring legacy of slavery that might surface were addressed almost exclusively as problems of conduct and character (p.133).

In the liberal scheme of things, freedom and slavery actually presuppose one another and are bonded together, in as much as slavery is the constitutive outside of freedom. As historian Catherine Hall helpfully explains, 'identities are constructed within power relations and that which is external to an identity, the "outside", marks the absence or lack which is constitutive of its presence' (Hall, 2002, p.9). Identity 'depends on the outside, on the marking both of its positive presence and content and of its negative and excluded parts'. So in 19th century metropolitan discourse, for instance, the supposed 'excitability' of the African, signalling an incapacity for self-restraint or self-government, was counterpoised to the Englishman's rationality, and the African's 'indolence' was contrasted with the Englishman's capacity for hard work (Hall, 2002, p.9). The genealogy of freedom discloses a promiscuous intimacy between liberty, domination and subjection that reveals how the 'the bounded bodily integrity of whiteness' is 'actually secured by the abjection of others' (Hartman 1997, p.123). As for the much-extolled precepts of liberal universalism, this is really no universalism at all, for this is far too flimsy a notion to embrace the vast disparities between bodies that throw into sharp and dismal relief what Hartman terms the 'castigated particularity of the universal' – in other words, the particularities, and above all the differences and inequalities, between human lives that call into question, and ultimately give the lie to, these liberal doctrines and ideals.

The question of what emancipation amounted to, and the status of the emancipated, is hugely germane to the moment in which the 'crisis' of the Kingston Lunatic Asylum erupted, which was expressive of a wider crisis in Jamaican society in the aftermath of slavery that forms a constant reference point in the events that took place in, and around, the asylum. Put very succinctly, we can say that the inmates of the asylum were being punished for both the audacity and the 'failures' of emancipation. During the time of slavery, slaveholders were largely indifferent to the pain they caused to the enslaved. Although abolition brought with it a dramatic change in sensibility, forcing slaveholders to confront the question of how civilized people could be so careless of the terrible suffering they caused fellow human beings, we can read the regime at Kingston Lunatic Asylum as a bullish assertion of business as usual in this respect, and as aggressively repudiating any concessions from the planter class to their habitual norms and reflexes (Burnard, 2004, p.136). Since the end of the 18th century, Jamaica's privileged position in the empire had gradually weakened, and the West Indian planter as a social type had increasingly been denigrated by missionaries, abolitionists and humanitarians (Burnard, 2004, p.242). As a result, by the middle of the following century, the planters were a bruised and embittered class, disinclined to take hostages and prone to lash out at any suggestions of slight or challenges to their standing as the rightful upholders of racial supremacy.

The traumas of colonial modernity

As Trevor Burnard and other scholars have shown, the reach and impact of slavery were manifold, bringing with them enormous prosperity that touched the lives of most Britons and Americans in the 18th century in innumerable ways. Yet all this political influence and economic power was forged out of trauma, for 'the period when white Jamaicans most prospered was when black Jamaicans endured especially miserable lives in a particularly vicious and all-encompassing slave system' (Burnard, 2020, p.11). Burnard endorses the classic portrayal of Jamaica by the distinguished scholar of slavery Orlando Patterson (1990) as a Hobbesian society where planters sought to dehumanise slaves and obliterate their personal histories, inflicting a 'reign of terror' on them and reducing them to a condition of 'social death' (p.13).

Historian Vincent Brown also portrays enslaved people as cowed and psychologically terrified by instruments of 'spiritual terror' invented and deployed by white slave owners, though at the same time he cautions against 'pathologizing slaves by allowing the condition of social death to stand for the experience of life in slavery', suggesting that 'it might be more helpful to focus on what the enslaved actually made of their situation', and to identify and explore forms of protest or resistance (Brown, 2009, p.1236). Both these dimensions are actually hugely relevant to a consideration of the human experience at the Kingston Lunatic Asylum in the late 1850s, but we should recall as well, lest we shed any crocodile tears over these maltreated mental patients, that for two centuries the prosperity of Britons at all levels of society had depended on the continuing misery of Jamaican slaves in conditions not unlike, and frequently worse, than these.

In her widely-acclaimed study *The Intimacies of Four Continents*, Lisa Lowe (2015b) introduces a number of narratives and examples to illustrate what she terms the mutual entailments of, variously, freedom and subjugation, privilege and degradation, and possession and expropriation. We can quickly recognise how Kingston Lunatic Asylum, through its institutional dispositions and routines, enacts just these kinds of mutual entailments. The maintenance of our 'comfort stations' at the imperial centre requires that we also maintain all these deprived people shitting at the periphery. And we would err to suppose that this is merely the by-product of an aberration, or deformity, in a local welfare culture somewhere in the colonial hinterlands. Quite the contrary: it signifies loudly and widely across a plethora of imperial spaces. This is, in actuality, the engine room of colonial modernity into which, by force of circumstance, we have been granted a privileged insight. What is notably at stake here is how liberal regimes constitute the 'human', for, as Lisa Lowe writes:

> It is the pronounced asymmetry of the colonial division of humanity that is the signature feature of liberal modes of distinction that privilege particular subjects and societies as rational, civilized and human, and treat others as the labouring, replaceable or disposable contexts that constitute that humanity. (Lowe, 2015b, p.16).

The engine room of colonial modernity

'What is the state?' asks Diana Paton in a consideration of its formation in Victorian Jamaica (2018). She proposes in answer that the state does not exist and that we should investigate, instead, the 'state idea' and 'state systems'. Thus in Jamaica, 'the state, was formed through everyday encounters' in 'reformatories and prisons, in dispensaries and on the streets', where its 'claim to authority required the imaginings of networks of power projected across large blocks of space and backed up by the regular use of violence' (Paton, 2018, p.127). In the Kingston Lunatic Asylum, we are vouchsafed just such a vantage point. We are in the engine room, permitted – dare one add, privileged? – to experience it at work and see the powerlessness of those who find themselves in its maws. What is this 'state'? Henrietta Dawson wonders how to ascertain 'the real state of the Lunatic' in a marvellous turn of phrase, rich in ambiguity, in which she is surely reaching beyond nosology to hint at a concern with the lunatic state, or condition, of the imperial polity.

What we discover is reminiscent of the tradition of grotesque realism associated with the satirical creations of the Renaissance physician and writer Francois Rabelais, in works such as *Gargantua* and *Pantagruel*. Here, as the Russian literary critic Mikhail Bakhtin highlights in his critical study of Rabelais' work (Bakhtin, 1965/1984), the essential principle of grotesque realism is, above all, the degradation associated with defecation, or sometimes also with an aggressive, predatory sexuality and the deflation or lowering of all humanistic ideals, and of anything that is abstract or spiritual, to an organic level of basic bodily functions. In such a place, activities such as reading or writing and the possession or use of instruments of writing, or of personal hygiene, or indeed of paper for any purpose, whether for writing or even, and far more basically, personal hygiene, or of pieces of cloth that might do as sanitary towels, along with all expressions of private or personal sensibility and dignity, are all expressly prohibited, derided and punished.

Succinctly stated, the vantage point from which we are being permitted to experience the workings of the state in this mode is, incontrovertibly, that of the state's arsehole, or the state as an arsehole, considered diversely as an indifferent, hostile or punitive outlook or frame of mind, as a physical organism, and as an institutional order for the political regulation and chastisement of detractors, or violators, from the official norms of the collective body. Envisaged and performed in this way, the 'state' is a latrine of a kind in which the boundaries that are normally maintained between different kinds of human spaces and activities, such as the 'clean' and the 'dirty', or the individual and the collective body, are all the time being sluiced, breached and tested. Tread a step or two beyond the porter's lodge at the entrance to the public hospital, and we enter abruptly, as Henrietta Dawson discovers when she is admitted, into a different world, baffling and disconcerting, like a dreamscape, as in the novel *The Unconsoled* by the contemporary British writer Kazuo Ishiguro (1995) – one that today we might be inclined to call surreal. At the same time, we should observe that the constraints of the collective body did sometimes provide scope for individual initiative and protest – so, for instance, Henrietta Dawson felt emboldened to play the 'mad woman', and to strip off and sit naked on the bench, as the situation seemed to allow.

5

The 'beneficent despotism' of racial liberalism

The limitations of liberal imperial thought and ideology

Thomas Laqueur has described the emergence and exercise of humanity as an ethical 'sentiment', a process linked to a conjoining of the human and the humane brought on by a newly felt obligation to treat fellow humans as connected in an enlarging circle of moral inclusion (Laqueur, 1989). The nascent humanitarian sensibility of the late 18th and early 19th centuries was incubated through diffuse narratives testifying to a preoccupation with the suffering of individual bodies – slaves above all, but also the abused, sick, exploited and neglected in early industrial Britain itself. However, for all its resonance and power, there was a distinct limitation to such humanitarian enthusiasm or attention; it did not, for the most part, open or expand opportunities for the marginalised to discover their own voices, viewing them as moral objects rather than as potential political subjects. And here, once again, we are brought face to face with the tensions, contradictions, paradoxes and hypocrisies in liberal imperial thought and ideology: on the one hand, reaching out a hand to extend the circle of moral inclusion, opening a door to welcome newcomers; on the other, quickly withdrawing it through the application and assertion of tough-minded and frequently unattainable, or unsustainable, criteria of admission and inclusion.

As Anne O'Connell has shown, the figure of the pauper was inextricably linked with those of the slave, the ex-slave and the Aboriginal, all of whom were considered fit subjects to be tutored and readied to participate in conduct befitting the new economy (O'Connell, 2009). The New Poor Law of 1834 and the movement for the total abolition of colonial slavery deeply influenced one another, meriting closer consideration and comparison, even though generally they have mostly been treated separately, with their own specialised literatures. Social scientists, Christian evangelicals, political economists and others attempted to document the daily lives of the slave and pauper populations, and to measure their ability to become improving economic subjects. Depicted as anti-social and degenerate, and as insinuating themselves into the natural order of political economy, paupers were not considered to be rational subjects or granted fully human status, and were, instead, viewed as a separate, contaminated and contaminating race (O'Connell, 2009, p.181).

Though the abolition of slavery has been projected as a triumph of British justice and morality since the early decades of the 19th century, in actuality the British nation was deeply implicated in, and violently supportive of, colonial slavery, as historian Michael Taylor has recently shown in a riveting account of the West India Interest (Taylor, 2020, pp.xiii, xvii). Few interests in this period were as wealthy and powerful as the West India Interest, which sought to protect and promote the British Caribbean. As Taylor observes, it 'did not simply have connections to the British establishment; it was the British establishment' (p.xvi). It was not just a handful of planters and merchants; it involved hundreds of MPs, peers, civil servants, businessmen, financiers, landowners, clergymen, intellectuals, journalists, publishers, soldiers, sailors and judges, and all of them went to extreme lengths to preserve and protect colonial slavery (Taylor, 2020, p.311).

Perhaps the most reactionary of Britain's major periodicals, *Blackwood's Magazine* was a declared ally of the Interest, and from 1823 onwards became a bastion of the pro-slavery resistance. Indeed, in most of Britain's major press and publications slavery was favoured over emancipation (Taylor, 2020, pp.59–60). Images were purveyed of contented slaves and of an idealised landscape in which slave houses were dotted about like cottages in the English countryside (pp.39–41). The plantation was represented as a 'nursery for [Africans] in their youth, and an asylum in [old] age', where the elderly were allegedly treated with reverence as a 'reward' for years of service (p.41). In reality, concludes Taylor, the liberated slaves of the West Indies 'were subjected to four years of apprenticeship, which was slavery in all but name, and then to the same violence, inequality and rapacity that blighted the lives of the hundreds of millions of other victims of the British Empire' (p.311). The Foreign Secretary, George Canning (1770–1827) proved deeply duplicitous. Nominally wholly supportive of emancipation, in actuality he was all the time intent on introducing restrictive caveats that created impossible obstacles to emancipatory aspirations. As Taylor describes, 'he consistently rubbished abolitionist attacks on the government and discussed slavery in the language of racial contempt'; 'I send you', he wrote to the Colonial Office, 'a plan for ameliorating n****rs' (Taylor, 2020, p.64).

As a visible public form and modality of power, the commission of inquiry increasingly came into prominence in this period, through Royal Commissions, parliamentary investigations and other official reviews, helping to entrench white bourgeois power through such forms of scrutiny and the reform of designated populations (O'Connell, 2009). In the 19th century, developmental thinking was integral to imperialism, taking the form of a hierarchical ordering of races and cultures along developmental gradients stretching from savagery to civilization and barbarity to modernity. For Social Darwinists, relations of domination between human groups reflected, and were warranted by, different stages of human evolution (McCarthy, 2009, pp.1–3). By the end of the 19th century, argues the philosopher Ladelle McWhorter (2005), race had been utterly transformed from a morphological to a developmental category, excavating most of its meaning from developmental discourses, accompanied by the vigorous confirmation of whiteness as the norm of health and functioning, and attesting to a recognition of 'race' as a special kind of abnormality requiring careful monitoring and management (McWhorter, 2005, p.543, Lorimer, 2013).

The 'rule of colonial difference'

All this was to culminate, declares Stoler, in an outlook in which race became the 'organising grammar of an imperial order in which modernity, the civilising mission, and the "measure of man" were framed' (1995, p.27). By 1914, argues Thomas McCarthy in a startling observation, three-quarters of the globe was governed by colonial relations (McCarthy 2009, p.3). Still today, many of the theories and concepts of the mental health sciences continue to reflect a Eurocentric epistemological structure of human understanding and human existence in which Eurocentrism is naturalised as common sense and as scientised variants of an 18th century colonial moral language (Shohat & Stam, 2014; Stam, 2001). The 'rule of colonial difference', contends political theorist Partha Chatterjee, positions backward or colonized subjects as different from, inferior to, and temporally behind civilized modern Europeans (Chatterjee, 1994). For instance, British officials in the 19th and early 20th centuries were sometimes inclined to describe travel across the geographical space of empire as a journey backwards in time (see also McClintock, 2001).

In a speech in the House of Commons in 1833, historian Thomas Babington Macaulay had argued for benevolent despotism as the most appropriate form of rule for a backward society in need of civilisation, approvingly describing the Government of India as taking the form of 'an enlightened and paternal despotism' (Hall, 2009, p.514; Macaulay, 1833). 'A good government', Macaulay asserted, 'like a good coat, is that which fits the body for which it is designed.' In a similar vein, John Stuart Mill argued that, whereas representative government was undoubtedly 'the most perfect polity' for all mankind, unhappily some societies were not yet ready for it:

> There are… conditions of society in which a vigorous despotism is, in itself, the best mode of government for training the people… to render them capable of a higher civilization. (Mill, 1861, p.329)

As the historian of British colonial violence Elizabeth Kolsky acidly comments, notions of colonial tutelage such as these were by no means as benign as they appeared, for implicitly they provided a justification for the exercise of colonial violence. Just as a father had a right to discipline his child, so the coloniser had the right to discipline his subjects from time to time (Kolsky, 2015).

A political order of 'beneficent despotism'

As a number of historians have shown, notably Thomas Holt in *The Problem of Freedom* (1992), the brief interlude of hope, in which abolition and emancipation opened a window onto the prospect of genuine equality for freed slaves, was soon clouded over and erased by a torrent of invective that was gaining ground in the 1840s and 1850s, in which black people were portrayed as inveterately lazy and suffering, above all, from a racial defect. Somehow, they:

> were missing that drive for material self-improvement innate in Europeans. Incapable of self-direction and inner restraint, they must be subjected to external controllers. Having failed to master themselves, they must have masters. (Holt, 1992, p.280)

This outlook was communicated most vociferously, and venomously, one might add, by Thomas Carlyle in his 'Discourses on the N****r Question', first published in *Fraser's Magazine* in December 1849. Pondering how one might 'abolish the abuses of slavery, and save the precious thing in it', Carlyle imagined saying to black people:

> You are not 'slaves' now; nor do I wish, if it can be avoided, to see you slaves again; but decidedly you have to be servants to those that are born wiser than you, that are born lords of you; servants to the Whites, if they are (as what mortal can doubt they are?) born wiser than you. (Carlyle, 1849)

Carlyle's correspondence exhibits a constant deprecation and vilification of black people for, as Thomas Holt tersely remarks, they had become 'his emblem of denigration, of the level to which whites could sink' (Holt, 1992, p.282). Yet, it would a mistake to suppose that Carlyle was painting himself into a solitary corner by his rhetorical excesses for, as Holt underlines, what is actually striking about his polemic is the extent to which it confirms, and actively contributes to, an evolving official debate that was, increasingly, amenable to accommodating 'racial realities' (Holt, 1992, p.283). 'The Negroes', asserted Sir Henry Taylor at the Colonial Office in 1846, are like children and 'require a discipline which shall enforce upon them steadiness in their own conduct and considerations for the interests of others' (Holt, 1992, pp.284–285). Like Carlyle, Taylor himself was now becoming disposed towards a political order of 'beneficent despotism', as he came to style it (Holt, 1992, p.285). The general

'Sir Henry Taylor from life', photographed by Julia Margaret
Cameron in 1865 © National Portrait Gallery

tenor of the racial ideology of the late 19th century was that 'the natives' lacked inner controls and stood greatly in need of external controllers. Though the dominant classic liberal ideology embraced the liberal democratic presumption that all men, black men (but not women) included, shared certain innate traits and values, it was at the same time unforgiving towards those who, once they had been granted conditions of freedom, failed to make good.

By general consent, work discipline was the established test of internal control and, as early as 1833, Henry Taylor was already admonishing all those slaves who failed to respond to market incentives as an 'idle and spendthrift residue, whose liberation from arbitrary control could be duly retarded'. By the end of the 1850s, few dissented from the view that ex-slaves had miserably failed the test of work discipline and, as a consequence, were now ripe subjects for being brought back under the governance of their betters. Charles Kingsley, the writer, a conservative and a friend of Carlyle, explained that the denial of 'congenital differences' between races that Mill and his friends insisted upon was something that he had been 'cured of… by the harsh school of fact', which had taught him that 'the differences of races are so great that certain races, e.g. the Irish Celts, seem quite unfit for self-government' (cited in Holt, 1992, p.308).

The capacity to self-govern is seen to depend on the assimilation of internal controls, and in the rhetoric of colonial officials like Henry Taylor the social relations of colonial reality – the ways in which black people are perceived and represented – come to be framed through the lens of moral treatment and the management of lunacy. The racialised terrain of politics now abuts, and imbricates with, that of psychological medicine, for it is as if, in the official mind, ex-slaves and the black population in Jamaica are largely indistinguishable from mental patients, all of them fitting candidates for 'an enlightened and paternal despotism'.

On display here is a failing, or failed, therapeutic cadre on the brink of relegation to the back wards as hopeless cases, although the scope and depth of the 'enlightenment' that may be produced by the 'paternal despotism' of psychiatry is, of course, open to contention. In a stimulating discussion, historian Jordanna Bailkin draws attention to the variety of ways in which, in the 20th century, during the post-war period at the end of empire, psychology and psychiatry became a basis for governance in Britain, drawing on a prototype for co-opting a psychiatric perspective into colonial governance that had been assayed much earlier, albeit in a more rudimentary fashion (Bailkin, 2012, p.37).

Abolishing the 'savage banquet'

The entanglement between politics and madness may also be discerned from a vantage point inside the asylum in these years for, in the wake of the scandal at the Kingston Lunatic Asylum, Dr Thomas Allen, a reputed alienist and asylum superintendent from Britain, was dispatched to Jamaica to restore order, sanitation and, above all, moral discipline to that benighted institution. Allen disembarked at Kingston in 1864, at a critical moment in the fortunes of the lunatic asylum and of the incarcerated mad population in Jamaica, certainly, but also in the fortunes of the emancipated, Jamaica's freed ex-slave population. Amidst these volatile circumstances, Allen was shortly to discover a kindred spirit in Governor Edward Eyre, and forge a sympathetic bond with him that resulted in both men uttering, and disseminating, racial sentiments that could be taken for reflections of each other. Hastening to the male asylum soon after he had disembarked, Allen's initial encounter with the inmates was less than salutary:[1]

> The dinner appears to be ample. This carving takes place in the midst of the patients. They are very noisy. A patient is now fighting and others are chatting and quarrelling. A patient comes up for a piece of meat, it is given to him and he walks away. The patients sit, or not, at the table as they choose. They come up and walk off with their food, and take it when, and where, they please; they are now eating distributed about the Airing Court, in all places and corners, some on the steps of the single rooms, some in the East portion of the Airing Court, others on the top of the water closet wall, others near the pump and the fence of the Airing Court. They all eat with their fingers. No grace is said. No table-cloths were used, nor the slightest social decency observed. It is a most savage banquet and a dreadful sight.

And thence to the women as they also were having dinner:

> Patients takes their meals in all directions, all eat with their fingers, and like savages. There is terrible disorder, some are standing on benches, others are carrying their food on their heads. At this moment a male labourer is endeavouring to induce some patients to go to the dining table. Some of the women have on only a shift which is filthy and stained black with menstrual fluid. Some of the women are very indecent.

From a cursory review of the mental state of the patients in the asylum, he concluded:

> it is but too apparent that a large number of them are hopelessly incurable. In many instances their inclinations, habits and uncontrollable passions are evidently as much the result of a naturally savage and uncivilized condition, as of mental unsoundness. In others, the profane, foul and unnatural language, thoughts and acts, betoken a mind totally unimpressed with religious teaching or elevating influences and demonstrate the evil effects of unsuitable dwellings and the want of proper marriage obligations, and responsibilities, in producing a low physical and moral state... Much of this intellectual and moral debasement of the patients is also the result of long standing disease.

---

1. Dr Thomas Allen's descriptions of his experience at the Kingston Lunatic Asylum are taken from Colonial Office files, CO 137/382 & CO 137/388, in the National Archives. See under Archives Consulted in the references for more details.

Allen disposed of an intrusive psychiatric gaze, sometimes verging on the misogynistic, remarking in one instance on how 'female lunatics do make use of the vagina as a receptacle for improper things', after one patient had 'concealed some lucifers [matches] either in or about the vagina'. Notwithstanding the unpromising human material by which he is surrounded, Allen soon sets about a moral and behavioural transformation of the regime:

> Every endeavour is made to induce the patient to look, think, act
> and speak like persons of sound reason. They are individualized and
> surrounded by such kind and civilizing influences as will break up their
> morbid trains of thought, tend to exercise their self-control, as well as to
> excite their feeling of self-respect.

Before many weeks have passed, he has achieved a passable result:

> It affords me the greatest pleasure to refer to the marked improvement
> in the conduct and habits of the patients. In place of the distressing
> turmoil, and insubordination, which formerly prevailed among them,
> order and tranquillity have been to a great extent established. This is
> particularly the case on the male side. Instead of patients dining without
> table cloths, or grace being said, or social decorum observed, and all
> more or less disorderly, eating their food with their fingers, many of them
> being scattered about the airing court, they now dine decently and with
> the strictest propriety. The table is covered with a cloth, every patient is
> provided with a spoon, grace is said, to which all reverently attend, and
> the meal passes off comfortably and quietly. At the evening meal, the same
> order and control is maintained, and the patients, after hearing a portion of
> the Bible read to them, and singing a hymn, quietly disperse and go to bed.

There is, obviously, a measure of self-congratulation in this description but, even so, at this time, Allen was attracting plaudits for his reforms, even from naturally rather sceptical journalists. The irony is, and although it was not to last for long, it is a moment to be savoured that the mad black population of the lunatic asylum appears to hold more promise in Thomas Allen's perhaps rather self-infatuated clinical gaze than does the colonised population of Jamaica as a whole in the gaze of the Colonial Office in the metropole. Indeed, Allen's firm approach to the management and reform of the 'savage' and 'uncivilised' lunatics may well have bolstered Governor Eyre in his resolve to take a firm line with the rebellious 'natives'. Demonstrably, Allen was restoring and maintaining public order, and that was what Eyre approved. In 1864 already, in his communications to the governor, Allen was writing about the 'naturally savage and uncivilized condition' of the natives, and 'their uncontrollable passions', with 'moral depravity, religious fanaticism and gross superstition' prevailing among them. He was, in effect, feeding Eyre an image of the 'madhouse' of Jamaican society in which 'society' and 'madhouse' had been collapsed into each other. In December 1865, Eyre wrote to the Secretary of State describing 'the Negro' in very similar terms, as 'creatures of impulse and imitation, easily misled, very excitable… all the evil passions of a race little removed… from absolute savages' (see also Olusoga, 2016, pp.384–385).

Allen remained consistent in his opinions over the years that he served in Jamaica, still maintaining in 1872 that the asylum inmates were 'vindictive and savage' and that any opposition would throw them into an 'ungovernable rage'. If anything, his views became markedly more racist over time, latterly unleavened by any sense of a mitigating or compensating therapeutic hope or promise (Smith, 2014, pp.154, 163). As Leonard Smith underlines (pp.153–154), perspectives that linked 'negroes' to savagery and barbarism were increasingly absorbed into white ruling class belief systems, and colonial common sense, especially after the Morant Bay rebellion. The lunatic asylum and Jamaican society became increasingly indistinguishable, and the 'reform' of the asylum was forever waiting on a social reform that never took place.

Conceding failure, a disillusioned Thomas Allen eventually went home to England to die, and within decades of the Kingston Lunatic Asylum scandal, the asylum was once again notorious for its abominable conditions (Fryar, 2016). However, as late as the 1870s, the asylum band still regularly played on some of the wards, including that for 'refractory' patients, and twice weekly a group of patients marched out to the sea shore, accompanied by the band, where they engaged in singing and dancing. In the 1880s, however, the departure of attendants to work on the Panama Canal resulted in the break-up of the band, and Leonard Smith recounts how, by 1914, the asylum 'had become little more than a vast impersonal warehouse for the chronically insane', in which therapeutic aspirations 'were now little more than a forlorn hope' (Smith, 2014, p.96; Heuring, 2011; Altink, 2012).

Dashing the nascent hopes of freed Jamaicans

For the black body in Jamaica, the abolition of slavery marked the passage from slave to native: ex-slaves now became subjects and not property, and power shifted from absolute coercion to forms of tutelage. However, although ex-slaves were now subjects and possessed certain rights as such, they were not citizens; in the British colonial mind, citizenship could only be bestowed after a period of learning for which, in the original vision of the preparation for emancipation, the apprenticeship system was to be a key instrument. For a brief moment after the abolition of racial slavery, writes African studies scholar Anthony Bogues (2018), there was a discernable shift in colonial policy concerning colonial rule, as slaves became subjects not property. Though the planters still regarded the ex-slave as an object or thing, in the minds of colonial officials like Henry Taylor and the political economist Herman Merivale, post-emancipation Jamaican society could be envisaged as an experiment in liberal imperial rule that potentially provided some space for opposition to hegemonic colonial rule (Bogues, 2018).

It may be doubted, however, how far the Colonial Office was ever truly committed to rethinking modes of governance and to reassessing the social and ontological status of the ex-slave. Behind the scenes, officials were now more and more inclined to endorse Thomas Carlyle's position in his infamous essay (Carlyle, 1849): emancipation had been a disaster for the colonies. As the historian of the Caribbean, Gad Heuman, has argued, overall the vision of the Jamaican population entertained by the Colonial Office was profoundly negative, and shaped by the increasingly racist thinking of the time that black people's idleness and poor character lay at the root of the problem (Heuman, 2018, p.139). And by 1865, in the immediate aftermath of the Morant Bay rebellion, Henry Taylor was singing loudly from the official song sheet in support of Governor Eyre's actions in authorising the massacre of 'Her Majesty's subjects'. If there is a lesson here, it is that liberal imperial politics is inevitably hobbled by a colonial power that can never transcend its 'arche-violence', or 'originary violence', to use Jacques Derrida's term (1967/2016, p.112; Bogues, 2018, p.169). Through repeated re-enactments of just that 'originary violence', the regime at Kingston Lunatic Asylum in the 1850s was, in major part, a perverse attempt to cauterise and repulse the nascent hopes of freed Jamaicans, in what the Jamaican scholar and social critic Rex Nettleford has called their cultural, psychic, spiritual and physical 'battles for space' (Nettleford, 1997).

The brutal putting down of the 1865 insurrection certainly saw an abundance of 'originary violence'. Though the flogging of women had been banished by law in 1838, on the orders of Governor Eyre, many women were flogged by the colonial authorities in the wake of the disturbances, maintaining, according to their forthright critic Charles Buxton MP, 'that all this hanging, shooting, and flogging that went on for more than a month was necessary, because otherwise the negroes would have shaken off the Queen's authority, and driven the white inhabitants into the sea' (Hansard, 1866, para.1771, cited in Winter, 2012). At the upper end of the social scale, Colonel Thomas Hobbs, the commander of British forces in St Thomas, received an order from Lt Colonel Elkington, the deputy adjutant-general, that possessed a distinct echo of Mrs Ryan at the Kingston Lunatic Asylum: 'Hope you will not send in any prisoners… Do punish the blackguards well!' The Reverend Henry Bleby, a Methodist missionary in Jamaica at the time, recalls of this instruction:

> Colonel Hobbs shot thirteen men at Monklands, all at once, thinking no doubt it was a capital sport to make a battue [indiscriminate slaughter] of his fellow men.(Cited in National Museum Jamaica, 2015)

'Victims of the Jamaica Rebellion of 1865' from *Photography Album Documenting the Morant Bay Rebellion in Jamaica*, courtesy of Special Collections, Princeton University Library. Colonel Hobbs, 'Died mad', features in the third row, second left.

The prisoners were all shot with their backs to a trench that Hobbs had ordered to be dug, but at Hobbs's behest one prisoner, who remained alive, was finished off with a pickaxe. A charge of cruelty was brought against Hobbs by the Royal Commission of Enquiry into the rebellion, following which, overwhelmed by guilt, 'his mind became unhinged', and on the journey home, accompanied by his wife and three children, he slipped away from his escort off the coast of Haiti and threw himself overboard. Described by those who knew him as a cultured and sensitive man, he is shown in a surviving photograph (above, bottom row, second from left) seated with a small child balanced on his lap, looking like a harassed and distracted single parent (National Museum Jamaica, 2015; Report of the Jamaica Royal Commission, 1866, Part II, p.23[2]).

---

2. For details of the Report of the Jamaica Royal Commission, see Bishopsgate Institute, under 'Archives Consulted' in the references.

At the other end of the social scale, again as reported to the Jamaica Royal Commission (1866), Richard Clark, a black master baker and journeyman, was going about his business when he was arrested by a group of soldiers, who alleged that they heard him say: 'Tonight will be worse, because he is going to kill every white man and every brown man.' To this accusation, Clarke replied:

> I said, 'I never did say so'. He said, 'Silence you, not a word, I am not going to talk to a rebel. We soldiers did not come here to play.' And he shoved me down, lashed me, fixed a rope round my neck, then raised me up and shoved me two yards, and jerked me up again by the rope.

Clarke ended up in a prison, where he was sentenced to 100 lashes by Colonel Alexander Nelson, deputy adjutant general, who was responsible for putting down the rebellion. Then, as Clarke described:

> I went to seek my clothes; all my clothes were gone; what money I had was all gone; so I remained at the Bay, begging bread, and begging to get home. After that I went to Dr Philippo, and he says the kidney is injured. If I was in a private place, I could show you the situation I am in. I am a poor man.' 'Are you not able to work?' 'The doctor says I am not able to support even myself.' 'Then how have you been living since then?' 'I have been obliged to live off my family.' 'Was no reason assigned for the flogging?' 'None. I cannot account for it. There is no account I can give. I am breaking out all over, enough to face the dead. I am very poorly. I am under the doctor and I am now taking medicine.' (Report of the Jamaica Royal Commission, 1866)

By 1865, Whitehall had already put paid to any notion of an alternative economy in Jamaica organised around black ownership or initiative:

> Indeed, black was no longer a credible adjective to modify initiative or enterprise. A powerful tradition had taken hold in which the ex-slaves were characterized as endowed with relatively simple material aspirations, easily satisfied in a tropical environment. (Holt, 1992, p.279; see also Olusoga, 2016, pp.384–396)

Both in England and in the colonies, legislation was being enacted to reform prisons, poor relief and the police, producing institutions such as penitentiaries, mental hospitals and reformatories that enforced regularity, punctuality, uniformity and routine, and which, in their discipline and governance, bore an uncanny resemblance to the slave plantation. 'Slavery is dead! Long live slavery!' (Holt, 1992, p.37).

6

Revivalists, Rastafari and psychiatry

Psychiatry confronts challenges to the colonial symbolic order

The real kickback against the colonial order in Jamaica came from the Revival movement in its numerous varieties in the closing decades of the 19th century through into the early 20th, and later from Rastafarianism, all of which the colonial authorities, together with their sycophants and allies at all levels, from the colonial governor down to the provincial journalist, subjected to remorseless derision as manifestations of a form of religious madness, meriting confinement or punishment in the lunatic asylum, the prison or the house of correction. Though some of this was simply rhetorical declamation, it is also the case, as we shall see in the discussion that follows of two ground-breaking and unorthodox Jamaican religious leaders from this period, Alexander Bedward, founder and leader of the Bedwardites, and Leonard Howell, a foundational Rastafari leader, that the colonial authorities resorted to the lunatic asylum and the disciplinary apparatus of psychiatry on numerous occasions over a number of decades as an instrument to control and attempt to discredit what they perceived to be untoward and threatening forms of spiritual behaviour. As Diana Paton, the historian of the Caribbean, has helpfully explained, the concept of 'religion' has served as 'a race-making term with multiple, complex, and power-laden meanings' and 'a marker of the line between supposedly "civilized" peoples (who practice religion) and "primitive" peoples (who practice superstition or magic)' (Paton, 2009, p.2).

With all 'the barking and howling', claimed R. Edward Foulkes in an article under the satirical title 'The Bark Religion', published at the turn of the 20th century, Revivalist meeting places were 'a never-failing means of ensuring inmates for the Lunatic Asylum or the Public Hospital' (cited in Moore & Johnson, 2004, p.362, n.88). Congregations of the Revival movement were frequently dominated by women presenting in scenes of 'inconceivable confusion'. 'It is by no means strange that females only are subjected to the "convulsions" for which Revivalism is remarkable,' reported the *Falmouth Post* in 1861, 'as nervous excitement is part of the composition of the weaker sex, to be reduced to a great state of nervousness by constitutional disorganisations' (cited in Moore & Johnson, 2004, p.73). Emanating from 'the very lowest class', these women should be punished with hard labour in the house of correction, fulminated the *Post*, as this might deter others from 'making indecent exhibitions of their persons… by shouting, yelling and using obscene and filthy language in the public streets' (cited in Moore & Johnson, 2004, p.74). As historians Brian Moore and Michele Johnson remark, in a patriarchal society such as Victorian Jamaica, bound by a gender ideology according to which women were expected to be pious, obedient and submissive, 'that Revival created a space for women is partly what made it so potentially powerful and disruptive' (2004, p.74).

According to the Caribbean intellectual historian Anthony Bogues, it is on the terrain of the triumph of Afro-creole religious practices and norms in giving birth to religions such as Myal and Kumina that 'the contestation about what the Afro-Jamaican slave would become was sharpest'. Afro-Jamaicans humanised the cultural landscape by peopling it with gods and spirits, demons and duppies and a lot more, and, as Bogues convincingly argues, such a humanisation on the Afro-Jamaican's own terms succeeded in creating a symbolic order that ran counter to the colonial symbolic order (2018, p.168; see also Paton & Forde, 2012). Myalists believed, as Monica Schuler writes, that 'all misfortune, not just slavery, stemmed from malicious forces, embodied in the spirit of the dead'. All problems, including physical illnesses, were thought to derive from spiritual sources, requiring the performance of rituals to exorcise the problem and prevent recurrence – notably the Myal dance, sometimes described as violent because it involved the frantic movements of all parts of the body (Schuler, 1979). As Moore and Johnson emphasise, the real significance of Afro-Christianity resided in its independence from the colonial religio-cultural power structure: the fact that 'it placed itself outside the control of the Euro-Christian religious complex' and its supporting secular institutions, and managed to 'render it *impotent* where it tried to impinge on what they believed was their superior spiritualism' (Moore & Johnson, 2004, p.95, original emphasis). The appearance of the new Myal religion in 1760, writes Monica Schuler, symbolised 'a spirit of cooperation among enslaved Africans of various ethnic backgrounds that had not hitherto been the case in Jamaica… Indeed, Myalism may actually have fostered pan-African cooperation where once only ethnic division had existed' (Schuler, 1979). By the turn of the century, Revival street preachers were being perceived not simply as 'nuisances' to the respectable public but as potential political agitators (Moore & Johnson, 2004, p.75).[1]

Alexander Bedward (1848–1930)

Revd Alexander Bedward

Alexander Bedward was born in St Andrew Parish in south-eastern Jamaica in 1848. Nothing is known about his father but his mother was supposedly a healer. He never learned to write and read only haltingly. As a youth, he raised provisions on a plantation and then, apart from the years 1883 to 1885 when he was a migrant labourer in Colon, a seaport on the isthmus of Panama, he worked on Lord Verley's sugar estate in Mona, St Andrew, as a cooper and a foreman. In 1891 he decided to devote himself full-time to his ministry. He dated the onset of his spiritual odyssey from the massive fire that swept through the lower half of Kingston in December 1882, when he began to have persistent disturbing dreams and to exhibit erratic behaviour, which perturbed his family, who considered committing him for lunacy. However, regarding these experiences as possible signs of divine election, as the Afro-Jamaican worldview encouraged him to do, Bedward felt the urge to channel them into a religious vocation, and in 1889 the hermit H.E. Shakespeare Wood, a reputed African American, inducted him as one of 24 elders of August Town's Native Baptist Church. In October 1891, by now convinced that God had called him

---

1. For more on Revival as an indigenous religion and spiritual healing practice in Jamaica, see Wedenoja & Anderson (2014). On Kumina, see Stewart (2018).

to become a saviour of Black Jamaicans, Bedward resigned from his plantation job and began performing healing ceremonies with water drawn from a spring beside his property on the Hope River.

By 1893, his healing rituals were becoming widely celebrated, and Bishop Enos Nuttall, the Anglican Bishop of Jamaica, issued a statement on the 'Hope River Observances', with the purpose of reassuring 'the thoughtful public'. As reported in *The Gleaner* on 3rd October, he revealed that as many as 6000 souls (on later occasions the estimate would rise to 12,000) were now gathering at the river every Wednesday morning to hear Bedward's emotional homilies, and to bathe in or drink the water of the healing stream, the water being 'drunk on the spot and also carried away in bottles, and… taken direct from the stream while bathing operations are proceeding'. While acknowledging a public health concern, the Bishop was reluctant to condemn the proceedings, since 'there is great excitement but nothing that can be called disorder'. To interfere with them would, he believed, 'be wrong in principle, practically useless, and likely also to create resistance that would involve danger to the general peace'.

In his homilies, Bedward vocalised a traditional African and biblical abhorrence of commercialism in the healing vocation, prophesying the imminent end of the world and excoriating his mainly white, clerical and medical critics and competitors as mercenaries who charged for their services. As Monica Schuler has put it, in view of his prophetic persona and self-description as one of the Book of Revelation's 'two witnesses', Bedward could not help but be dissatisfied, continuously assailing the injustices that confronted downtrodden Jamaicans. Consisting primarily of small farmers, casual and household workers, higglers, craft workers and the unemployed, his followers were drawn to his religious message and to the critical appeal of the moral economy of blackness that he enjoined on them, which forefronted above all the injustices associated with white rule, the need for land, and the necessity for setting up social welfare schemes that addressed the needs of the aged, infants, sick and illiterate. In the meantime, British missionary advocates launched their own programmes for the spiritual reformation of Jamaica's new black subjects of the British Crown, aiming to produce, in Schuler's words, 'sober, working-class Victorians' (Schuler, 1980, p.31; Stewart, 2018, p.605).

Like Paul Bogle before him, Bedward advocated for black people to establish their own institutions, such as courts of law to administer justice and protect fair play. Charles Price has remarked that Bedward's confidence in his own authority as a black saviour, and his capacity to call God to his side in the struggle to overturn the injustice inflicted upon black people and indict whites for slavery by calling them robbers and thieves, was unquestionably aggressive (Price, 2009, p.44). *The Daily Gleaner* newspaper took umbrage over such socio-political utterances denouncing the rich for grabbing 'the substance of the poor', which it regarded as a potential threat to social order.[2] In the same year, Dr Bronstorph, a local medical practitioner, threw medical confidentiality to the winds, issuing a statement following his examination of Bedward that declared him insane, 'dangerously so and suffering from religious monomania'.

Bedward was brought to trial on a charge of sedition in 1895. In his deposition, Henry Blake, the Governor of Jamaica, averred that 'as in such a movement among a black and coloured population, there is always an element of possible danger'. Blake had had the movement watched carefully by the police. It was reported in the ever-assiduous *Daily Gleaner* that Bedward was 'exciting the people by seditious language', and calling on them:

> to drive out the white population who were oppressing them, holding
> out to them the fires of hell as their doom if they neglected to do it, and
> reminding them of the Morant Bay rebellion. He referred to the black
> population as the 'black wall' and the white as the 'white wall', saying that
> the white wall had long enough oppressed the black wall and the time
> had now arrived when the black wall must knock down and oppress the
> white wall. (1895, p.3)[3]

At the trial, Philip Stern, the white Jewish lawyer who was defending Bedward, charged that the seditious utterances attributed to him had largely been made up by a *Gleaner* reporter, one John Lanigan, from whose article the indictment before the court had been taken, and who had taken notes from Bedward's speech at the Hope River on his shirt sleeves, later copying them in his lodgings. However, the 'grand language which appeared in the *Gleaner* newspaper' never actually 'fell from the lips of the man', argued Stern, since Bedward had a been speaking in a Jamaican patois (or patwah), called Jamaican creole by linguists, and he was in any case simply 'a poor half-witted creature', given to incessant rambling, who 'could only string together a few disjointed sentences', and who may have used cheeky, but definitely not seditious, language.

Dr Jasper Cargill, as medical witness for the defence, was of opinion that Bedward was a weak-minded man, a vain fanatic who was not responsible for his language but suffered from a type of mental intoxication that he called amentia (an archaic medical term, formerly used to refer to people with marked mental deficits):

---

2. *The Daily Gleaner* was the daily English-language newspaper founded in Kingston, Jamaica, in 1834. Generally known as *The Gleaner*, it formally changed its name to this in 1992.

3. See CO 137/ 566/32 Report on the proceedings of the case of Alexander Bedward (1895), in Archives Consulted.

Dr Cargill cross-examined: 'Bedward speaks disconnectedly.'

His Honour: 'That is no uncommon thing.'

Witness: 'No.'

His Honour: 'I have heard a lot of it since I have been on the bench without amentia.'

The jury, however, were not persuaded by the defence's scepticism over what Bedward had actually said on the Hope riverbank, and evidently did not find him to be anything like as inarticulate or 'half-witted' as Stern and the medical counsel professed. They were satisfied that he did use the seditious language with which he was charged. They acquitted him on the grounds of insanity, but the judge ordered that he be confined 'during Her Majesty's pleasure', which, *The Gleaner* concluded, 'has the effect of placing Bedward in the Lunatic Asylum where he will be kept until further notice'. However, this was not to be, for Philip Stern's tenacious endeavours on Bedward's behalf were not concluded just yet. An appeal was lodged, and it was found that the provisions of the Lunacy Laws that 'empowered a judge to confine a person of unsound mind applied only to felonies and did not to extend to misdemeanors'. Bedward was accordingly discharged from the asylum, much to the chagrin of the colonial authorities.

His release from confinement was heralded by his followers as a great miracle and succeeded only in augmenting his lustre. Between the mid-1890s and 1921, his Revivalist movement grew in strength. His congregations were now organised into 'camps' under the guidance of a 'shepherd', and Bessie Pullen-Burry, who visited Jamaica at the turn of the 20th century, estimated that there were 6000 Bedwardites in these camps. Over these years, there were frequent clashes between Bedwardites and the colonial authorities, and whenever possible the British colonial authorities used the vagrancy laws to arrest racial activists, brand them as mad and delusional, and remand them to the asylum (Price, 2009, p.45).

In 1920, believing that his powers were failing, Bedward identified another Jamaican, Marcus Garvey (1887–1940), who was now very much prominent, as Moses, and himself merely as Moses' spokesman. He announced that he would undertake a spiritual ascension into heaven at the end of December, leading between 3000 and 6000 of his followers to dispose of their belongings and gather to join him. When his ascension failed to occur, Bedward declared that his followers had misunderstood him and that he had ascended in spirit. In April 1921, flouting a ban on marching, Bedward gathered together nearly 700 of his supporters, who were surrounded by an armed force, arrested and tried under the Vagrancy Law (Post, 1978, p.8). Sir Leslie Probyn, the Governor, had given instructions for the charges under which Bedward was to be arrested to be pre-arranged, and many of his followers were sentenced to hard labour on trumped-up charges, much to the delight of *The Gleaner,* which over many years had been waging a symbolic battle against Bedwardism, maligning the religious practices of the group, calling for their repression, and setting itself, by reporting and sarcasm, to stifle and ridicule it out of existence (Lewis, 1987, p.39).

As though, in the colonial mind, the lunatic asylum was really just an adjunct of the penal system, Bedward was detained and remained there until his death on 8 November 1930, although it has been claimed that he showed no evidence of the madness with which the colonial regime charged him (Reynolds, 2000, cited in Price, 2009, p.46). King Ras Tafari had been crowned Emperor of Ethiopia just six days before Bedward's death, and legend has it that Bedward died a happy man, taking the news of the coronation when it reached him for a sign that the redemption of African people was at hand and that his earthly mission was now concluded. Contrary to what some critics have alleged, Alexander Bedward was an Old Testament-style prophet and millenarian, who never advocated armed rebellion and was reportedly always accessible to white visitors.[4]

Leonard Percival Howell

'The First Rasta'
Leonard Percival Howell

As the black anthropologist Charles Price has shown, Alexander Bedward and his followers were among the first Jamaicans to make Blackness meaningful and significant, and to reconfigure black identity into 'a collective identification

---

4. www.encyclopedia.com/history/historians-and-chronicles/historians-miscellaneous-biographies/alexander-bedward

and social movement capable of posing an organized challenge to White and colonial hegemony' (Price, 2009).[5] There are numerous connections between Bedwardists, Myalists, Native Baptists, Kumina, Revivalists and the emergent Rastafari, in which cultural resources were passed on and transformed into new identities. For instance, some of the earliest Rastafari were once a part of the Bedwardite fold – notably, Robert Hinds and also Rasta Ivey (born 1906–12), who was baptised by a Bedwardite and recalled defending her faith, despite being ridiculed and sent to an insane asylum in the 1960s (Price, 2009, pp.43–44, 188). Price also reports that the political threat posed by Rastafari agitation was fully recognised by the colonial regime as early as 1933–1934. The incantation of the Rastafari cult prayer, after which 'the cultists are thrown into a fanatical frenzy not far removed from the throes of pocomania', has been likened to the Pentecostal 'gifts of the Spirit', or 'speaking in tongues' (referred to by one commentator as the 'tongue movement' in Jamaica) (Price, 2009, p.41). As Robert A. Hill noted in his seminal study *Dread History*, first published in 1981, the association between Rastafari eschatology and pocomania caught the attention of a colonial official as early as 1940, who suggested that Leonard Howell's Ethiopian Salvation Society 'has probably developed doctrines combining sedition with pocomania' (Hill, 2001, p.45).

Leonard Howell (1898–1981) was a foundational Rastafari leader who was harassed and persecuted by the colonial and post-colonial authorities over several decades. He oversaw and inspired the founding decades of the Rastafari religion and movement and must be counted among the most persecuted of the first generation of Rastafari preachers, having throughout his lifetime been incarcerated in jail, or the Bellevue Lunatic Asylum, for a total period that far exceeded the incarcerations of the other three first-generation Rastafari preachers put together (Hutton et al., 2015, loc.1538). Though the precise number and dates of Howell's admissions to the asylum are open to dispute, it is certain that his career as a Rastafari leader was punctuated by intermittent confinements. As the Black Studies scholar Daive Dunkley has graphically described, the notoriety that Howell achieved by promoting the message of Rastafari and black nationalism, and the continuing threat that he posed, threw the colonial regime into a state of frenzy, provoking them into launching 'one of the longest, and most consistent, campaigns against any opponent of

---

5. For a nuanced overview of Jamaican psychiatry from the 1980s that includes some remarks about Rastas or Rastafarians, see Wedenoja (1983). Today, it can be said that Rastafari has moved from being a negatively stigmatised identity, as it was through to the 1950s, to a positive exemplar of moral, religious and cultural blackness – from 'outcasts to culture bearers', to echo the title of a recent study by Ennis Barrington Edmonds that showcases this burgeoning and enthusiastic area of scholarship (Chevannes, 2000; Edmonds, 2003; Price, 2009; Niaah & MacLeod, 2013; Hutton et al., 2015).

colonialism in British Jamaica during the twentieth century', in which their 'rage and eagerness to see Howell undermined continued unabated as he was in jail, and condemned to the lunatic asylum at Kingston' (Dunkley, 2013, p.66; see also Hoenisch, 1988; Van Dijk, 1995).

Ironically, however, Howell's upbringing and early development gave no hint of his subsequent trajectory. Born into an affluent Anglican family, he was educated in colonial schools operated by the church, where the history of slavery did not figure, and he was fed stereotypical prejudices about black people and a positive attitude towards the British. At the age of 13, however, after witnessing the murder of a young woman by her boyfriend, Howell refused to testify against the accused man, who was represented by Jamaica's first black lawyer, provoking the anger of the colonial administration. To avoid the persecution of his son by the state, Howell's father, who was a major stakeholder in the Jamaican banana export industry, arranged to smuggle his son aboard a banana boat that left for America in 1912. Dunkley contends that the young Howell's departure from the island marked the beginning of his contempt for colonial Jamaica, which would only deepen and remain with him for the rest of his life (Dunkley, 2013, p.69). In New York, he met Marcus Garvey, enlisted in the Universal Negro Improvement Association and began to develop a positive Afrocentric identity.

As with many other episodes in Howell's life, controversy hangs over the circumstances of his departure from the United States for Jamaica in 1932. Shortly after his return, *The Gleaner* published a story alleging that he had been deported from the United States as a degenerate or a career criminal – outright falsehoods and fabrications that in due course Howell was able to dispel but that signalled the start of what would turn out to be a relentless campaign of vilification and disinformation against him by *The Gleaner*, much as they had pursued Alexander Bedward. In 1933, however, Howell was already achieving some success in mounting a challenge to the colonial symbolic order. According to an undercover police report, at a Rastafari meeting in April, he declared, 'The negro is now free and the white people will have to bow to the Negro Race', and he concluded the meeting with the incendiary exhortation:

> You must sing the National Anthem, but before you start, you must
> remember that you are not singing it for King George the Fifth, but for
> Ras Tafair, our new king! (Hill, 2001, pp.29–30; Lee, 1999/2003, pp.63–66)

At this point, the colonial authorities contemplated pressing charges for sedition, but decided instead to guide Howell on a path to 'the Lunatic Asylum' since, as the crown solicitor declared: 'The man is a stupid ranter who puts forward an imaginary being or person who he calls "Ras Tafari" and whom he describes as Christ as well as King of Ethiopians'.

In the following year, however, the colonial authorities did put him on trial for sedition, and in court Howell read from Thessalonians and Revelations in support of his claims of black divinity, evoking guffaws from the court audience at the idea that black people could have their own history and their own God. As *The Gleaner* grudgingly acknowledged, however, both Howell and his co-defendant Robert Hinds were completely undaunted by such ridicule, staying firm in their belief that the 'God of righteousness' had returned to earth to redeem black people and lead humankind. Howell insisted that his speech was religious, but the government countered that it was political. Significantly, several of Howell's witnesses were women, indicative of the visible presence of women from the earliest days of the Rastafari movement.

Officially, Howell was sentenced to prison by the court on this occasion but, as Rasta Ivey remembers it, he wound up in the lunatic asylum, testifying (as with Bedward) to the elision between the asylum and the prison as interchangeable components of the penal system. He returned to preach about the Rastafari in Kingston and St Thomas soon after his release the following year:

> Him tell them [the court] 'bout Rasta and them send him asylum, and
> when him go asylum and come out [he] come preach every night…
> Them time, me live a town, you see. (Price, 2009, pp.59–60)

By this time, Howell had transformed himself into a Hindu mystic named for Gangunguru Maragh, or Gong Maragh, or 'The Gong' for short, which is how he was known until the 1960s (Lee, 1999/2003, p.98).

Howell's short but powerful book *The Promised Key* (Maragh, 1935/2014) read like a declaration of war against colonialism and white rule, prophesying the replacement of 'White supremacy' by 'Black supremacy'. Despite its brevity, the book was perceived as a liability by the colonial regime, fuelling the urge for a more systematic suppression of the Rastafari movement. Drawing on a number of accounts, Robert Hill concludes that there was a 'very real likelihood that Rastafarian millenarian ideology functioned as an active catalyst in the developing popular consciousness that led to the labour uprisings of 1938 by virtue of its radical vision of black dominion' (Hill, 2001, p.33). The colonial authorities evidently took a similar view because, in October 1937, Howell was dispatched to the Bellevue Lunatic Asylum by the Court.

By then, he had already served a term of imprisonment with hard labour and, initially, the authorities hoped that this would suffice to dampen the ardours of Rastafari enthusiasts. Quite quickly, however, they were forced to revise this assessment, and Howell's detention in the asylum was a confirmation of the continuing threat he still posed to the colonial symbolic order and to the security of the colonial regime (Dunkley, 2012, p.9). Initially, he was discharged from the asylum on 11 January 1938, and was able to resume his preaching. However, on 15 February, in the wake of a big labour strike that had started at Serge Island in the previous month, right in the middle of Howell's preaching territory, with an angry march by 1500 workers brandishing machetes and sticks, heralding the start of a 'campaign of union actions that rolled through Jamaica like a social hurricane' in that year, subsequently transforming the old colonial system, Howell was again removed to the Bellevue Mental Hospital, and this time was held there for about 12 months (Lee, 1999/2003, p.117). Legend has it that, when his wife visited him at the asylum, she was told that he was in a coma, though in actuality he was playing unconscious until his wife arrived, to avoid the electroshocks and sedation injections that the asylum administered (Lee, 1999/2003, p.117).

He was to be readmitted to Bellevue again in 1960, though his family and followers claimed that he was actually sent to the asylum on several occasions in the intervening years. According to his son, Monty, his father was sent to prison or the asylum more times than he could remember. 'The situation in Jamaica at the time, when a black man was thinking in the form of a Black God and King, this was so outlandish that they branded him a mad man,' the 74-year-old Monty Howell recalled (Walker, 2014). However, since the colonial authorities were always clandestine in their machinations over a figure like Howell, hiding behind silence and mendacity, it has not been possible to retrieve documentation in support of such claims (Dunkley, 2013, p.71).

In July 1939, Alexander Bustamante, a politically ambitious trade union leader and a brown-skinned, middle-class Jamaican who, in essence, identified as 'white' and believed that Howell was subverting 'whiteness', urged the Colonial Secretary to return Howell, the 'leader of this terrible thing that is called "Rastafari"', to the mental asylum. 'It seems to me that the only right and proper place for this man is the Asylum,' declaimed Bustamante; 'He is a danger to the peace of the Community, I think he is the greatest danger that exists in this country today' (Dunkley, 2012, p.7).

The legacy of the legendary Pinnacle community is controversial. It was the first self-sustaining village for members of the Rastafarian faith, founded in 1940 in Sligoville, St Catherine's, on a 500-acre site that Howell had purchased. It attracted 700 people in the year it started, and eventually embraced more than 3000. Accounts of the undoubted achievements of the community, at least in its heyday, in becoming a self-sufficient and thriving agricultural and crafts community, a place of non-violent agitation and an expression of Leonard

Howell's ideas regarding self-government and self-reliance for black people by providing members with plots on which they were able to build wooden houses with thatched roofs and to cultivate food crops for subsistence and sale, are potentially undermined by allegations and slurs about the extremist and punitive methods of Howell himself, and the aggressive behaviour of Pinnacle members towards the neighbouring community. Yet, as Dunkley astutely remarks, 'almost nothing was printed in the press which stated that the Pinnacle community was itself under attack'. Instead, 'Howell's methods were presented as evidence of extremism, and the kind that only an unstable mind would adopt, and further proof that the Rastafari movement was lunacy' (Dunkley, 2013, p. 85).

In 1944 Pinnacle began its ascent to becoming a major hub for ganja cultivation, yet although this business yielded great wealth and hugely enhanced the self-sufficiency of the community, allowing Rastas to organise their own banking and, according to Howell, even to have their own currency, it over-reached itself. Ganja became the catalyst for Pinnacle's eventual decline and demise, attracting unwanted attention to the community and culminating in a raid in 1954, when a government militia invaded the settlement, setting the ganja fields alight and burning the houses to the ground (National Museum Jamaica, 2013).

Howell's last confinement in a mental asylum was in 1960, for about a year, in the wake of another intensive police raid that finally put an end to the Pinnacle community. Afterwards he continued to live at Pinnacle some of the time, still engaging in the cultivation of ganja and providing support to the small number of followers who remained there and still active outside Pinnacle as the foundational leader of the Rastafari movement (Hutton et al., 2015, locs. 3054, 3159). Striking throughout his career was Howell's indefatigable energy, and his capacity to inspire with confidence and hope those who had been brought down by hardship and stigma. Philosopher and political scientist Clinton Hutton positions the praxis of Leonard Howell within the trajectory of the New World's ontology of resistance, exploring the genesis of Rastafarian thought through the prism of Garveyism, Revivalism/Myalism, Kumina and other expressions of African spirituality (see Chapter 1 in Hutton et al., 2015).

For all their 'excesses', it is worth remarking that both Alexander Bedward and Leonard Howell cultivated rather respectable, one might almost add conformist, personas. Howell always wore his hair short – not for him the trademark Rasta dreadlocks – and rarely appeared in public in anything other than a three-piece suit and tie. Bedward was frequently attired in a black and white clerical gown and surplice, in which he could have been taken for an Anglican chaplain. It must be admitted that it is difficult to get a handle on the psychiatric profiles of either Bedward or Howell, mainly because the decisions that were taken about them were largely political, administrative and legal, rather than medical. Psychiatry as a profession or discipline appears only to have played a very supine role in the mental health trajectories of both these personalities, who were celebrated and maligned in equal measure, though it is, of course, also true that the particulars of what was done to both of them in the institution, how they were treated and what was said and, presumably, written about them has either been withheld or destroyed. From the 1930s right through to the 1950s, Rastafari was a negatively stigmatised identity, exemplified strikingly in a series of classic papers produced by social psychologist George Eaton Simpson, mostly in the 1950s and early 1960s (Simpson, 1955, 1962a, 1962b, 1985) describing the movement in such terms as 'escapist-adjustive' and 'pseudo-religious in nature', and presenting an image of the brethren as social cripples (Simpson, 1962b, p.43; Yawney, 1978, p.64).

The relationship between psychiatry and the Rastafarian movement has also been ambivalent at times. For instance, transcultural psychiatrist Raymond Prince, who worked in Jamaica in the late 1960s, became interested in the movement because of his contact with mentally ill or distressed Rastafarians, and in the first instance regarded it as a 'delusional' system. He did allow that the belief structure provided meaning and self-esteem in the midst of degradation, even if the result was group psychosis. When he advanced these opinions at a conference of the American Psychiatric Association held in Jamaica in 1969, the brethren who attended the sessions accused him of racism, and threatened to picket the proceedings if he did not amend his views. This Prince reluctantly agreed to do, presenting a revised version of his paper in which he accepted that, while the views of members of such movements might be unrealistic, they were not psychotic, and moreover, because of their socially integrating role, the appearance of such cults was to be regarded as a symptom of social health rather than illness (Prince, 1970; Yawney, 1978, pp.64–67).

PART 2

'Poor whites'

Part 2 – Prologue

At the dawn of the 20th century, the state of public health in Jamaica was abysmal. The medical service, stated William Manning, the newly appointed governor in 1913, was 'a relic of the conditions which prevailed when human beings were chattels'. Back in 1854, in a report to the Colonial Office on the cholera epidemic, Dr Gavin Milroy had complained vociferously about the want of medical care in Jamaica, declaring that 'entire parishes and extensive districts of many thousands are entirely without any doctors'. Fifty years later, nothing much had changed. The 'welfare' services of the plantation system, such as they were, had been replaced by a poor-relief system, which in its structures and attitudes reflected the Poor Law system in Britain. Margaret Jones, the historian of Jamaican public health, notes that in Jamaica 'racial stereotyping could be added to this customary notion that recipients of state aid were responsible for their own fate because of their lifestyle, irresponsibility and weakness of character' (Jones, 2013, loc.712). Such health care as existed was often delivered in the poor house. In 1916, a report on the Kingston & St Andrew Poor House, with 701 inmates, revealed that, in addition to its nominal function, it also served as an infectious diseases hospital, an orphan asylum and a maternity hospital. 'All colonial governments sought to provide services as cheaply as possible,' comments Jones, 'but arguably Jamaica's medical services represents one of the worst examples of such parsimony' (Jones, 2013, loc.663).

Even though the lustre of Jamaica's former reputation had long faded and it was now a rather marginal colony, perceived by many as a hopeless case, with alarming signs that its black population was becoming increasingly restive, in the teeth of all this accumulating misery, resentment and simmering protest, the colonial authorities and their allies determined to seize the public relations initiative and to project a reassuring, and domesticated, image of Jamaica as a benign and healthful paradise, a kind of English village writ large. A British missionary, explorer, photographer and doctor who had taken up residence in

Jamaica, James Johnston (1851–1921) had been giving lectures and slide shows for more than a decade, paid for by the Elder Dempster Shipping Company, explaining the benefits of visiting and migrating to Jamaica, and concluding his presentation on a defiant note by extolling Jamaica as 'the brightest jewel in the British Crown' (Johnston, 1903; Burnard, 2020; Carby, 2019, pp.203–210; Thompson, 2007, pp.33–34). In 1903 Johnston published one of the first guides to Jamaica as a tourist destination, *Jamaica: The new riviera*. There is 'a short but very pleasant trip from Kingston' that should be taken, he enthuses, 'along

Top: Cover of *Jamaica: The New Riviera,* published by James Johnston in 1903.
Below: Johnston's photograph of 'Domestics with yams, cocoanuts & c.' from the book © the Caribbean Photo Archive

the windward or shore road that leads to Morant Bay, following the car line, past the Lunatic Asylum'. On reaching Rock Fort the 'view of the harbor and Palisades from this point is very fine'.

As Hazel Carby explains, Johnston's photographs were skilfully curated to erase any suggestion of Jamaican belligerence. Rural Jamaicans are depicted 'in the neat, clean attire that everyone in Edwardian Britain would recognize as the attire of servants', all posing as subjects who had been suitably 'managed, tamed, and domesticated' (Carby, 2019, p.210). From the image of *'Domestics, with Yams, Cocoanuts, & c.'* (see previous page), one might be forgiven for supposing that Dr Thomas Allen's fanciful ambitions for tranquillising the restive 'natives' in the lunatic asylum had miraculously borne fruit across the whole of Jamaica. In rather similar terms, Mimi Sheller remarks on how early 20th-century photographs of Jamaica 'recuperate the Jamaican working class into safe poses of productivity and law and order which had been so severely fractured in 1865' (Sheller, 2011, p.557). As if to conform obligingly with the image of submissiveness conveyed by Carby and Sheller's commentaries, Johnston concludes his tour by recounting how:

> there is a huge quarry close by where the prisoners from the Penitentiary are brought every working day to put in their time of 'hard labour', their Osnaburg garbs abundantly testifying by sundry brands to the number of years they are 'doing'. (Johnston, 1903, p.38)

In the two chapters that follow, the spotlight shifts from the mad and poor in Jamaica to the poor and mad in Britain. For the 'respectable' classes in Britain in the 1880s, there was not much to choose between the 'white rabble' who had been demonstrating in London in 1886 under the Reform banner and the black population in Jamaica. Exactly the same questions were posed, and much the same answers returned, about the capacity for self-government among the working classes and the inmates of lunatic asylums in Britain as were being asked about their counterparts in Jamaica. As I review in the first of these chapters, fears were being stoked up across disparate media that various population groups were failing to uphold the standards of the imperial race, and that the stability and future of the empire were coming under threat. As a consequence, the mad poor in late 19th century Britain (by which we can understand the great majority of the contemporary insane) became racialised as what I term 'poor whites'.

Historian Anna Stubblefield has invoked the term 'tainted whiteness' to convey a complementary emphasis on contemporary concerns with varieties of white impurity, several of which are brought together under the umbrella of 'the feebleminded', which by the early 20th century had come to function as a sign of racial taint (Stubblefield, 2007). Here we can discern the impulse and outlook that was to confirm the status of the 'mentally ill' as 'damaged goods', morally, socially and biologically, from this time onwards. I sketch briefly the controversies that culminate in the landmark, though now discredited, Mental Deficiency Act of 1913. And I review briefly what was at stake for the mad poor in this period, how they fared in life and in death, the discourses in which they were dissected and displayed, and the pits in which their remains were deposited.

It is not incidental that, in James Johnston's photographs, the Jamaican poor were posing in the attire of servants – as historian Geoff Eley has argued, there are strong grounds for 'seeing servitude and slavery as the social forms of labour that were foundational to the capitalist modernity forged during the eighteenth century' (Eley, 2014, p.7). At the turn of the 20th century, domestic servants formed roughly 40% of the female labour force in Britain. In the second chapter in this section, I tell in some detail what was at stake in these years for a young woman having to manage the transition between one mode of social subordination, or servitude, and another – between that of a mental patient, or lunatic, on the one hand, and that of a residential domestic servant on the other. Born into poverty, Alice Rebecca Triggs found herself drawn into the triangulated destinies of war, madness and migration, her parents both dying when she was young, her sister emigrating to Australia, and her brother meeting his death in the First World War on the first day of the Somme offensive, leaving Alice to fend for herself alone.

There is an unmistakeable resonance here with Saidiya Hartman's description of the situation of the emancipated ex-slave, nominally a 'free individual' but in actuality lumbered with 'an abased and encumbered individuality', all the time castigated and made blameworthy (Hartman, 1997, p.6).

'A blot on her race! Away with her, down the hold!' Within the acutely and fervently discriminatory racial consciousness of the period, as a single woman of limited education from poor circumstances, who appeared to lack the capacity and required skills for self-government (though arguably she possessed them in abundance on her own terms), Alice found herself stigmatised as a 'poor white' and was consigned into the darkness of the psychiatric equivalent of a slave hold. We must try to comprehend critically the circumstances and the ardour that gave rise to, and impelled, this type of medico-moral outlook, focused on mental and moral defect and promoted an ideal of white racial superiority by disavowing persons or groups considered blemished or defective. Alice Rebecca Triggs was reviled and shut away for more than 40 years by the supine psychiatric authorities of her time – custodians of a narrow and punitive ideology of racial whiteness – and never allowed to tell, or become, the narrator of her own story.

7

The mad poor as poor whites

Sociologist and author of the book *Racism After 'Race Relations'* (1993), Robert Miles captures an important theme when he proposes:

> it was not only the European *exterior* that was racialised by certain classes of Europeans: there was also a racialization of the interior of Europe... A central theme of colonial racism during the 19th century was the claim that colonisation has as one of its objectives the *civilisation* of 'backward' or 'childish' races... In such instances, colonial exploitation was achieved, *inter alia*, by means of a civilising process which entailed an inferiorisation of the colonial subject and practices of cultural imperialism. (Miles, 1993, pp.88–89)

The 'white rabble' who demonstrated in London in 1886 under the Reform banner seemed to the 'respectable' classes to be pretty much indistinguishable from the 'Negro' and the 400,000 blacks in Jamaica, all of them 'tainted from birth and irredeemable, their unhappy condition an inevitable result of laziness, drunkenness, and want of thrift '(Semmel, 1962, p.87). In his classic account of the aftermath of the Governor Eyre controversy, historian Bernard Semmel points out that, while the comparisons were not always made openly, the English governing classes in the 1860s were inclined to regard the Irish, the Jamaican black population and other 'native' peoples much as they had traditionally regarded their own labouring classes:

> ... thoroughly undisciplined, with a tendency to revert to bestial behaviour, consequently requiring to be kept in order by force and by occasional but severe flashes of violence; vicious and sly, incapable of telling the truth, naturally lazy and unwilling to work unless under compulsion. (Semmel, 1962, p.141)

Openly dissenting from John Stuart Mill and his denial of congenital differences between the races, the writer and historian Charles Kingsley, Mills' contemporary, was now driven to the conclusion that the English working man, along with the Jamaican black and the Irish, was 'quite unfit for self-government' (Semmel, 1962, p.105). In the service of furbishing a more pessimistic outlook on the capabilities and prospects of the subordinate classes or races, in all these debates there was a constant back and forth between the condition of the ungovernable classes in Britain and the condition of the African or the emancipated ex-slave. 'It was within the exploding nineteenth century city,' anthropologists Jean and John Comaroff write, 'that the bourgeoisie met with its own most immediate experience of primitive unreason... coupling the pauper and the primitive in a common destiny' (1992, pp. 255–256). And as the transnational agent of the civilizing mission, the Salvation Army worked tirelessly to reclaim 'savages' in 'Darkest England' as much as in 'Darkest India' (Fischer-Tiné, 2012, pp.125–164).

In his magisterial study of the hegemonic sway of 'the White Man', historian Bill Schwarz remarks on the importance of 'the symbolic transaction between the idea of the residuum and its like at home and of the native overseas' (Schwarz, 2013, pp.170–171). He goes on to elaborate how, both in his home country and overseas, the figure of the White Man is mobilised to provide the norm against which refractory individuals can be tested. We must grasp, insists Schwarz, 'the conjunctions binding the normative with the perverse or the primitive... the structural, relational connections between the masculine and the feminine, manly and unmanly, white and non-white, rational and irrational, the fit and the unfit', and attend to what he terms 'the shifting dispositions of racial whiteness' (Schwarz, 2013, pp.170–171). Political scientist Robbie Shilliam has recently argued that, for a long line of thinkers, from Edmund Burke, Thomas Carlyle and William Cobbett through to Beatrice and Sidney Webb, the African or ex-slave has been a formative referent for the imaginary that they have all deployed in support of a racialised moral economy where some workers are integrated and made over into citizens and others are cast out as 'primitive', threatening and undeserving (Shilliam, 2018).

Arising out of encounters with 'natives' abroad, and with the 'uncivilized' urban poor in Britain, there were intense imperial concerns to demarcate between 'deserving' and 'undeserving' population groups. As historian Jose Harris has observed, in the second half of the 19th century British politics became 'increasingly caught up in the politics of empire', with the result that 'British citizens, both male and female, were viewed as the raw material of a new imperial race', raising fraught questions as to whether the conditions of life in contemporary urban Britain were at all adequate to meet the expectations, and demands, of imperial aggrandisement (Harris, 1993, p.181). By the turn of the century, the family was being cast as the breeding and training ground for a modern imperial race, with the result, as Harris describes, that 'bad mothering was no longer seen merely as a private failure, but as subversive of community, nation, Empire and race' (1993, p.80). Formerly, a sense of racial identity as primarily a cultural and historical, rather than biological, phenomenon had prevailed, but this was now in tension with anthropological opinion emphasising the immense evolutionary gulf between the 'backward' and 'advanced' races. Overall, Harris argues, the massive expansion of empire, which drew an increasing number of Britons into master–servant relationships with foreign peoples, undoubtedly served to promote a consciousness of racial superiority (1993, p.234).

Observers frequently applied racial metaphors to the poorer classes of Britain themselves, referring to them as a 'backward people' and 'a race apart'. 'Large sections of the British poor would not have been classified as white,' remarks Anoop Nayak, for 'the designation of the British working classes as white is a modern phenomenon' (Nayak, 2009, p.29). The white poor 'have long existed on the boundaries of whiteness', comments David Gillborn, inhabiting a condition that Ricky Lee Allen terms 'White but not quite' (Gillborn, 2010, p.14; Allen, 2009, p.214). Historian Dorothy Porter describes how doctors, in their encounters with barely 'tolerable human types' inhabiting the slums, 'frequently had to remind themselves that the poor belonged to the human species at all' (Porter, 1991, p.159; Wohl, 1977/2017, pp.43–79). A black American academic visiting Britain in the 1900s 'observed that "racial" segregation between rich and poor in London was more profound than anywhere else in the world, even including the southern United States' (cited in Harris, 1993, pp.235–236).

From the 1840s onwards, concerns over threats to white superiority and the imperative to protect the quality of white stock found heightened expression across the empire, from India to Malaya to Australia to South Africa, in anxieties over a population group identified as 'poor whites'. This was manifested most audibly in Britain in the clamour over racial degeneration and national decline that followed the military disasters of December 1899 at the hands of a few thousand poorly organised Dutch farmers in what became known as the Boer War. This gave rise to the widely debated *Report of the Interdepartmental Committee on Physical Deterioration* (1905), to be followed a few years later by the Royal Commission for the Care and Control of the Feeble-Minded (1908), and then by the landmark, though some will say infamous, Mental Deficiency Act of 1913. In the meantime, all of this gave an added spurt to eugenics, turning it from a fledgling 'science' into a 'movement' (Larson, 1991). By 1912, Havelock Ellis (1959–1939), a Fabian, psychologist and sexual radical, was urging 'the eugenic guardianship of the race'. As historians have remarked, 'in the early twentieth century it was difficult for even liberal-minded psychiatrists to escape the racist biases of that era or the racial framing of psychiatric inquiry in Africa' (Akyeampong et al., 2015, p.3). Racial science had become the norm, to the point that contesting racial science meant contesting science itself (Cleall, 2022, pp.215–245).

Though it was constantly being revised, imperial ideology always retained an affinity for metaphors of child growth and development – or, in a more polemical guise, for notions of retarded development and primitive regression. Much favoured in early Victorian England was the term 'residuum', used to signify two classes of 'refuse': sewage, and the lowest classes in the urban population. In its latter meaning, residuum was widely believed to consist of inveterate and irredeemable incompetents, whom a number of reformers, including Alfred Marshall, William Booth and (briefly) William Beveridge, favoured segregating permanently in disciplinary labour colonies (Jones, 1971). Drastic and punitive though such proposals may seem, they are not so surprising when viewed in the context of the outlook that typified the socialist social reformers Beatrice and Sidney Webb, for example, who attached the disparaging moniker the 'average sensual man' to the ordinary person or 'man in the street'. At its most benevolent, the notion of a colonised subject as a childlike innocent in need of humane care and civilizing influence had supplied a common thread between the 'native' and the 'lunatic'. But now this compact had been expanded to include the 'average sensual man' as a being who was, apparently, incapable of exercising self-control over his affairs, least of all over his 'sensual' nature', and who, as the cultural historian Gertrude Himmelfarb observes, 'was little more than a child, a "non-adult" incapable of controlling his appetites or judging his own best interests' (Himmelfarb, 1991, pp.372, 375).

Himmelfarb quotes from Beatrice Webb's diary: 'That was a brilliant suggestion of H.G. Wells that we should divide the world into adults and non-adults', alluding to what was actually by now quite a standard high imperial trope. The non-adult races would either die out, it was assumed, or take an awfully long time to reach a capacity for self-government and self-determination. Only a minority of Britons counted as adult, or civilised; a considerable part of the population, alleged alienist Joseph Mortimer Granville in 1877, 'labour under diseases destroying the powers of self-control and self-help in the individual and deteriorating the race' (Granville, 1877, p.326). Lunatics must be 'trained afresh in the ways of life' and the first step in their re-education 'ought to commence in placing the insane on the footing of children. The whole policy and system of treatment hinges on this presumption: lunatics are not only irresponsible, they are incapable of self-control' (Granville, 1877, p.22).

For the writer H.G. Wells, the 'common people' were mostly an inferior bunch, morally, politically and physically: a 'great swollen, shapeless, hypertrophied social mass', the 'people of the abyss', to be replaced in the utopian new republic that he envisaged by a class of 'modern efficients' (Himmelfarb, 1991, p.371). Similar sentiments feature in his contemporary George Bernard Shaw's play *Man and Superman*, written in 1903. In the first decade of the new century, when drafting a Minority Report for the Poor Law Commission, Beatrice Webb was to moot, quite without irony, a proposal for 'a great social drainage scheme'. One scents a faint but unmistakeable whiff of the 'seepage' at the Kingston Lunatic Asylum in Jamaica. Advocating that the poor law now be broken into separate authorities, the Webbs envisaged, among other institutions, a dedicated asylum authority for the mentally ill, and also a special authority to provide for the permanent segregation and governance, 'under reasonably comfortable conditions, and firm but kindly control', of the entire population of the feeble-minded, even those who were not destitute, along with detention colonies for recalcitrant workers, or idlers, whose 'morbid states of mind' arrested their ability to contribute usefully to the industrial order (Himmelfarb, 1991, p.369).

It is against this background of widespread fears that various population groups were failing to uphold the standards of the imperial race that the mad poor in late 19th century Britain (by which we can understand the great majority of the contemporary insane) became racialised as what I term 'poor whites' to convey the idea, above all, of morally stigmatised identities. Historian Anna Stubblefield has invoked the term 'tainted whiteness' to convey a complementary emphasis on contemporary concerns with varieties of white impurity, several of which, such as poverty and lack of civilisation-building skills, are brought together under the umbrella of 'the feebleminded', which by the early 20th century had come to function as a sign of racial taint: a feeble-minded white person was an impure white person who posed a threat to the supremacy of the white race (Stubblefield, 2007, pp.168–169).

Here we can identify the impulse and outlook that was to confirm the status of the 'mentally ill' as 'damaged goods', morally, socially and biologically, at one and the same time. Those who succeeded in exhibiting emotional self-control and self-mastery might sometimes be considered to have recovered, but for many of the 'abject others', the prospect of a re-entry into society was not on the horizon. Increasingly, madness was drawn into a racial and eugenic discourse where the mad were cast as racial deviants or anachronistic humans, outside the time of imperial modernity (McClintock, 2001). Obsessed with identifying the unfit, eugenicists were forever haunted by uncertainties over whether 'deficiency' entailed a biological failing or just social incompetence and, above all, until well into the 20th century, by the chimera of a 'social problem group', the existence of which could never be convincingly established (Macnicol, 1983; Thomson, 1999).

Some of the notions that were current may have been Social Darwinist but, as Dorothy Porter adroitly remarks, Social Darwinism was frequently just a matter of dressing longstanding prejudices in a new guise (Porter, 1991, p.160). In contemporary discourse, paupers, and least of all pauper lunatics, were not considered rational subjects, or granted fully human status, but, together with the slave and the ex-slave, were seen as emblematic of 'problem' populations requiring discipline in order to learn how to conduct themselves in the new market economy (O'Connell, 2009, p.172). Foisted on the asylum system in ever-greater numbers, the mad poor faced increasingly grim prospects. The foundations on which, henceforth, the destinies of the mad poor in Britain were to be managed, portrayed and stigmatised had been laid by the New Poor Law of 1834. Though the conditions in asylums were not necessarily harsh, just as in the workhouse, it was the stigma attaching to confinement that constituted the cruelty, making the very idea of the asylum shameful and disgraceful. In John Arlidge's *On the State of Lunacy* (1859) – a remarkable commentary by a sensitive medical observer – we discover a threnody for a vanishing humanitarian era in his belief that the mad poor were being 'pauperised' under a law that 'inflicts injury and social degradation'. His prediction of a calamity in which the asylum would become a 'monster' and a 'manufactory of chronic insanity' proved prescient indeed.

J. Mortimer Granville, lead investigator for the *Lancet Commission on Lunatic Asylums*, reported in 1877 how at Colney Hatch Asylum in London (later to be renamed Friern Hospital – one of the largest such institutions in Britain), 'it is difficult to describe – and perhaps impossible to formulate – the treatment of mental disease', since the 'vastness of the institution, and the multitude of its inmates, are… overwhelming obstacles to treatment in the true sense of the term'. In many of the wards, 'moral measures of control are manifestly of small avail':

> It would be as easy to tame a wild horse in the midst of his herd as to control an insane virago by stern kindness under the conditions that exist, and the surroundings created by the system extant at this asylum. (Granville, 1877, pp.180–181)

Yet all is not lost:

> the majority of the inmates, regarded *individually*, are, however, plainly amenable to moral treatment. Even the parties in the attempted fights we

witnessed were coherent in their rage, and gave plausible reasons for their animosity when passion was partially appeased. (Granville, 1877, p.181)

He was also able to report that, at Hanwell Asylum in West London, where in the late 1830s alienist John Connolly (1794–1866) famously abolished mechanical restraints, replacing them for a time with a regime of 'moral treatment', the institution has 'within the last few years emerged from a period of darkness and empiricism', during which, it is implied, the shower bath was being used as an instrument of discipline. The institution had now 'entered an era of scientific progress and enlightenment' in which, once again, 'the treatment is becoming more essentially moral'. But such improvement remained precarious and continuously under threat. As Granville discerned:

> the difficulties which psychologists doomed to labour in a building like
> the asylum at Hanwell, and with attendants dressed as prison warders,
> must encounter and contrive to surmount, can scarcely be over-
> estimated. (Granville, 1877, p.83)

To throw light on what was frequently at stake for the mad poor in this period, we may turn to the correspondence of inmates of the Royal Edinburgh Asylum between 1873 and 1908 (Beveridge, 1997). Roughly three-quarters of them suffered the degradations of pauper status and were compelled to wear asylum-issue pauper uniforms and subjected to taunts from their social 'superiors' among the inmate community. Tellingly, many of them had reached the conclusion that the very nature of being an inmate in an asylum rendered nugatory any aspiration to meaningful personhood, and that escape was the only recourse left to them.

A defeated outlook was thrust upon the mad in this period, and in some contemporary documents the reader can almost see it happening. In Glasgow, for instance, driven by spectres of degeneration and hereditary taint, 'racial' and 'class' fears intermingled, resulting in the total exclusion of pauper lunatic patients from the Glasgow Royal Hospital (Andrews, 1999). At Hanwell Asylum, once again, the efforts of the mad poor and their families to attribute their distress to their social circumstances were derided by middle-class physicians, who were mostly inclined to moralise the predicaments of their working-class patients in the language of idleness, moral depravity and lack of will (Suzuki, 2007). The deaths of black patients in colonial lunatic asylums may, generally, have been sparsely reported ('Died' was a typical entry), as historians have remarked, but the deaths and burials of the mad poor in Britain were no less brutal and unceremonial: their bodies were frequently sold for dissection to repay their welfare debts to society, their names simply entered in an 'Abnormalities and Dissections' book, and their remains disposed of in a common paupers' grave (Hurren, 2011).

In manufactories and foundries across Britain, industrial modernity was on display, taking its cue from the slave systems and economies driven by chattel slavery, which, in the new historiography of the Black Atlantic, are now understood as large-scale capitalist systems in which slaves were the first modern proletariat. To the modernity of the enslaved mass worker, historian Geoff Eley adds the complementary importance of domestic servitude for the overall labour markets. There are, Eley asserts, 'strong grounds for seeing servitude and slavery as the social forms of labour that were foundational to the capitalist modernity forged during the eighteenth century' (2014) and to the modes of social subordination that enabled it to thrive:

> The search for a 'pure' working-class formation from which forms
> of enslavement, servitude, indenturing, impressment, conscription,
> imprisonment and coercion have been purged, remains a chimera. (Eley,
> 2014, p.7)

Servitude is at the heart of it, and at the turn of the 20th century domestic servants formed roughly 40% of the female workforce in Britain.

Philosopher and novelist William Godwin (1756–1836), founder of philosophical anarchism, thought hard and long about the condition of servants and the meaning of servitude, noting the 'monstrous association and union of wealth and poverty together' that the co-habitation of servants and masters, as distinct classes in a single household, represented. Servants, he wrote in 1797:

> must either cherish a burning envy in their bosoms, an inextinguishable
> abhorrence against the injustice of society; or, guided by the hopelessness
> of their condition, they must blunt every finer feeling of the mind, and
> sit down in their obscure retreat, having for the constant habits of their
> reflections, slavery and contentment. They can scarcely expect to emerge
> from their depression. They must expect to spend the best years of their
> existence in a miserable dependence. (Godwin, 1797, pp.201–211)

Servitude, he concluded, was akin to slavery. Although it had been alleged that servants could not be considered as slaves because the engagement into which they entered was voluntary, Godwin strongly disagreed: 'It is the condition under which he exists, not the way he came into it, that constitutes the difference between a freeman and a slave', though he acknowledged that 'the slavery of an English servant has its mitigations, and is, in several intelligible and distinct particulars, preferable to that of the West-Indian Negro' (Godwin, 1797, pp.201–211).

Historians such as Lucy Delap (2011), Alison Light (2007), Carolyn Steedman (2007) and Selina Todd (2009) have taken domestic service as a foundational narrative among the varied stories that may be told about the 20th century and the making of modern national identity. In doing so, they inevitably part company in some respects with the austerity, and divisiveness, of Godwin's portrait, revealing instead a diversity of experiences of domestic service in which young women in service did not necessarily internalise inferiority and servility, or experience an abject sense of self. Unquestionably, much has been achieved here, but at the same time, when engaging with the experience of servitude in British society at the end of the 19th century and in the early years of the 20th, the asperity of Godwin's vision is, I believe, an indispensable guide to the condition of a moral, emotional and libidinal economy, with a high premium on emotional self-control, beset by profound anxieties about the future of the race. Strictures from the superior classes were being laid ever more harshly on states of being among the lower or inferior orders, who were perceived as posing a threat to the vitality and stability, and hence to the future, of the white race. In what follows, I am going to tell the story of a young woman who, though she is by no means representative of the overall experience of domestic service in this period, at the same time offers an intimate and revealing portrait of what was at stake in these years for those like her in having to manage the transition between one mode of social subordination, or servitude, and another: between that of a mental patient, or lunatic, on the one hand, and that of a residential domestic servant on the other.

8

Alice Rebecca Triggs: War, madness and migration

At the end of December 1916 an advertisement was placed in *The Times*:

> As Cook-General, situation required for respectable young woman, excellent references. London or suburbs preferred. Has been mentally ill, now perfectly well and strong. Apply by letter care of Miss Vickers, Church House, Westminster.

The 'young woman' in question was Alice Rebecca Triggs, born in Islington in July 1885, and now in the care of the Mental After Care Association (MACA), founded in 1879 and originally named The After-Care Association for Poor and Friendless Female Convalescents on Leaving Asylums for the Insane. Needless to say, 'respectable' vied with other epithets on the slate of Alice's track record over the previous 10 years or so.[1] Her father, Joseph Triggs, a printer's compositor, had died of pneumonia age 50, in March 1899, in the presence of his wife, Alice Mary Triggs. In the census for 1901, Alice Mary Triggs is identified as head of the household at 145 New North Road, Shoreditch, East London, where she was now living with her son Joseph, age 17, a solicitor's clerk; her daughter Alice Rebecca, age 15, a general servant domestic, and her younger daughter, Florence, age 13. Sadly, they were not to be together for much longer, for in June of the following year Alice the elder died a lonely death from chronic intestinal ulceration at the Shoreditch Infirmary, identified merely as 'Trigg' on the death certificate, middle name not given, no known rank or profession. So Joseph, Alice the younger and Florence had now lost

---

1. My discussion of Alice draws mostly on the records of the Mental After Care Association that are held by the Wellcome Collection, and also on her case records from Colney Hatch Asylum and other Poor Law institutions, held by the London Metropolitan Archives, as itemised in Archives Consulted listed at the end of the book.

both their parents and were left to make their own ways in the world. Here, as it turned out, they would quite soon find themselves drawn into the triangulated destinies, or career paths, very much of their time, of war, madness and migration.

Soon after their mother's death, the household broke up and Joseph, Alice and Florence went separate ways: Joseph into lodgings and Florence and Alice into service. Alice found a situation as servant with a cousin on her father's side in Muswell Hill, where she was to stay for seven years. It appears that Florence, through contact with, and quite likely the support of, two or more uncles on her mother's side who had already emigrated to Australia, decided after a few years in service in London to follow in their path. On 23rd September 1911, at the age of 23, she boarded the *Norseman*, bound for Brisbane, never to return to Britain again or to clap eyes on either of her siblings, though she held them both dear and did not lose contact with them. On the passenger list, her occupation is given as 'domestic servant', but it seems likely that, in embarking on her journey, she was already intent upon transcending the destiny that appeared to have been chosen for her in Britain, for she was never to work as a servant again. The colour of her skin and her apparent respectability also counted for a good deal, for she sailed for Australia during the heyday of the controversial 'White Australia' policy, embodied in colonial legislation starting in 1888, which underscored the status of Australia as a 'white' nation, laying down strict criteria and guidelines as to the kinds of immigrants who were acceptable to the Australian state (Tavan, 2005).

We do not know exactly what happened to Alice in the years leading up to the First World War, but she seems to have come to the attention of the authorities in about 1913, after she had left – or been dismissed from – her situation with her cousin in Muswell Hill. Thereafter, having developed a dependency on alcohol, she fell into an unsettled life: short periods of service interspersed with bouts of drinking, occasioning the predictable aspersions that she was also working as a prostitute. There is no evidence given for this, and it is more likely that she had one or more ill-considered casual liaisons, with the result that she contracted venereal disease (VD), for which she was soon vilified as a 'fallen' or 'immoral' woman by the Poor Law authorities. All the same, she made a good impression on some of those who had dealings with her, who regarded her as warm, talkative and friendly. 'There is something very nice about the woman,' one MACA worker remarked.

It was an inopportune moment in which to fall prey to VD, for in the febrile atmosphere of a gathering climate of national emergency, the disease was fast assuming the status of a canker in the national body and a threat to the war effort. The 'Great Scourge', as the militant suffragist Christabel Pankhurst

(1880–1950) had recently termed sexual diseases, was widely regarded as 'the great cause of physical, mental and moral degeneracy, and of race suicide' (Pankhurst, 1913). After extensive lobbying, a Royal Commission on venereal disease had been set up in 1913, reporting in 1916 and estimating that up to 10% of the urban population in Britain had syphilis, and a higher percentage was likely to have gonorrhoea. The Contagious Diseases Acts of 1864, 1866 and 1869, had been repealed in 1886, marking the end of a 20-year experiment in which the British state had attempted, but failed, to coerce targeted groups to submit to treatment for venereal disease. After 1916, the system of treatment was nominally voluntary but, as historian Pamela Cox has shown, in actuality certain categories of people, like women considered sexually transgressive, were still subjected to more traditional forms of coercion, and many Poor Law infirmaries continued to operate old-style 'lock wards' as dedicated treatment spaces for male and female pauper patients with sexually transmitted diseases, (Cox, 2007).

Right on the cusp of the new legislation, Alice was herself treated in the lock ward at Islington Infirmary, before being sent to 'The Haven' in Ely, one of an extensive network of mainly Christian charitable 'rescue homes', as they were then known, that occupied a significant place in a mixed economy of coercive governance. These sought to control their inmates by discouraging them from leaving, and taught them skills (Alice was said to have learned to cook) that instilled in them the virtues of domestic service. Alice remained there for 10 months until, early in February 1915, she allegedly 'lost her reason there suddenly in church one morning' and was promptly sent back to Miss Alice Bardsley, the superintendent of the rescue home in Islington who had previously supported her. Alice Bardsley took her back to the Islington Infirmary, where she reportedly made a rather curious statement that 'the patient dances, is not mentally strong, screamed out in church & said she must chop wood, the Germans were coming, and was foolish and dazed'.

Alice denied to the medical officer at the Infirmary that she had ever been 'immoral', earning her the rebuke that she was 'apparently morally irresponsible'. 'Immoral' ('has been immoral', 'denies being immoral') was a standard trope in the poor law universe, conveying an intentional ambiguity between a single transgressive act and the surrender to the depravity of prostitution. Alice, in her 'denial', may well have been intending merely to limit the significance or extent of her 'misconduct', but such was the inescapable stranglehold of the label that she succeeded only in aggravating her perceived transgression. The following day she was conveyed to Colney Hatch Asylum, where her temperament was described as cheerful but very obstinate, and she was said to be rather talkative, easily upset and impertinent when spoken to.

Moral imbecility

At Colney Hatch, Alice was brought before Dr Samuel Elgee, a well-regarded and ambitious alienist, who served as deputy medical superintendent at the asylum during the war and would become medical superintendent at Cane Hill, another London County Council asylum, in 1919. Elgee had read the reports of Alice's supposed transgressions and did not take to her at all, seeing in her an opportunity to promote, and take advantage of, the newly-minted diagnostic category of moral imbecility that had been spawned by the Mental Deficiency Act of 1913. As briefly noted above, this legislation had arisen after intensive lobbying and prolonged debate, together with a Royal Commission on the Care and Control of the Feeble-Minded, to address concerns over racial degeneration and the sapping of the national strength by 'weak' or 'degenerative' groups, and, practically, to provide for the segregation of people deemed to be 'feeble-minded' or 'moral defectives', in the interests of the 'purification of the race' (Walmsley, 2000).

The diagnosis is inscribed in bold letters on the case record against her name: MORAL IMBECILITY. She was suffering, it went on, 'from Congenital Mental Deficiency of the moral variety'. Her comprehension, Elgee admitted, was good; there was no clouding of consciousness, and she could orientate herself correctly. Her memory for all events was also good, for she conversed rationally; no delusions or hallucinations had been elicited from her, and she gave a moderately connected account of herself. All pretty convincing so far. She was obviously not mad, or psychotic, in a conventional sense. So what was the problem then? Her deficiency, it turns out, was exclusively in the moral and sexual domain, for 'she is untruthful, she has been immoral, and her sense of right and wrong is not well developed'. Most tellingly, as far

Alice Triggs photographed in 1915 (l) and 1916 (r) on her admissions to Colney Hatch Lunatic Asylum (photos courtesy of London Metropolitan Archives)

as Elgee is concerned, 'when questioned about herself, she is evidently lying all the time.' By this Elgee intended to convey that, in her statements to him, Alice lamentably failed to satisfy or comply with the 'truth' that he powerfully imagined about her circumstances and conduct – a truth that he clearly felt he knew to be true, in which Alice was most certainly a serial sexual transgressor, guilty of all manner of sexual misconduct, even though the evidence for this conjecture, wilfully denied or withheld by Alice herself, as he believed, eluded him, and was nowhere to be found. If Elgee was privy to something ('evidently lying') about what Alice had been doing that she was disavowing, he was very coy about it; he certainly did not declare what it was, simply assuming that his authority could be taken on trust, even though his declarations were rhetorical through and through, and lacking in substance. Most likely, in her exchange with him, Alice had evinced no particular regrets ('she is without shame as to her past life') over her sexual encounters and, perhaps, even hinted at the pleasure they afforded her. Unquestionably, in her self-presentation, she had failed to conform to Edwardian norms of how women, especially those of a lower class, were supposed to behave, for she was inclined to talk too much, to be cheeky and impudent, to exhibit a deficiency 'of the moral variety', to deny that she was, or had ever been, 'immoral', and in her exchanges with Dr Elgee to wilfully abscond from the 'truth' that he knew about her. And it was this, above all, that now heaped all this diagnostic ordure on her head.

The Mental Deficiency Act of 1913, in an admirably clear and unadorned statement, defines moral imbeciles 'as persons who from an early age display some permanent mental defect, coupled with strong vicious or criminal propensities, on which punishment has had little or no deterrent effect'. One may feel aghast to read this, as I certainly was when I first saw the diagnosis appended to Alice's case, against the background of what I already knew and we will shortly learn about her. Could this really be Alice, we might wonder? However, looking beyond questions about the diagnosis in this individual case, apposite though that may be, we need to remember also that moral imbecility was always a controversial diagnosis, even in its own time, and try to comprehend critically the circumstances, and the ardour, that gave rise to and impelled this type of medico-moral outlook. Admittedly, to do this is exceedingly difficult, because we are, in effect, dealing with a creedal system, rather than a formal diagnostic one – one that, by our contemporary lights, is pretty much inaccessible to us as a way of thinking, and above all feeling, about life and relations between different groups of human beings.

In 1921, at a meeting of the section of psychiatry at the Royal Society of Medicine, Alfred Tredgold (1870–1952), the neurologist and psychiatrist who may be considered one of the prime movers behind the Mental Deficiency Act, provided a helpful critical commentary on the diagnostic category of moral imbecility (Tredgold, 1921). After anchoring the meaning of 'sexual misconduct' in a moral universe in which 'amongst civilized peoples, the sexual instinct is no longer manifested in rape and promiscuous intercourse, but within the bonds of wedlock', he addressed the question of what was to count as vicious sexual misconduct, which was integral to the diagnosis of moral imbecility. It was, he proposed, 'misconduct that is persistent and outrageous', and by way of example he distinguished between a woman who pursues her calling as a prostitute in 'what may be termed a decent, respectable manner' and one who 'openly and persistently flaunts herself in an offensive and outrageous manner', in what amounts to 'vicious conduct'. Tredgold, to his credit, did not shirk from the controversies that hung over the diagnosis, especially the idea of a permanent mental defect. In the discussion that followed his presentation, one Dr Stoddart referred to patients whose 'moral defect' could be cured by psychoanalysis, arguing that such cases, being curable, should not be brought under the Mental Deficiency Act. A Dr Shrubsall mounted a similar argument, maintaining that, by means of psychotherapy, 'hidden springs of trouble may be tapped and the psychic energy released to more normal routes of operation', and concluding:

> Who was prepared to say with the brief opportunities for diagnosis available to most certifying officers which cases could be relieved and which could not? (Tredgold, 1921)

Indeed, but such queries were unlikely to qualify the certitudes, or stay the hand, of Dr Elgee and his like in reproducing a discourse that, as John Macnicol (1983) has remarked, is rife with confusion between moralism and scientific categorisation. For Alice, and others of her class, such discriminating psychotherapeutic options were, in any case, wholly inaccessible, thus revealing and affirming the extent to which the whole diagnostic apparatus of mental and moral defect was deeply and inextricably embedded in the apparatus of social class, with its attendant ideologies, which itself supported the imperial project, promoting an ideal of white racial superiority by marginalising, or disavowing, persons or groups considered blemished or defective.

So what was to be done with Alice? In the first instance, rather little, for once all the rhetorical mud-slinging had settled down, she was transferred to Napsbury Asylum, near St Albans (spelled as 'Napsberry' by the Islington Guardians), and spent much of her time working in the laundry until, in February 1916, she was discharged when the War Office decided to requisition Napsbury, and a number of other asylums, as war hospitals (Barham, 2004, pp.55–57). And at this point, a new calamity entered her life – around the middle of 1916, her brother Joseph, who had enlisted in the London Rifle Brigade and been sent to France with the expeditionary force, was posted as missing in action. Some weeks were to pass before it was finally declared that Rifleman Joseph Triggs, service number 301759, had died on 1 July 2016, the first day of the Somme offensive. Joseph was later to be listed at the Thiepval Memorial among the missing who would for ever after be remembered, although tellingly it is the younger sister, Florence, at an address in Australia, who is named as his surviving next of kin, not Alice of the Colney Hatch Lunatic Asylum. For, in the meantime, Alice had been readmitted to Colney Hatch.

This time round, she was placed under the care of Dr Ernest Reid, who gave her a diagnosis of 'melancholia' ('She states that she has been depressed about her brother in the trenches, she has been out to service but could not work, she was so miserable and cried all day'). This diagnosis, up to a point, respects the integrity of her emotional state as reflecting a reality that is understandable and not to be gainsaid, thus positioning her within a normative moral world of grieving or anxious human subjects in a country at war, rather than as a deviant or freak. Significantly, over the entire course of this admission, no mention was made of 'moral imbecility'. She was initially placed on suicidal watch but, by the end of August, this was withdrawn and she was declared 'very much improved, bright clean and tidy, conversing cheerfully and working regularly'. In November she was sent out on trial to the Mental After Care Association, and formally discharged as 'recovered' on 15 December 1916.

Alice goes into service

So, this was the 'respectable young woman', the recovered 'moral imbecile', who was 'now perfectly well and strong', whom readers of *The Times* were invited to receive into their homes as 'Cook-General' (meaning a general servant who also acted as cook). After some false starts and mix-ups, in February 1917 Alice was eventually placed – initially for a trial month – in a situation with a Mrs A.S. Baxter, a widow aged 61, who lived in Streatham, south London. Soon after Alice moved in, Mrs Baxter was confined to her room for three weeks with a cold, so requested that Alice stay for another month so she could make her mind up about her.

Alice Sarah Baxter had no children, but her step daughter, Gertrude, a draper's assistant, had been living with her until quite recently. She always signed herself 'Mrs A.S. Baxter' and so could avoid having to concede the intimacy of sharing a first name with Alice the servant. She took upon herself the responsibility for inducting Alice into the appropriate mode of servitude for a domestic servant in a respectable middle-class household, as the MACA annals record:

I am very sorry for the poor girl's sad circumstances, and will do my best for her to get on should she stay, especially if I can teach her to be less rough & noisy & more methodical generally... I find she is very excitable and a great talker & evidently has not been well-trained in early years. Certainly she needs to replenish her wardrobe in order to keep a decent place. She has only two morning dresses both of which she brought here soiled. Nevertheless she has several good points and seems anxious to please.

A week or so later, however, doubts were creeping in:

She really is not at all fit for genteel refined people. She knows not how to do anything nicely, & her cooking of vegetables is simply awful. She is more fitted to trades people, who have things rough & ready & could treat her as one of the family, I think.

Shortly after this, Alice was obviously starting to hover on the edge of abject territory:

I am very sorry to be obliged to say I cannot keep Alice Triggs unless there is a great change in her the next few weeks. She says she has never been used to getting up till 7.30 or after. I require her up at quarter to 7 & bring early tea at 7 o'clock. She has not done it once yet. She is always late with every meal & all her work. She is also a great procrastinator. Something left every day! I have been very patient and forbearing as it was a new place to her, but she gets later and later, and most tiresome and rude. I am so sorry, I am ready to be such a good friend to her, but it seems perfectly useless. She certainly must be off her head more than is certified. She will not go out at all on Sundays, shuts herself up in the kitchen with a big fire, windows and doors all closed, it is a most wretched experience for me.

And then there was the matter of Alice's laundry and Mrs Baxter's intrusive comments on the state of her undergarments:

I put her dresses, aprons, caps & collars out to the laundry but her undergarments she wears too long. She does not care to wash them though she has plenty of time and convenience.

It is to be wondered how Mrs Baxter became privy to the condition of Alice's knickers, although her remarks might also be a proxy for her suspicions, or apprehensions, over the 'unclean' or soiled state of Alice's morals.

Alice's condition of 'servitude' is perhaps best symbolised by the box that always accompanied her from one situation to another, as it would any other domestic servant. Tied around with ropes for ease of transport and to secure the lid, it can be seen as containing her 'props' for the 'clean and proper self' that she must become in order to perform in polite society, and thus as representing not so much a straitjacket as a constraining apparatus (hence the ropes to hold the lid on) to maintain her in the harness of civilized bourgeois life, and ensure that she knew, and stayed in, her proper place. It represents not only Mrs Baxter but also the Mental After Care Association, who tutored Alice in how she should keep her place. 'It is very good of the doctors to give me another chance,' Alice confided at one point. 'I do so hope you will keep well and be able to stay out of the institution for the rest of your life,' answered Miss Vickers, the Secretary of the Association, 'I was so glad you appreciated all that has been done for you by the doctors and nurses as I know how very good they are to all the patients.'

All along the way, Miss Vickers admonishes Alice in a relentlessly patronising tone to do her utmost to please the employers who have been gracious enough to offer her a situation. Alice, however, appeared reluctant, or unable, to permit herself to be cajoled into accepting her place as it had been taught, or assigned, to her by her 'superiors'. She was clearly painfully aware that, in taking a situation as a domestic servant after leaving the asylum, she might merely be trading one form of servitude for another. In this regard, the box that she was shortly to abandon in Mrs Baxter's house, leaving Mrs Baxter to wonder what she was to do with this item which Alice 'never unpacked, only opened the lid and left the rope on', represents an aborted foetus – Alice's abject failure to grow, and mature, into a viable human being who can discover a path to resolve and move beyond the dilemma of these competing forms of servitude. In the immediate circumstances of April 1917, it is also expressive of Alice's grief and abandonment – a ghastly desolation that she was unable to communicate. The ongoing slaughter on the Western Front, summoning waves of emotion that Mrs Baxter was vainly attempting to disavow, remained the elephant in the room in the brittle atmosphere of Mrs Baxter's household, where the mistress was battling to maintain an atmosphere of business just as usual with her servant, fearful lest mistress and servant, the one Alice and the other, should both become unbuttoned.

Alice's sojourn with Mrs Baxter ended quite abruptly when Mrs Baxter returned home to experience 'a fearful fright':

> I rang the bell several times & no reply. Suddenly I remembered I had
> my door key so I came in, went in the dining room & rang the bell. No
> response. Then I went out in the kitchen and found all doors locked &

windows bolted & all the place left dirty, nothing done at all! I went then upstairs & called Alice! She replied, saying she had a fearful fit of nerves & had to leave all the work & stay in her room. I begged her to come down, I said staying in your bedroom will not cure your nerves. She said, 'I can't & I won't!'. I then said if you do not come down and light up the kitchen fire and clear up, I shall get a policeman in, and he will make you! But she would not. I said, 'are you ill?' 'No'. 'Are you sure?' 'Yes. I am alright, only I have nerves'. I waited half an hour, at last in desperation & fright I went for a police. Then an inspector came & they said, as she was not violent, they could do nothing… Then I sent for my doctor who immediately wrote an order for her to be removed to the Wandsworth & Clapham Infirmary… so we had to get a cab and send her there.

A day or so later Mrs Baxter dispatched Alice's box to the workhouse on St John's Hill in Wandsworth, 'glad & relieved she is away from my home', for 'it has been a very unpleasant experience for me. I sincerely regret the poor girl's illness and all the worry and expense it has caused me. I am bitterly disappointed'. Nursing her own narcissism, and recoiling from the intrusion of raw human emotions that Alice had enforced on her, perhaps putting her in mind of 'tradespeople' with their rough manners, Mrs Baxter seemed more vexed by the inconvenience that had been done to her than concerned for what might be distressing Alice.

Returned to Colney Hatch on 5 April 1917, Alice found in Dr Reid a reasonably sympathetic ear to whom she could confide her grief. In her admission photograph this time round (though it appears to have been taken 10 days or so after her admission), she looks drawn and distraught. She was said to be:

depressed and sad, for she still mourns, she says, for the brother who was killed in the war. It makes her so miserable that she cannot do her work as a domestic servant… She is so depressed at times that life is not worth living, and she does not hesitate to admit that she has contemplated suicide. Her conversation is coherent and connected.

Alice was placed under close supervision, but towards the end of the month, although still 'little inclined to speak, she will reply cheerfully, and is already occupying herself, but not much', and shortly after the suicide watch was withdrawn.

'We were indeed sorry to hear that you were ill again and obliged to go back to Colney Hatch,' Miss Vickers ventured in May, in a double-edged tone that resolutely disavows Alice's bereavement, alludes to moral failing ('obliged'), classes her distress as a pathology ('ill again'), and cajoles her to square up to her personal responsibility to 'do everything you can to get strong and well quite quickly'. In September Alice was 'conversing readily – quite cheerful and working regularly', although she was still said to lack confidence in herself and to be 'readily depressed by trifles of no importance'. All the same, she now wrote a breezy letter, counting herself among the 'fit', to Miss Vickers at MACA:

> You asked me to let you know how I get on. I am doing all I can to get out and earn my own living again, which I am so longing to do… I am wondering if you will be able to help me again as I am sure there is plenty of work for women now, I shall do all I can this time to keep out, I have seen the doctor and hope it means something for me, as I feel so well and fit.

'She treats me as if I am silly and a lunatic'

In the middle of October she was sent out on four weeks' trial, and was discharged as 'recovered' a month later, to stay at a MACA rehabilitation home in Sussex. From here she wrote to ask Miss Vickers to send her down some walking shoes and stockings, as 'the boots the Asylum people gave me are so big and heavy to get about', and expressed gratitude to Miss Vickers for her 'kind help' and to the doctors for giving her 'another chance'. The shoes, when they arrived, 'fit very well', and by now she had been reunited with her box, 'so that is alright'. Shortly after, Miss Vickers wrote that 'we have found you a very nice situation at St Leonards, where I think you will be very happy and comfortable'. By the beginning of December Alice and her box were moved into her new situation at St Leonards-on-Sea, Sussex, in the home of Mrs Emmeline Quick – like Mrs Baxter, a widow in her early 60s, but with a much larger house and five adult children, who appeared to visit quite frequently. It was, perhaps, to be doubted that Alice's new situation would fit quite as snugly as her new shoes. Miss Vickers had told Mrs Quick that, previous to Alice's first illness, 'she was not particularly steady, but that was attributable to her illness coming on, and now she seems a most respectable hard-working woman'. In agreeing to accept Alice, Mrs Quick ventured that 'the doctor would not allow anyone to enter a situation unless he considered the patient quite recovered from her misfortune'.

Miss Vickers asked that Alice be paid direct for her wages 'as she is considered quite recovered and we sincerely hope she will make good use of her money. Perhaps you would talk to her about trying to save some of it in the Post Office or War Bonds.' 'Quite recovered' Alice might have been, but still there is the sense that she was on probation and that the Poor Law waited in the wings. 'Should she relapse at any time,' Miss Vickers advised Mrs Quick, 'you will have to send for the nearest Relieving Officer saying you have a person in your house who has had a mental illness and you will find they will send almost at once.' 'I find her a well trained servant,' Mrs Quick reported in early January, 'and I am sure she is anxious to do well, but she needs careful and constant supervision, as at times she is quite inexplicable.' By the end of the month, Alice seemed to have got the measure of Mrs Quick, reporting to Miss Vickers:

> Mrs Quick is a very nervy woman herself, she as [sic] been in bed all last week and had the doctor and now one of the daughters are in bed. I think it is the flu but she is getting on alright again. There is three daughters here, and one son, home all day, and the Mother and the other son from France as [sic] been here now nearly 3 weeks, so there is plenty do but I go out for walks a good bit, so I am feeling well.

Trouble was brewing, though, for early in February Mrs Quick wrote to Miss Vickers:

> I am extremely sorry to be obliged to write you but Miss A. Trigg has been so rude & unruly & giving way to fits of temper that unless she behaves better, I fear I cannot keep her. She cannot realize the untrue things she says. I have overlooked this so many times during the last three weeks & done my best to help her. Ever since she has been here I have sent her out nearly every day or so & giving her little outings. I also tried to persuade her to join the YMCA and go to the social evenings, as I know the ladies who help there. Last week I told her I would willingly let her have any afternoons off.

Miss Vickers ventilated her disappointment to Alice that she was 'not doing quite as well' as when she first went to Mrs Quick. She trusted 'you are doing your best to improve... so you can earn a good reference', thereby conveying the unequivocal message that Alice was blameworthy and culpable in this situation, since 'Mrs Quick has taken you on our recommendation, and it is up to you to prove yourself worthy of all the nice things we said about you' and 'I very much hope that I shall receive a good report of you soon.'

Here it is apposite to remark on the resonance between Alice's situation and Saidiya Hartman's description of the plight of the emancipated ex-slave, nominally a 'free individual' with a 'nascent individuality', but in actuality lumbered with 'an abased and encumbered individuality', a 'travestied liberation', in which their expressions of their agency are constantly castigated and the individual made blameworthy (Hartman, 1997, pp.6, 9, 117). Matters came to a head for Alice towards the end of the month, as expressed in an emotional but forceful letter to Miss Vickers ('I know this is an awful letter,' Alice has scrawled at the top) that actually conveys very succinctly the 'truth' of her predicament. Caught between one form of servitude and another, pretty much powerless to influence her situation, she is evidently intent nevertheless on making known her desire and determination to regain control of her own personhood ('I am supposed to be free now!') as a capable agent who is not to be treated as a 'lunatic':

> I am just writing to let you know that if I am not to be trusted with a few shillings, well I mean my month's money, which was due nearly a fortnight ago, and she as [sic] not yet paid it, this is a fine way to go and treat a girl after being away eighteen months! As she treats me as if I am silly and a lunatic, I should think my place is away with the lunatics, not out in the world with a nine roomed house to do! Up till last week, she had me taken out, the girl next door had to take me to the pictures, I asked her if I could go alone but she would not let me, I had to be quite rude to her, she is an awful woman, and I am always at her, as I have told her I am supposed to be free now, and not to be watched about anyway, & would rather be away than be here like this, no money given, I am in a fearful temper over it & can hardly be decent to her, I would like you to fetch me away from her as soon as possible, before there is any trouble, I remain yours truly, Alice Triggs

Shortly, Mrs Quick issued her own rebuke: 'I am very grieved to write that Alice has again been so defiant and rude I can no longer keep her & shall be obliged if you will arrange to send for her as soon as possible.' Fortuitously, and fortunately for Alice, the next-door neighbour to Mrs Quick was a Miss Ethel Chown, a woman in her late 30s, a nurse and also a boarding-house keeper, who was already known to MACA and who now stepped in to play a role as intermediary in this fractious situation. She reported to Miss Vickers:

> Mrs Quick has been constantly coming to me with complaints about Alice. The latter I think has some cause for complaint. No doubt there are faults on both sides. Last night I had a long talk with Alice, and she seemed quite reasonable, but this morning Mrs Quick said she was so impertinent that she must leave today. I have been sent for so often by Mrs Quick that I thought the best thing I could do was to bring Alice here until I heard from you what you wished done as the girl had nowhere to go.

Mrs Quick had, in the meantime, already written to Miss Chown:

> Alice has been so abominably rude this morning and utterly defied my
> wishes, that I cannot keep her any longer. I'm afraid she made un-true
> statements about the kitchen fire, which is her latest grievance.

For her part, Alice was perhaps trying to do the impossible – to reconcile her
desire to be acknowledged as a free and independent woman with the strictures
and duties of a life in harness as a domestic servant. Realising, however, that
there was no end on the horizon to her subordination, she now wrote to Miss
Vickers, grateful for her support, and hopeful that she could be found another
situation, since right now this was her only recourse:

> I am sorry I could not stop until the 13th March with Mrs Quick. I really
> should have done, but she was nasty over it and told me to go at once, so
> dear Miss Chown took me in with her and as [sic] been very, very kind to
> me indeed, I can better explain if I see you sometime about it, of course I
> was upset over it, and did a bit of weeping, but I am quite alright now and
> quite happy that you are getting me another place soon now, I do hope I
> shall get on this time and make you better pleased, thanking you for all
> the trouble you are taking.

Initially, Mrs Quick refused to pay Alice's wages for the last weeks of her service,
complaining again about Alice's 'insubordinate and untruthful behaviour', and
telling Miss Chown 'that she has not the time to bother about it'. Finally and
reluctantly she did so, and in the meantime, Miss Chown proved herself a
doughty advocate for Alice, discretely indicating where her sympathies resided.

'A blot on her race, away with her!'

A new situation was soon found for Alice in Surbiton, Surrey, a suburb of
London, in the family of a Mrs Marriott, who wrote in late March 1919 to
report on how Alice was faring in the domestic economy:

> She is a very nice girl, quiet in manner and very obliging, and I think she
> is settling down with us, but as soon as I can I will get another girl to take
> the house parlour work, she [Alice] wants to take the cooking and kitchen
> work, and she does not like having to come into the room and wait at
> table, she says it makes her nervous. So I have not let her wait at table at
> all. It is a pity, for she is a good house maid, & house parlour maids are
> more difficult to get than cooks at present, & I want to try and get a really
> nice girl. Please accept the enclosed small donation towards your funds.

What this friendly but slightly ambiguous letter augured for Alice's future in the Marriott household, or anywhere else, we will never know, as this is the last encounter we have with Alice in the historical record. All that we know subsequently is that, on 15 April 1920, Alice was admitted to Napsbury Lunatic Asylum, suffering from an attack that had lasted 11 days, and was discharged on 31 August. On 23 December 1920, she was again admitted to Napsbury, and this time she was to remain there, under a compulsory detention order, until her death in 1962, 42 years later, at the age of 77, although she was re-graded as a voluntary patient in December 1957. These sparse details are all that is recorded of the last four decades or so of Alice's life. Her case notes and any other documentation for this period have all been lost or destroyed. There are no grounds for supposing that anything sinister lies behind the disappearance of these records but we may consider that their loss is, at the very least, a sign of a lack of care or concern for, or indifference towards, Alice's memory, and perhaps even an indication of a measure of official relief that this unbecoming history has been got out of the way and thrust into oblivion.

We do not know for sure why Alice was detained, but it must have been under the Mental Deficiency Act of 1913, since there was no other legal instrument that would permit detention for such a long period (the Act was not repealed until 1959). Perhaps by this time Alice was persuaded that, between the competing servitudes of the mental asylum and domestic service, the mental asylum was preferable. Whatever was the case, she was to join a population of around 65,000 people who were placed in colonies, mental hospitals or other institutions for the remainder of their lives, with no legal rights to petition against prolonged detention (Walmsley, 2000). Quite possibly, Dr Samuel Elgee's diagnosis of moral imbecility from 1915 had come back to haunt her, even though it is difficult to comprehend how it could have been justified by the criteria for the diagnosis that are set out in the Act.

Between 1957 and 1972, the social anthropologist and later psychoanalyst Elizabeth Bott undertook a classic study of the workings and culture of a large mental hospital on the outskirts of London that was later revealed to be Napsbury. There existed an enormous pretence, Bott concluded, that mental patients were in hospital entirely for medical reasons when actually they were there largely for social reasons. Chronic hospitalisation occurs when the hospital appears to offer a more viable social place for the patient than can be found outside in the community, she concluded. Nurses had to engage in considerable self-deception 'because the care they provide for social reasons is regarded by society... as a medical rather than a social necessity' (Bott 1976, p.135).

This is, indeed, an apt summary of what appears to have happened to Alice. Within the acutely and fervently discriminatory racial consciousness of the period, as a single woman of limited education from poor circumstances, who appeared to lack the capacity and required skills for self-government, Alice found herself stigmatised as a 'poor white' and consigned into the darkness of the psychiatric equivalent of a slave hold. This outcome was quite adventitious, it should be said. Had Joseph survived the Great War, for example, or Florence chosen not to emigrate to Australia in 1911, Alice would have had a family support system that might have helped spare her such a bleak fate. There is a sad irony to this tale in that, in 1919, and again in 1920, Alice's sister, Florence, writing from Australia under her married name as Florence Jarmson, tried unsuccessfully to advise her that a bequest was due to her and 'there is a fair sum of money waiting for her from an uncle here'. Sadly, at this point the Mental After Care Association had already lost contact with Alice and was unable to pass on the message. If Alice had had an advocate of some sort, perhaps the situation could have been retrieved in some way, but as it was, she lacked even that. The diagnosis of moral imbecility, as it most likely was, was achieved all the more readily because there was no one to challenge it. Undoubtedly, Beatrice Webb would have heartily approved of the decision.

George Szmukler is a psychiatrist who has broken ranks with his own profession to write critically and trenchantly about psychiatric coercion. In commenting on the inexorable consequences of segregation, he has remarked on the historical invisibility of the coerced, and the fact that, until very recently, people with a mental illness subjected to involuntary detention have had practically no 'voice' or standing in society (Szmukler, 2018, p.12). Remarking on the exclusion of the voice of the servant in multiple social histories, Carolyn Steedman reminds us that Emily Bronte's *Wuthering Heights* is actually told by one of the great servant narrators of modernity, Nelly Dean, and 'here the servant certainly has a voice: large swathes of the text are the (invented) voice of one of the Pennine working class'. 'It is the servant,' insists Steedman, 'who must tell' (2007, p.11–12).

From the surviving photographs of Alice taken by the asylum photographer at Colney Hatch during her admissions (see p.106 for those from 1915 and 1916) – and these photographs are very probably the only ones that were ever taken of her – she does not in the least conform to any stereotype of an asylum inmate. Rather, she comes across as sweet, clever, contained and determined, in the words of a female respondent to whom I showed them, all of which is borne out by the snippets and glimpses of her person – her vivacity, energy and insubordinate character – that we can extract from her record, in which, for the most part, she is being told 'about' or told 'to', rather than 'telling' for herself. But we know that she had a voice, and liked to talk, because employers and hospital clinicians sometimes rebuked her for it.

Victim of the custodians of a peculiarly narrow, punitive and obnoxious ideology of racial whiteness, Alice Rebecca Triggs was reviled, shut away and denied a life of her own by the supine psychiatric authorities of her time, and never allowed to tell, or to become, the narrator of her own story. And that, certainly, was her abiding pain and remains our irreparable loss.

PART 3

Pathologies of empire

Part 3 – Prologue

Historians have recently been uncovering some of the ways in which, between the First and Second World Wars, psychoanalytically-inclined observers, among them former colonial civil servants or advisers, started to expose some of the traumas of colonial oppression and the pathological irrationalities of the imperial project, and to cast light on the racialised narratives of mainstream psychology. One such was physician and ethnologist Charles Seligman (1873–1940), whose explorations of the role of dreams had the effect of blurring the boundaries of the 'primitive' and the 'civilised' in ways he did not, perhaps, entirely anticipate. His revelation was that the same kinds of concentrated meanings, inner conflicts and irrational drives were to be identified in the inner worlds of subjects in Britain and equally among 'native' populations in British colonies (Linstrum, 2016, p.37, 43–44; Thomson, 1999, pp.236–237, 241–242).

Here was a trove of rich examples of how psychoanalysis could open up new ways of thinking about colonised minds and provide ammunition for anticolonial thinkers and activists. The equally remarkable, and sadly overlooked, Bernard Houghton (1864–1933), who had a long career in the Indian Civil Service in Burma, working in the vast, sprawling and intimidating Secretariat complex in Rangoon that reputedly kindled the idea of Big Brother in the imagination of the young Eric Blair (aka George Orwell), published a number of pamphlets and books under titles such as *The Mind of the Indian Government* (1922/2018) and *The Psychology of Empire* (1921), which denounced the aggression, violence and, above all, the madness and hypocrisy of imperialism. In the Great War, for example:

> Each nation firmly believed it was acting on the defensive, blindly
> swallowed the particular lies its chiefs thought best for their own ends,
> refused to hear any arguments of its adversaries, scoffed at the idea that

they had any, was roused to madness by their wickedness and their cruelty. Each nation thought that the happiness of Europe was bound up with its own victory. The atmosphere was that of a lunatic asylum. In all that hell of passion and welter of blood, where was reason? Where was justice? Where in fact was our boasted civilisation? It was the group or nation first, foremost and all the time. Nothing else mattered. In a flash, man was back in the Stone Age, tribe fighting against savage tribe, no thought but to hold closely together, no aim but to kill without pity and without remorse. (Houghton, 1922/2018)

So irked were officials at the India Office by Houghton's sentiments that they contemplated prosecuting him for sedition (see https://bernardhoughtonblog. wordpress.com/2015/11/; Linstrum, 2016, pp.66–67; Saha, 2013).

Another former colonial administrator, but from Nigeria, Sylvia Hope Leith-Ross (1884–1980), who subsequently trained as an anthropologist, returned to Nigeria to study the origins of the 1929 Aba Women's Riots. She discovered that it was just one in a series of 'profound, and in different ways, terrifying experiences', including the Anglo-Aro War of 1902, that had impacted on the 'psychological life' of Nigerians following the 'coming of the white man', and, as a consequence of this lengthy history of imperial violence – and here she was ahead of her time in bringing to light the deferred action of past traumatic events – ignited a long fuse of traumatised memory that was to burn slowly over many years (Linstrum, 2016, pp.70–72; Callaway, 2004).

However, it was Frantz Fanon, the Martinique psychiatrist and revolutionary, who most eloquently and trenchantly turned imperialism's own arsenal back on itself by giving expression to the idea that it was itself a form of mental pathology. Arguably, as Erik Linstrum intimates, ideas like this first emerged in the inter-war British Empire, and in an even more embryonic form at the dawn of the 20th century, bringing into the light 'the complex intermingling of power and pathology' that Jordanna Bailkin has discerned in the co-option of psychology and psychiatry as a basis for governance that was later to be demonstrated more intensively and forcibly towards the end of empire (Linstrum, 2012, p.213; Bailkin, 2012, pp.37, 124).

In Part 3 of this book, I shall explore two episodes that indubitably enjoin reflection on the irrationalities and pathologies of imperial governance. The first involves a colonial agent in Central Africa, in the territories of contemporary Uganda and Malawi, around the turn of the 20th century, which provoked vexing questions as to whether it is one person's madness or the madness of colonialism itself that we are dealing with. The second concerns a controversy over the successor to the head of the ruling family in Khairpur, one of the princely states in India, in the 1930s. In the first case, a number of ideas are in play around a memorandum that was produced in 1903 that may hint at a familiarity with Freud's *Interpretation of Dreams*, first published in 1900. Though the author does declare an interest in the subconscious, it is rather unlikely that he could have read Freud's book, since it was published in an edition of 600 copies that did not sell out for eight years, and the first English translation (by A.A. Brill) did not appear until 1913.

The second case reveals the mobilisation of psychiatry for political purposes and also, perhaps, the simultaneous application of psychoanalysis both to expose the underbelly of hegemonic forces and equally to reveal its own inability to cross cultures and acknowledge their differing expectations of masculinity. As the historian Catherine Evans (2016) has remarked, in considering the history of the mind sciences in the British Empire, it is notably difficult to separate pathology from normality, for the lines between the diseased and the healthy, the normative and the normal, were all the time shifting, along with social attitudes, and the mind of the archetypical 'primitive' subject of colonial rule could be, and frequently was, viewed as normal and pathological at one and the same time (Evans, 2016, pp.475–476; Evans, 2021; Richards, 1997; Thomson, 1999).

Denzil Forrester's painting, 'Funeral of Winston Rose' (1981) © the artist; photo © Mark Blower

'Three Wicked Men' by Denzil Forrester MBE (1982) © the artist; photo © Tate Images

J.M.W.Turner's painting 'Slavers Throwing Overboard the Dead and Dying, Typhoon Coming On', commonly know as 'The Slave Ship' (1840); photograph © Museum of Fine Arts, Boston (see pages 31 and 34)

9

The strange career of R.R. Racey: Mad at his post or the madness of colonialism?

Between 1890 and 1902, an area of eastern Africa inhabited by around two million people and distributed across some 30 or more hereditary rulerships was transformed into the southern core of the new British colonial polity of 'Uganda'. For some decades already, even before the arrival of the Europeans and the initiation of colonial rule, the rulerships had experienced convulsions wrought by the incursion of 'Arab' traders from East Africa looking to procure ivory and slaves in exchange for guns, cotton cloth and other goods (Low, 2009). At this moment, in what has been dubbed the 'scramble' for (or sometimes the 'partition' or 'rape' of) Africa, British colonial rule was still heavily contested and undecided between rival colonial powers – notably, Germany – and marked by protracted and violent regional struggles and wars.

Key players included the legendary Sir Harry Johnston (1858–1927), explorer, botanist, linguist and colonial administrator, an ardent enthusiast for British colonial expansion, who was dispatched to the Ugandan Protectorate as a Special Commissioner in 1899, tasked with establishing a civilian administration after years of disastrous and costly military rule. During his later travels in the Caribbean and the United States, where he had intensive contact with people of African descent, Johnston underwent a change of heart, and in publications such as *The Negro in the New World* (1910) espoused the equality between human beings regardless of race. But at this point in his life he was still a social Darwinist, deeply dyed in racism, who talked about 'savages' and wrote comic verses about cannibals (Oliver, 1957, 2004; Olusoga 2016, pp.440–441).

Johnston had succeeded in concluding an agreement with ruling chiefs that appeared to make them privileged allies of the British, thus enabling him drastically to reduce military expenditure. It was into this scene of tumult and struggle, in which guile and chicanery counted for as much as military strength in erecting a bulwark for colonial rule, that a young Canadian geologist, generally referred to as R.R. Racey (born in 1873), was appointed to an administrative position in 1896. Here, as he was soon to discover, his capabilities were going to be tested well beyond the more usual breaking of lances in the cause of colonial expansion.

By all accounts, Racey acquitted himself admirably, rising to the position of Collector within the colonial service, earning the appreciation and respect of his superiors, and in the meantime submitting a geological collection that added to the knowledge of the geology and mineralogy of the district and was lauded by the authorities of the British Museum.[1] Urged on by Johnston, by the turn of the century Racey was fixed on establishing a commanding British hegemony over the Bantu kingdom of Nkore. This he sought to achieve principally by persuasively incorporating a number of smaller rulerships through a succession of 'barazas' or palavers, or by force if necessary – an amalgamation that resulted in a redrawing of the territorial map. Choosing suitable euphemisms in his report, but hinting at a starker and darker reality, Racey summarised the outcome thus:

> It has been with the greatest difficulty that various chiefs of importance
> have been dealt with in order to bring about an acknowledgement
> of the superiority of Her Majesty's Government. This having been
> accomplished, it remains to gradually mould the whole into a coherent
> mass amenable to British rule. (Cited in Low, 2009, p.248)

This was formally recognised in the Ankole Agreement of 1901, which consolidated Nkore, and other states, into Ankole, its anglicised name, under the auspices of the Uganda Protectorate (Low, 2009, p.274), to which Racey was a signatory.

It was against this background that there took place, in July 1901, what the historian Anthony Low (2009) describes as an 'appalling encounter' involving Ndagara, the Mukama (or ruler) of the hilly kingdom of Buhweju. Racey, pursuing an aggressive 'forward policy', and leading a party of 60 of his recently formed armed police, had succeeded in surprising the aged Ndagara, together with many of his kinsmen and followers, gathered in a small village (Low, 2009, p.273; Steinhart, 1977/2019). Racey 'sent in [an] account of the butchery – I can use no other expression – of a lot of natives by the Police

---

1. My discussion of R.R. Racey draws largely on Foreign and Colonial Office sources in the National Archives – see Archives Consulted for details.

under his immediate command,' reported Mr F.J. (later Sir Frederick) Jackson (1860–1929), ornithologist and explorer, then Commissioner of the Uganda Protectorate (and later Governor of Uganda). It appears that:

> a hand to hand conflict took place in which the chief, his son, and 70
> of his followers including 24 smaller chiefs were killed, and 51 others; a
> total of 123 casualties at an expenditure of 879 rounds of ammunition…
> It sounds to me like the butchery of a lot of poor panic-stricken, possibly
> unarmed creatures, who couldn't run away and were shot at close quarters.

Moreover, to cap it all, in the aftermath of this slaughter, many of the women at Ndagara's court then took their own lives.

Only three weeks before this horrendous bloodbath, Racey had already attracted the attention of his superiors for his impetuosity in striking one Lieutenant Mundy to the ground in the presence of a group that included several native African people. Exactly what had riled Racey so much that he invited Mundy to 'fight it out' is open to question. 'It is clear to me,' concluded Sub-Commissioner George Wilson in his subsequent report, 'that the feeling which culminated in the assault had risen to fever pitch from a multitude of collisions on departmental subjects.' Jackson hastily dispatched a telegram to the Secretary of State in London:

> Racey knocked Lt Mundy down in presence of British NCO and others…
> Action absolutely unjustifiable due to uncontrolled temper and to personal
> animosity. Will you sanction his being called to resign? Example necessary.

As Jackson was to elaborate in an accompanying letter, quarrels of this sort 'are nearly always noticed and commented on by native employees, and the natives themselves, and it is scarcely possible to exaggerate the harmful effects that such scenes, and the often exaggerated native account of them, have on the prestige of Europeans and of the Administration generally'. Racey, in his loss of self-control, was guilty of breaching a cardinal rule of colonial discipline and etiquette: 'Not in front of the natives!' To aggravate the offence still further, he had apparently also been in the habit of sanctioning the execution of natives guilty of offences by spearing them to death, as was the local custom. Amidst all of this consternation, Racey himself remained implacable (*vide* his dispatch of 7th August 1900):

> I have been placed here by Sir H.H. Johnston, KCB 'to do my utmost to
> keep peace and order' and I have endeavoured to carry out these orders.

George Wilson (1862–1943), born in Glasgow but brought up in a rough background in Australia, was a music hall entertainer and a big game hunter before commencing a colonial career as a transport officer under Sir Frederick Lugard, and ending it 15 years later as Uganda's Deputy Commissioner. He was at the time Sub-Commissioner of the Western province, and so was called up to inquire into Racey's conduct. Although, predictably enough, he castigated Racey for his behaviour, he was quick to add: 'I feel that I have full cause to regard the work done by Mr Racey in this District, and that pending, as of so excellent a character as to justify the use of every effort on my part to retain his services in the District'. As to the native executions, 'spearings were a common practice… and excited no comments among Europeans in Ankoli [sic], not even amongst missionaries themselves'. Moreover, they 'were not as barbarous as was at first inferred… the manner of execution has not been regarded as over-painful, the sentence being carried out by "professional" executioners in one thrust and, I am told, death is almost instantaneous'. Wilson acknowledged that Racey possessed a 'very peculiar bent of mind', but concluded that even so he was 'a most zealous officer', who 'has suffered really from an ultra conscientiousness that has made him almost entirely forget that he is responsible to his employers as well as himself'. Overall, 'whilst his self-sufficiency has irritated me almost beyond endurance, his work has readily invited more than counter-balancing approval'.

No longer scrambling for Africa, and now residing in the depths of rural Surrey, Sir Harry Johnston was called upon for his opinion of Racey's conduct. For 'the assault on Lieutenant Mundy he certainly deserves enforced resignation or dismissal,' Johnston averred, since nothing can 'condone an action which must have seriously affected the prestige of the Administration in that remote part of the Uganda Protectorate'. However, the far more serious behaviour of Mr Racey was first, 'the infliction of the death penalty on natives without the confirmation of the Commissioner, and the infliction of this penalty by barbaric methods'; second, 'his outrageous attack on a chief and slaughter of natives, equally without authority from headquarters.' In Johnston's opinion, there were grounds here for a criminal charge which 'it might not be just or prudent to evade', though he was conscious at the same time that the Imperial Government might conclude that 'such action might entail too grave a public scandal'.

Whatever the outcome, he was strongly of the opinion that 'the retention of Mr Racey in the public service of Uganda is an impossibility: 'I use this word with the greatest regret, as I have a great personal liking for the man, who is of marked ability'. Until about a year previously, he wrote, Racey had shown himself 'patient and considerate with the natives', steering the Administration 'through a very trying period of transition in Ankole during which a reactionary party who favoured persecution for witchcraft and a re-establishment of the old pagan beliefs by force, was very nearly at war with the other sections of the chiefs and population who desired the introduction of Christianity'. The missionaries who were active in the district, both Catholic and Protestant, were 'loud in their praise of Mr Racey for the tact with which he had dealt with this business'. Yet, over the ensuing 12 months, Wilson had 'noticed a tendency on Mr Racey's part to resort, somewhat unnecessarily, to violent methods to compel allegiance to the British Administration on the part of chiefs dwelling very near the German borderland' and he now declared himself driven to the supposition that Racey's 'mental balance' had been disturbed by the strains of the situation, bringing about an 'extraordinary change' in his behaviour that could only be attributed to 'mental alienation'.

All the colonial officers who knew Racey appeared to be unstinting in their praise and affection for him, even though they havered over what should be now be done with him. Intimations of mental strain and alienation pointed the authorities in the Ugandan Protectorate, and in London, towards the sort of reprieve they were seeking. As Anthony Low remarks, all the outrage over butchery of natives was soon whitewashed in a concerted retreat from the moral brink (Low, 2009, p.274). The original storyline, and above all Racey's part in it, was now drastically amended and re-scripted by Wilson and Jackson, with Racey recast as a peacemaker rather than as an antagonist, and the native chiefs made over as 'the enemy'. Jackson now telegraphed to London:

> Racey was not present at actual fight. His report to Commandant was founded on statements by Sergeant Wood and police regarding killed and wounded, both greatly exaggerated. Racey did all he could to prevent a fight, which was begun by the enemy. Racey's only fault in this affair was acting without permission.

Not surprisingly, such a volte-face among the hierarchy in Uganda produced some confusion and bewilderment among colonial office staff in London. 'A full official report was promised by Mr Jackson,' wrote one official, but:

> what we now receive is not in any sense a full report, in fact we are left completely in the dark as to what really occurred. The original charges are stated to have been much exaggerated but what are the real facts is not said… One would almost have thought, from the present report, that the incident of firing volleys into the natives had no basis in fact, and belonged entirely to the categories of 'exaggeration' in the sense that no incident ever occurred.

Though this last observation was, of course, made from inside the colonial system, it pinpoints very succinctly and accurately what is at stake here. The message was, these incidents must all be disavowed; these events never happened on such a scale; the account that was originally given was a gross exaggeration by the natives – who were in any case prone to exaggeration, as was well known – and the lower ranks. Moreover, what was being disavowed here was more, much more, than these specific incidents, for it included also any suspicion, or suggestion or insinuation, that the project of colonial annexation and expansion was in any way intrinsically associated with violence. When it started to dawn on the hierarchy that an account of Racey's actions might be regarded as a mirror in which not just Racey himself but the collective enterprise of colonial expansion might be made publicly visible, any residual inclination to moralise about his misdeeds was quickly toned down. Through his 'ultra-conscientiousness', Racey risked exposing not just himself but the lineaments of the colonial enterprise writ large.

However, any question about his criminality, or criminal liability, cannot so easily be neatly separated from the question of the criminality of the colonial project as whole. Through his contributions to colonial knowledge, and above all the part that he played in redrawing the territorial map in this area of eastern Africa, and in establishing a commanding hegemony over what would later become Uganda, Racey had become part of the fabric of colonial achievement in the region and so could not easily be isolated as a pathology and disowned. Talk of mental alienation might seem apposite, but here again the maladies of a soul may, after all, reflect the maladies of a culture or society.

It was decided in the late summer of 1901 that Racey must return to London and that his position at the Foreign Office should be reviewed. Racey himself submitted a brief memorandum at this point, redolent with understated meaning, confiding that, in the matter of the incident with Lieutenant Mundy, 'my nerves had become somewhat overstrained, owing to anxiety and climatic influence'. Nevertheless, he had succeeded, he stressed, 'in completing the task given me by Sir H.H. Johnston in August 1900, namely that of amalgamating the various principal independent chieftainships of Ankole'. Moreover, 'I have prevented severe concussion in the same district through the meddling of French Fathers with politics… I have handled savage natives in a satisfactory manner… I have introduced wheat culture in Ankole for the payment of hut taxes', and finally, 'I should like very much to be permitted to return to Uganda.'

Confronted with the enormous pressures among the agents of colonialism to disavow the nature and extent of the violence that projects of colonial incursion and expansion inevitably entailed, Racey, as Harry Johnson's protégé, could only hint at the burden (the psychic suffering, the day-to-day need to suppress and dissemble) of the brutality that necessarily underlay, and pulsated through, the task of 'amalgamation' that Johnston had enjoined on him.

When Racey reached London in October 1901, he was informed by Eric Barrington, Principal Private Secretary to the Marquess of Lansdowne, the Foreign Secretary, that the account of his quarrel with Lieutenant Mundy (his other 'indiscretions' were, apparently, overlooked by now) was before the Marquess, who was:

> willing to believe that his behaviour was to be attributed to the state of
> his health: that he was suffering from over strain and acted under great
> provocation. At the same time, it was impossible, in the interests of
> discipline, to pass over his offence, and allow him to return to Uganda.
> He must therefore place his resignation in Lord Lansdowne's hands, and
> take a long rest which he needed.

Racey assured Barrington that he would send in his resignation and return to Canada for a few months. 'I am afraid he is quite in an unusual state', Barrington observed, 'he has a very strange look in his eyes.'

Some six months later, Racey wrote to the Marquess requesting an appointment to serve again in tropical Africa:

> May I venture to hope it may be taken into consideration that while in
> Uganda my principal aim was to try and give loyal support to the Empire.
> I have the honour to be, with the utmost respect, your Lordship's most
> obedient humble servant, R.R. Racey.

Following some further exchanges, it was soon decided that Racey would sail from London in June 1902 to take up an appointment in the British Central African Protectorate (later to become Nysasaland, and subsequently Malawi). Though still displaying some eccentricities, he again distinguished himself in the field, impressing his superiors by his dedication and aptitude, until in December 1904 he produced a vivid but startling and disconcerting memorandum. Under the heading 'Mbona', it described his encounters with a native cult that revered a celebrated rainmaker of that name who, according to oral tradition and on account of his great popularity, came into conflict with the secular and religious authorities of the day, who in the end had him killed. The cult that subsequently developed in his memory and was named after him was supervised by local chiefs and headmen under the chairmanship of a high priest and a chief administrator. In addition, there was also a spirit medium, a man or woman who on occasion claimed to be possessed by Mbona and, while thus possessed, commented on a variety of urgent political issues. In previous times, the cult had also maintained a spirit wife – a woman consecrated for life to Mbona's service, who was believed to receive revelations from the deity in her dreams (Schoffeleers, 1987).

The circulation of his memorandum was to be Racey's undoing. Soon afterwards, at the behest of his superiors, his mental condition was examined by two medical officers, who concluded that he was suffering from a form of insanity, with delusions and hallucinations that were still developing and extending. The general appearance and behaviour of Mr Racey during their interview, especially his facial expression and preoccupied manner, only served to confirm their opinion. Believing that it would be dangerous to permit him to remain in the Protectorate any longer, as his duties, which brought him 'constantly in contact with natives', would be adversely affected by his condition, they recommended that he be invalided from the service and sent home to London.

It was 'a most extraordinary report,' observed E.J. Harris at the Colonial Office in March 1905:

> Mr Racey told me, before he went out last summer, that he was very
> interested in telepathy and the 'sub-conscious' but this 'memorandum'
> goes a great deal beyond any ordinary theories.

Indeed it did, for what he circulated, and what his colonial colleagues and superiors were to find so unsettling, was a kind of preliminary ethnographic record of his encounter with the spiritualised universe to which he submitted himself, or permitted himself to be submitted, as 'a spiritualist, or one in whom the subconscious nature has awakened'.

In her classic paper on madness in Nyasaland in the colonial period, the anthropologist Megan Vaughan reflects on 'the insecurity and psychological vulnerability of the Europeans themselves, in a situation where the segregation of cultures seemed necessary for the maintenance of their own sanity and the precarious myth of their superiority'. Any relaxation of the boundaries that led to an unstructured dialogue between the two groups could all too easily culminate in what were perceived to be the dire consequences of Europeans 'going native' (Vaughan, 1983, pp.232, 238). In obvious respects, Vaughan's remarks bear directly on Racey's arguably somewhat injudicious experiment in throwing caution to the winds and circulating his memorandum, for its readers were jolted and plunged into an experience of life that was beyond all colonial norms. Disclosing at points a psychotic intensity that is almost hallucinogenic, Racey's memorandum is unquestionably unsettling, and it is easy to understand why it was treated as evidence of his insanity. I do not mean to divest it of its strangeness, or to downplay the difficulty its content may present for the reader or listener, but – as with engaging with the narratives of psychotic patients in mental hospitals (Barham, 1984/1993, pp.100–129; Barham, 2023) – I believe there is value in probing in some detail the alternative forms of human affinity or connection it might disclose.

What is the nature of this spiritualised universe to which Racey has submitted himself? Mbona, we learn, was said to possess a spiritual power to enter into a person and cause the one possessed to speak, act or do his behests. So, for instance, while travelling home from a journey, Racey felt a sickening sensation, a pain in the back of his head, and a feeling as if an invisible creature was trying to get him into its power. Mbona was reputed to draw out the spirit of anyone not strong enough to oppose him, as well as put his spirit into an individual or group of individuals. If Mbona wished to speak to anyone, even at a distance, his spirit was said to go through space to them and speak to their inner consciousness. Racey recounted that he had himself discovered that this telepathic power could extend to most minds through the use of mind fluid, akin to using a telephone.

Describing himself as a spiritualist, or one in whom the subconscious nature had awakened, Racey declared that he had been enabled to do many things that could not be seen by other human eyes. Thus, he had witnessed creatures of various descriptions attack people, either by jumping on their back and clinging to them or, more commonly, by 'obsessing'. Obsession, or obsessing, he explained, normally denoted the visitation or control of a person by an evil spirit from *without*, in contrast to possession, which denoted the control, or tormenting, of a person from *within*. Obsessing was achieved in several ways – whether by entering the body of a victim through diverse orifices or by entering the spirit of man via the connecting links between flesh and mind, with the result that, at times, the attacking force swallows up the victim's whole mind. Obsession by a crocodile meant that one became possessed of, or by, the spirit of a crocodile and consequently acted as one. Racey said that he himself had been obsessed by many creatures – hippopotami, most notably – and very frequently by men and women spirits, some white and some black. Obsessing, he reported, often caused intense pain, both in the head and elsewhere, and more especially in that place where the evil spirit, or spirits, have taken up their quarters.

To defend himself against an obsessing mind, Racey described how he used the Sword of the Spirit of God, which no evil creature could stand against, which could cause a spark to jump out and resolve itself into the perfect image of the one whose mind it was. At points in his narrative, there are intimations here of what seems to be the equivalent of the internet, translated to the spirit world. For instance, Racey explained that the mind could be sent world-wide at a second's bidding, and obsessing spirits (somewhat similar to today's internet trolls, perhaps) often sent their poison along with it or injected false messages into it (like today's 'fake news' reports). Alternatively, other spirits who were in the know might tap the extended telegraphic cord and inject false messages, or listen to what was being said and convey it to human minds.

There were controls that could be applied, both for good and ill. These controls largely used nets to ensnare others into their power. Control by net could only be avoided by keeping one's spiritual eyes open. Control by human spirits was very difficult to avoid, and once they were inside a person, it was most difficult to get them out.

Racey talked of having seen a spirit of unchaste love that caused many people to do things they later came to regret. Shaped like a dolphin, it absorbed the intelligence of its victims and created 'unlawful passions'. He described having experienced a spirit power so strong that it moved his feet across the ground against his will and so twisted his legs that, on several occasions, it took them out from under the table while he was eating.

Racey had concluded, he said, that the stronger and purer in essential quality the individual was, so much the greater was his influence, not only among the native and climatic conditions in Africa, but also the world over. Power could only be gained through the Holy Ghost inhabiting a person and guiding and strengthening those who were loyal to the cause of God. He said he had tried here to note what he had observed that might be useful from a spiritualist point of view and place on record what had been shown to him up to the present time, although of course there remained, without question, great vastnesses he had not yet charted. But his intense encounters with the Mbona cult had, he averred, brought back into his awareness hidden, or suppressed, levels of connectivity and intermingling between human beings and human spirits that were doubtless disconcerting but might also be potentially profoundly renewing. As he candidly admitted, 'it has been difficult to separate my individual experiences from those coming directly in touch with Mbona'.

I suggest this rather extraordinary narrative is only intelligible when viewed in the context of what had happened to Racey three years previously on his tour of duty in the Uganda Protectorate. His adversarial engagements with local chiefs and their followers may have stirred up deep animosities that might subconsciously have haunted him, making him fear that he could be in the grip, or become a victim of, vengeful or retributive spirits. Historian Markku Hokkanen makes a sensitive and helpful comment on the considerations that disturbed or extreme states of mind in past times present for historians:

'Mad' is a powerful word with multiple meanings that is hard to ignore, yet our craft as historians may require sidestepping it in attempts to understand the crises of past minds. Recourse to a vocabulary of emotions, particularly anguish, grief and fear, may in many cases be more fruitful. And in colonial contexts, attention to control, loss of control and fears of such a loss are recurrent, significant issues that connect crises of mind with both histories of emotions and those of violence. (Hokkanen, 2019, p.293)

This is entirely apposite to what happened with Racey: his encounter with the Mbona cult could be seen to have occasioned a kind of blowback or unconscious reprisal for his adversarial conduct in Uganda that was, at one and the same time, deeply unsettling and potentially also healing, in as much that it renewed his connection with, and participation in, humanity – 'the next plane of existence', to borrow his own phrase – from which he had been cut off by the exigencies of his job.

The potential among humans for alienation means that the elaboration of what the psychoanalytic theorist Jacques Lacan calls the *imago,* or the image-ego, as a fundamental structure of human existence can, neurologist and ethicist Grant Gillett (2015) explains, become bound by what seem to be illusions, and above all the illusion of autonomy. The individual, or a whole group even, may forget that their being is rooted in belonging, on which they necessarily rely to nourish and strengthen themselves to meet the challenges they will have to face. Instead, they become defensive, insecure, resentful and hostile, constantly anticipating betrayal and unable to achieve a good-enough mode of being in the world with themselves and others outside the group (Gillett, 2015, pp.3, 5).

In his first tour of duty for the Colonial Office, Racey had contributed formidably to building and enhancing colonial systems of administration and knowledge in Central Africa. Now, he was doing something utterly different – he was contributing, almost subversively, to the elaboration of a kind of counter-knowledge that engaged a conception of power that was potentially more powerful than colonial power itself – an entirely different order of power, on a different plane of human existence. Out of his intense engagement with the Mbona cult, he had produced, in effect, a kind of restitutive or reparative narrative.

The striking thing about the memorandum is Racey's awareness of the range and diversity of native spiritual powers, and his sense that these common powers were always going to be combative, and were not to be outdone by colonial might, even though Christianity might try to play a part. According to the anthropologist and former missionary Matthew Schoffeleers, who has intensively studied the Mbona cult, the cult's history reveals the impact of political and spiritual oppression in which the aristocracy and the commonalty were frequently at loggerheads. Catholic missionaries were making converts among the Mang'anja people at the time Racey was working there and, while this may on the one hand have emboldened him in supposing that Christianity could in some way triumph over indigenous belief systems, he might also have become uncomfortably aware that Christian beliefs were being assimilated and re-tooled within those same indigenous belief systems to produce variants on a Black Jesus. Schoffeleers has also drawn attention to communal healing systems in Nyasaland that were frequently conducted in public by healers who were themselves former sufferers, and did not isolate the 'patient' but instead brought them into contact with others who had experienced similar afflictions. It is possible that Racey had himself become aware of the power of this kind of healing, in association with, or adjacent to, the Mbona cult (Vaughan, 1983; Schoffeleers, 1975, 1992).

'In the early years of the twentieth century,' wrote Megan Vaughan in 1983, 'Third Assistant Racey went mad at his post in the Lower Shire Valley' (p.232). Well, did he? I do not think that that is how we should describe it. Without question, he put himself under great strain, and took his experience to a limit where, in the context where he was living and working, he would inevitably be considered mad and where, in consequence, it became imperative to corral and isolate the impact of his indiscretion. There is not the space to enlarge on such conjectures here. Briefly, my own construal of Racey's state of mind is that, although he certainly reports what we may characterise as 'mad' experiences, his account taken as a whole is not disorganised. Although it is punctuated by moments of peculiarity, and of intense emotion, it also exhibits control. In my opinion, Racey does not write like a psychotic.

It is also worth asking whether Racey might have been using drugs during the time that he was engaging with the Mbona cult, for there is an unmistakably hallucinogenic feel about much of what he reports. There is no indication that he was doing so, but the connection between disease, drugs and 'madness' or mental illness in the tropics was acknowledged by Victorian colonialists themselves, and by later historians, who have, for example, cited cases of illness, madness and morphine addiction (Vaughan 1983; Hokkanen, 2019; Fabian, 2000).

Although in the opinion of his superiors, and of the colonial medical authorities in the Protectorate, Racey had now crossed a line and gone native to the point of psychosis, at the same time he was not obviously mad at all, as Commissioner Sir Alfred Sharpe (1853–1935) acknowledged, allowing that, outside the subject of Mbona, Racey appeared to be quite sane, and he could find no fault with his work. Indeed, Racey's 'offence', it may be proposed, consisted precisely in the fact that his whole mode of being was *indeterminate,* thus making the official classifications and lines of demarcation look decidedly arbitrary and wobbly. It was, perhaps, the ironic achievement of Robert Ritchie Racey, to give him his full name, his Lordship's 'most obedient humble servant', earnestly lending his 'loyal support to the empire', that, quite beyond his own intentions and in a fashion that could scarcely have been predicted from his previous record of service, he contributed, in a small but not insignificant way, to the unravelling of that very segregation, and thus to the exacerbation of just that insecurity and psychological malaise among Europeans that Megan Vaughan has described, with a parting nod towards a new horizon identified by the dissolution of racial differences and barriers in the common melting pot of human emotions.[2]

The opinions of the colonial medical officers in the Protectorate notwithstanding, Racey was never formally certified as insane, and nor were any constraints placed upon him. Having been invalided from the service, he made his own way back to London to be examined by Sir Patrick Manson (1844–1922), the eminent Scottish physician and parasitologist, who was at that time the Chief Medical Officer to the Colonial Office, and who had been sent a copy of Racey's infamous memorandum to read in advance of their meeting. Sadly, nothing is recorded of Racey's encounter with Sir Patrick and what passed between them, but it does not appear that he left the Colonial Service in disgrace. Nor was he subjected to any further psychiatric interrogation or sequestration. His tempestuous experiences over the Mbona cult do not appear to have caused him irrevocable harm, for he shortly returned to his native Canada, where he married, raised a family of five children, and lived a long life before passing away in 1956.

---

2. For a discussion of some of the problems posed by the white colonial insane more broadly, see Jackson (2013).

10

The Mir of Khairpur: Imperial doubts about his 'fitness' to rule

It is frequently forgotten that the British Raj comprised only a portion of the territory, and population, of the Indian continent. Roughly two-fifths of the area, and one-third of the population, were made up of what were known in colonial parlance as the 'native' or the 'princely' states, of which there were more than 650 at the time of the First World War. When Lord Dalhousie was Governor-General of India, from 1848 to 1856, outbreaks of misrule were peremptorily dealt with by annexation but, following the revolt of 1857, the British authorities pursued a more conciliatory, and stealthy, policy towards the princes. Recognising the Princely Order as providing a 'ring fence' of friendly territories adjacent to provinces under British rule, they sought instead to groom the scions of the ruling princely families into the behavioural codes and mores of the British ruling classes (Copland, 1997).

But by the time of the First World War, with the constitutional reform process in India now under way, the princes were showing themselves to be rather less pliable; they wanted to be treated 'as somebodies... within the Indian Empire' (Copland, 1997, p.35). A small number of the princely states, notably Mysore and Travancore, were regarded as 'progressive' by the British, and on ceremonial occasions were accorded the highest number of gun salutes for which a 'native' state could be eligible. Other states were considered 'backward' or even 'despotic' – notably, the 24 or so former Orissa tributary states – and were not accorded any gun salutes (Ernst et al., 2019, p.256).

Although it was the 'settled policy of the Government not to incorporate this huge section in British India', and to view it instead 'as a huge field in which India can experiment and progress on its own lines' (Anon., 1916), still there were occasions on which experiment and progress seemed, to the perception of the British authorities, to be in danger of going awry, and where some form of intervention seemed warranted. Usually this was where there were doubts about the conduct, or capacity, of the incumbent ruler or of his successor.

This was especially so in the late 19th century, when a supposed feminisation of Indian males and their perceived excessive proclivity for masturbation became a focus of not inconsiderable colonial consternation (Sinha, 1995). And it was here that psychiatry, potentially, had a role to play as handmaiden to a political process, by supplying a narrative that would lend objectivity and legitimacy to what might otherwise be construed as partisan moral or political judgement or interference (Kapila, 2005).

To illustrate this phenomenon I shall in this chapter describe a crisis of succession that occurred in the princely state of Khairpur, in Sindh Province, in the 1930s.[1]

It is not known how many gun salutes, if any, Khairpur was thought to merit. Although the state had been permitted to retain its political existence after the British annexation of Sindh in 1843, the colonial authorities retained the power to intervene in questions of rulership, and had repeatedly exercised it in deposing 'unfit' Mirs. Indeed, they had already done so twice in the 20th century, even before the crisis described here (Kapila, 2002, p.168). By the early 1930s, serious doubts were being entertained about the capacity of Sahibzada Faiz Mohammad Khan (Faiz, or the Waliahad, as he was known, in a respectful honorific) to succeed his father as Mir. The matter was now becoming urgent as the ageing Mir was said to be in rapidly declining health.

The British authorities were much exercised by a report that arrived from Mr Burkett, assistant guardian to the heir apparent of Khairpur, who had accompanied Faiz, his wife, his mother and their retinue – six servants and a private secretary – on a visit to England in 1932. He wrote:

> Throughout the whole of our stay in England, the Sahibzada [a princely title roughly equating to the 'young prince'] showed interest only in the cinema, an interest which was encouraged by his wife. Exercise he would not take in any form until the last two months of our stay when he began to play some tennis… Of his personal habits I would prefer not to state in detail exactly how disgusting they were, beyond quoting the fact that while we were in Eynsham I had to practically force him to have a bath after I had discovered that he had not had one for several weeks… In Brighton I was requested by the hotel manager of the Grand Hotel to request the Sahibzada not to accompany his wife to the lavatory, which

---

1. The sources I draw on for my discussion of the Waliahad are all drawn from former India Office Records, now in the British Library, as listed in Archives Consulted.

was at the end of the corridor on their floor. Other matters reported to
me by the Doctor and nurses after his son was born are too revolting to
be put on paper.

It is notable that in Burkett's racialised expression of disgust, Faiz is 'abjected',
literally 'cast off' or 'rejected', to borrow from Julia Kristeva's complex
philosophical, psychological and linguistic analysis of the 'abject' in her book
Powers of Horror (1980/1984). For Kristeva, the abject refers to all those bodily
functions, or parts of the body, that disturb the self by provoking disgust, fear,
loathing or repulsion, since, as Kristeva comments, 'refuse and corpses show
me what I permanently thrust aside in order to live' (Kristeva, 1980/1984, p.3).

The Political Department of the Government of India now became
involved in the scrutiny of Faiz's background and habits, and Lt Colonel James
Fitzpatrick supplied a narrative in which a psychiatric diagnosis was invoked
to finesse a series of moral admonitions. The family history apparently showed
'taints of degeneracy' on both sides, he wrote: Faiz's father (the current Mir)
was 'an extremely dissipated character' and his mother was a former 'dancing
girl'. His upbringing had been deplorable, for he had 'never been controlled
by his doting father and mother, or learned the rudiments of self-control',
and he was now, as a consequence, 'an abnormal and most unprepossessing
youth'. As he grew to adulthood, 'it became apparent that he was suffering from
the mental disease known as schizophrenia or *dementia praecox*', Fitzpatrick
opined, although he did not state to whom this became 'apparent' or who made
the diagnosis.

Needless to say, it was not to psychiatric treatment that Fitzpatrick looked
for a remedy to Faiz's problems but rather to the character building that would
come from a period of military training, even though Fitzpatrick was not yet
fully ready to abandon the threat of psychiatric diagnosis. He had already
explained to Faiz that, in his opinion, the 'only hope of bringing out his latent
good qualities' was through separation from his wife and exposure to the moral
and physical discipline of a posting to a regiment. Faiz was 'vastly uxorious',
according to Fitzpatrick, and 'ruining his already weakened health by sexual
excesses'.

Faiz, it appeared, was unwilling to seize the opportunity. But if he
persisted in his refusal to sign up to a regiment, Fitzpatrick feared he would
have 'to advise the Government of India to give him up as a hopeless case'.
For, although Fitzpatrick still hoped that 'military training may make a man
of him', he rather doubted that Faiz had 'the guts to stick it out'. As historian
Emmanuel Akyeampong has remarked about Africa during the colonial
period, 'the process of committing a mentally insane person was political, as

chiefs and colonial officers mediated the diagnosis of insanity' (Akyeampong et al., 2015, p.28).

Historians such as John Tosh and Mrinalini Sinha have described the historical background to the ideals of 'manliness' that are being extolled here by Fitzpatrick. The late 19th and early 20th centuries saw a development in Britain of a culture of masculinity among the upper-middle classes especially – one that was characterised by a fear of female power, resulting in a flight from domesticity and feminised forms of ambience, the renunciation of the ministrations of women, an emphasis on learning to stand up for oneself in the company of men, and the avoidance of emotional closeness, all in the interest of instilling manly independence. The paragons of this kind of imperial manliness were men like General Gordon of Khartoum, Field-Marshall Kitchener and Lord Baden-Powell, who were generally represented as being without female ties (Tosh, 2005, p.107). The contours of colonial masculinity were shaped from within an imperial social formation that included both Britain and India, producing an ordering of masculinity in which elite colonial administrative and military officials, and other groups and classes to a lesser extent, shared in the characteristics of the 'manly Englishman', in sharp and striking contrast to politically self-conscious Indian intellectuals and others, who occupied the place of an 'unnatural' or 'perverted' masculinity, represented by the 'effeminate Bengali' (Sinha, 1995, p.2).

By the time Lt Colonel Harold Wilberforce-Bell took over the surveillance of Faiz's case from Fitzpatrick, Faiz had already been forcibly separated from his wife and placed under the care of a Major Grafton in a bungalow, in what amounted to a form of house arrest. A Dr W.L. Webster, specialist in mental diseases attached to the Indian Army, was in close attendance. In order to 'be in a position to consider the political future of the Heir Presumptive of Khairpur', Wilberforce-Bell was anxious to solicit medical reports from two doctors on Faiz's mental condition, and it is here that an unexpected twist was introduced into the narrative. A report was first of all requested from Webster, who provided a conventional case history of Faiz, confirming a diagnosis of *dementia praecox*, although he equivocated over the prognosis and stopped short of considering him certifiable at that point.

The second invitation to review Faiz's condition was extended to a Dr Guy Wrench, a British physician practising in Karachi. Born in 1877, Wrench was an experienced doctor who could perhaps best be characterised as an enthusiastic adherent of holistic medicine. As a student, he had studied under the psychiatrist Emil Kraepelin (who devised the *dementia praecox* diagnosis) in Munich for a semester, followed by a period in which he studied the methods of Professors Freud, Stekel and others in Vienna, and hence had had the opportunity to compare their very different approaches. Even before the First World War, he had already published a medical and psychological guide for wives, *The Healthy Marriage* (1913/2018), had contributed to 'alternative' magazines such as *The New Age*, and had published collections of philosophical essays with titles such as *The Mastery of Life* (1911) and *The Grammar of Life* (1908/2010). The latter were his attempts to engage sympathetically with the range of frequently conflicting philosophies and belief systems with which individuals were assailed at the turn of the century in a period of expanding global communication, and distil from them an 'exposition of the principles of life in all its bewildering vicissitudes'.

Since the mid-1920s, Wrench had lived in Karachi, drawn there not by any affinity with the British Raj, towards which he was largely disaffected, but in the hope that he might find in indigenous Indian culture deeper sources of wisdom than had been afforded him by the narrow outlook of Western science and medicine. Eschewing the Western obsession with disease, and influenced by the currents of holism that were much in the ascendant in the inter-war period (Lawrence & Weisz, 1998), Wrench wrote a book on the sources of health, *The Wheel of Health* (1946/2009), and a collection of essays on India, *Land And Motherland* (1947), and he was to remain in Karachi (latterly, the capital of the new state of Pakistan) until his death in 1954.

In exposing themselves to Guy Wrench's outlook on mental health and illness, Wilberforce-Bell and his officials can have had no idea what they were letting themselves in for, for the emergent illness narrative about Prince Faiz was at this point either diverted, or (depending on your point of view) liberated, into a perspective, and a wider current of thought, drastically at odds with the more limited purview of the regular medical specialists and the Political Department of the Government of India. If, to some extent, Wrench's appearance on the scene was adventitious and surprising, it also reflected the mutations of a rapidly changing cultural landscape in India in which alternative sources of authority were quickly emerging to challenge the hegemony of Western medicine in general, and of psychiatry in particular. Under these changing circumstances, the creation of a psychiatric narrative might now find itself open to multiple influences that could not always be anticipated or controlled (Kapila, 2005, 2007).

As Wrench recounts, his outlook had been greatly influenced by the teachings of psychoanalysis. As he wrote in his subsequent report:

> I think the teachings of the Viennese school are essential to the understanding of nervous and mental cases. I was in my student days deeply impressed with the profundity of Freud's teaching compared to

that of Kraepelin, and further experience over a number of years has only
strengthened my belief that Professor Freud and his pupils have given us
an understanding of neurosis and insanity such as Professor Kraepelin
and the older school at their most gifted periods never even approached.

Describing his interview with Faiz, Wrench first noted the strain inflicted on
the Waliahad by having to live among authority figures, not least his colonial
'benefactors', with outlooks much at variance to his own. To start with:

it was clear to me that he was on the defensive, that is to say that he had
for so long been surrounded by people, to whom he could not speak *his*
truth, that he would not speak it to me.

Before long, however, Wrench and Faiz established a rapport of a kind and
were able to communicate about the divergent attitudes towards marriage
prevailing in England and India, and Wrench was able to commiserate over
Faiz's deprivation 'of the natural companionship of his wife' – 'a grave error by
the authorities', he later remarked.

Wrench took issue with several of the claims and assertions made by the
imperial authorities. As a student in Munich, Wrench had on frequent occasions
seen cases of *dementia praecox* demonstrated by Kraepelin, and reported now:
'I can say at once that the Prince, as I saw him, was not in the least like a case
of that disease.' There were other misconceptions as well. Onanism and sexual
excess had been mentioned as possible causes of the Prince's condition; 'These
do not have such effects,' Wrench rejoined:

Everyone of us are composed of instincts, tendencies, bisexuality,
suppressions. Everyone of us, for example, according to Wilhelm Stekel,
has onanised in some form... As Stekel says: 'The psychical and organic
harm due to onanism exists only in the fantasy of the doctors,' and he
uses similar language about sexual excess.

As to the persecution complex from which the Prince was supposed to suffer:

I think if the Prince did not believe that he had enemies, and is the
subject of intrigue and persecution, I should think him so lacking in
natural observation and judgement as to be bordering on the insane.

Wrench implicitly accused the other specialists who had examined the Prince
of showing a lack of imagination and empathy in confronting his distress:

> It must be remembered that insanity is often nature's method of self-preservation, release, and rest from intolerable conditions. I could well imagine that nature, in order to give the Prince release, might rest him by shutting him into himself out of the world, but this is not now regarded as insanity, and is certainly curable, and is certainly not hereditary.

Overall, Wrench is convinced that 'in spite of these terrible strains upon the youth… he is fundamentally sane'. And finally, in an ironic riposte to Fitzpatrick's paean to military manhood, Wrench proposes that Faiz be 'sent to Vienna (where many psycho-analysts speak excellent English) with his wife and guardian', where he would 'then be permitted and enabled to become a man. He would then show to all concerned that he is no less than other men, and capable of filling his prospective position as ruler intelligently'.

The alternate visions of manhood and insanity that emerged from these commentaries proved rather too much for the colonial authorities to cope with. In an effort to forge a consensus, a third opinion was solicited from Colonel Charles Lodge-Patch, a distinguished British alienist of a decidedly traditional disposition and the long-standing medical superintendent of the Punjab Mental Hospital in Lahore. He predictably took umbrage over Guy Wrench's psychoanalytic leanings, above all 'the insinuations of Dr Wrench' that masturbatory and bisexual proclivities were a normal feature of manhood, his own not excepted, and he sought to disparage and sideline Wrench as lacking the expertise of a proper asylum alienist. He concurred entirely with Webster's diagnosis that the Waliahad was suffering from a simple type of *dementia praecox*:

> There is a history that he had previously been studying spiritualism, and I have known a great many cases in which the first indication of mental breakdowns was an unnatural interest in psychic research, spiritualism, yogi etc.

Although a meeting with Wrench had been proposed, after producing verbatim notes of a telephone conversation with Wrench, Webster declined the opportunity. Gratton, the Waliahad's guardian, also spoke to Wrench on the phone, subsequently relating to Lodge-Patch that Wrench had rather 'gone up in the air' and was likely to make trouble. In the face of Wrench's criticism of Faiz's enforced separation from his wife, Webster backed down somewhat and it was agreed that they would continue to live separately but that she could set up home nearby. However, even though (or perhaps because) the aged Mir and also the Waliahad's mother now seemed to have formed a relationship with

Wrench and expressed a desire to let him treat their son, the British authorities evidently wanted him removed from the case (after all, why should the colonial authorities take account of the opinions of a former Indian 'dancing girl'?), even if, as Lodge-Patch anticipated, he 'put up a squeal' as a result. Wrench did indeed bring his grievances in the way he had been handled before the Viceroy but the Viceroy declined to reply.

The road to Vienna and the form of manhood that it represented was now firmly barred, but the authorities were still lacking the degree of certainty and clarity that they believed they needed from medical specialists to reach a verdict on the Waliahad's capability and suitability to rule. Historian Ellen Samuels deploys the term the 'fantasy of identification' to denote the powerful belief in Western societies, originating in the 19th century, that embodied social identities, especially those of disabled people and racial others, are fixed, verifiable and visible through modern science:

> These fantasies of identification seek to definitively identify bodies, to
> place them in categories delineated by race, gender or ability status,
> and then to validate that placement through a verifiable, biological
> mark of identity… [for] the overpowering fantasy of modern disability
> identification is that disability is a knowable, obvious and unchanging
> category. (Samuels, 2014, pp.2, 121)

The power of this fantasy notwithstanding, even Lodge-Patch was reluctant to yield to the demand for certitude, strenuously refusing to lend psychiatric sanction to such a drastic form of closure:

> The boy has the hope before him that he will succeed as Ruler of
> Khairpur, and it is right that he should continue to hold this hope, as that
> will be the greatest incentive towards continued improvement or ultimate
> recovery.

When Faiz's father finally died, Wilberforce-Bell decided that Faiz had 'sufficiently improved in health to be sent for administrative training with a view to obtaining his ruling powers'. In the event, he succeeded as Mir only in an honorary capacity, without ever being granted any control over the state administration. In the meantime, the Indian press had got wind of the young Mir's predicament, and several newspapers took up his cause with great sympathy. In the opinion of the *Sind Observer,* His Highness' condition at Poona:

is that of one placed in a private mental home in charge of two European guardians – Major Grattan and Captain Burkitt... He is in the hands of people not of his race and colour. His wife does not live with him; his mother is far away in Khairpur and is not permitted to see her son at all; his own son is not allowed to go to him; the Mir has not even a single Khairpuri servant to attend on him; and he cannot see any old familiar face. A Medical Board, heavily paid, meets now and then at Poona, to make a report on the condition of his Highness and its reports do not show that the Mir is either on his way to recovery or will recover at all. Nobody appears to be interested in his recovery. Under such circumstances, granted he is really bad or mad, is it possible to think that he would make any recovery at all?

Another correspondent wrote:

When I was in Bengal, I was given reliable information from many sources, including the highest in authority, that the treatment meted out to the Mir Saheb was really cruel. I was told distinctly that any sane man would become mad with such treatment. They were distinctly of the opinion that he could be, and would be, a very able ruler if he was placed in the hands of sympathetic and kind persons. In the opinion of several friends, he was perfectly sane and able, but circumstances of life had forced him into this queer state of affairs.

It was reported by Major Grattan in 1938 that the Waliahad had been displaying a decided decline in his mental balance: he was said to be wandering at night, talking to himself, and gesticulating in front of the servants. Tiring at the prospect of having to endure Grattan as his guardian in perpetuity, at one point the Waliahad resolved to poison him using sulphuric acid, but was foiled in the attempt. His writings apparently tended to show that he was thinking a great deal about his 'powers' and how he might use them.

For their part, the British authorities were increasingly preoccupied with their own 'powers' and how they were in danger of losing them. As late as May 1947, with time running out on the British Raj, officials from the Political Department were still anxious to solicit medical opinion on the question of whether the Mir should be deposed on the grounds of insanity. For years, the authorities had been troubled by the continuing inability of the psychiatric experts to make their minds up robustly enough to give them a clear steer on how they should proceed. 'It does not seem that anything definite can be done regarding permanently disqualifying the Mir from obtaining ruling powers, until medical opinion is much more definite than it is at present', it was recorded in March 1937.

The authorities were searching for what Ellen Samuels calls 'biocertification' to describe the panoply of government and medical documents that purport to describe a person's social identity by reference to biology, even though generally, as is the case here, biocertification tends not to deliver the simple and straightforward answers that are wished for, and instead to produce documentary sprawl and increased uncertainty (Samuels, 2004, p.122). An apologetic note creeps in as acknowledgement is made of the limitations of medicine to deliver what was wanted: 'Stress should be laid on the fact that the study of Mental Disease was still in its infancy,' a report states. Colonel Thornton similarly cautioned that there could be no doubt, 'so far as modern medical knowledge was concerned, that the Mir was suffering from an incurable mental disease.'

In May 1947, in the final act before the curtain fell on the Raj itself, a letter was sent advising that the Crown Representative had decided to appoint a new commission of enquiry 'to advise whether or not His Highness the Mir of Khairpur, at present residing in Kodaikanal under the care of a guardian, Mr R.C. Meade, should be deposed on the ground of insanity'. The question of arranging for the production of medical evidence was still under consideration. Disdainful though the authorities were of Faiz's own 'truth', as Guy Wrench had alleged in 1934, the official 'truth' that the authorities had for so many years now been hoping to establish still eluded them. The illness narrative around Faiz remained strangely inconclusive, constantly in need of repair, always in danger of falling apart, and somehow always fated to be an accomplice to clandestine political machinations.

Guy Wrench may have been long banished, but the ghost of his commentary and verdict on the Mir's case still lingered years later. The last we learn of the Mir, in 1947, is that he was reported to be living quietly at Poona with Mr Meade, his current guardian, and that he was able to answer questions intelligently, 'but liable to break out into giggles without warning or apparent reason'. An alternative reading might equally be that, for compelling reasons, the Mir kept to himself but was unable to resist an occasional smirk at the antics of those who were forever trying to bind him in their webs while their authority to do so crumbled around them.

PART 4

Holds that kill: Winston and Orville

Part 4 – Prologue

In his calypso 'London is the Place for Me', composed on the eve of his arrival in London on the SS *Empire Windrush* in June 1948, Aldwyn Roberts (known popularly as 'Lord Kitchener'), was, in the words of historian Kennetta Hammond Perry, 'making a historical claim of belonging and attachment that anticipated the multifarious ways in which Afro-Caribbean migrants were to assert their belonging, contesting the power and prerogatives of the state, and articulating expectations of belonging within the imperial body politic' (2015, pp.3–4).

The *Windrush* moment inevitably looms large in any such narrative but, as Perry and other scholars have insisted, it is a mistake to equate the problem of race with the upsurge in postwar Caribbean migration since, in actuality, it is embedded in and reflects 'the longstanding imperial logics that fortified the relationship between Whiteness and colonial power' (Perry, 2015, p.13; see also Bonnett, 1998; Olusoga, 2016, pp.521–525).

Out of suppositions about imperial citizenship and belonging derived from post-emancipation colonial experience, a man like Aldwyn Roberts felt emboldened to refashion himself as Lord Kitchener and 'imagine that London, the urban epicentre of the British imperial enterprise that made him a colonial subject, could indeed represent a place of belonging to which he could lay claim' (Perry, 2015, p.7). However, in navigating the dynamics of being both black and British in metropolitan Britain, migrants soon found themselves beset by racialised visions of Britishness, and a larger racialised discourse of disenfranchisement that conflated 'immigrant' with 'outsider' and 'second-class citizen' status – labels that 'provided a public vocabulary of non-belonging that inherently denied Caribbean migrants the rights, respect, and recognition afforded them as British citizens' (Perry, 2015, p.22; see also Olusoga, 2016, pp.496–504). It was symptomatic of the historical moment that, four years after proudly singing 'London is the Place for Me', Lord Kitchener decided to record 'Sweet Jamaica', in which he sang of his disillusionment with life in Britain.

In the 1950s already, the black community in Britain was being made profoundly aware of the vulnerability of the Black body in British society, perhaps symbolised most tragically by the death by stabbing of Kelso Cochrane, a young Antiguan carpenter with aspirations to study law, in a street in Paddington in May 1959. His murder generated outrage among all sections of the community; at his funeral, more than 1000 people lined Ladbroke Grove in West London to pay their respects. Cochrane's assailants were never identified or brought to trial, and more than half a century later the Metropolitan Police files on the case remain closed to public access – a surprising level of secrecy, you might think, for an incident that, according to Scotland Yard, had 'absolutely nothing to do with racial conflict' (Perry, 2015, pp.126–128).

In the first of the two chapters that follow, I explore the tragic death of the Jamaican-born electrician and amateur boxer Winston Rose, who had been experiencing severe mental health issues and who, very literally, died at the hands of the police in 1981. The circumstances of his death and the attitudes adopted towards him by the authorities evince precisely that vulnerability of the Black body in British society that Perry and others have highlighted. As the chapter records, when the artist Denzil Forrester MBE, a close childhood friend of Winston Rose, learned of how George Floyd was killed by a police officer in Minneapolis in May 2020, he was at once reminded of Winston's death in very similar circumstances.

Thirty years later, in an equally shocking incident that resonates with Kelso Cochrane's death, five white youths set upon Stephen Lawrence and Duwayne Brooks while they were waiting for a bus in Eltham, chanting 'What, what, n****r?' Stephen Lawrence was stabbed to death and Duwayne Brooks had to flee for his life, yet the police refused to regard the incident as a racial attack. Indeed, they treated Brooks himself as a suspect and as a hysterical and unreliable witness. 'No one,' comments Stuart Hall, 'took Duwayne Brooks seriously' (1999, p.193).

'What does it mean to be "British" in a world where Britain no longer rules the waves?' ponders Hall, inquiring into the circumstances that stirred up such racial fears and hatred: 'There is a growing sense of defensive embattlement, particularly among some of the English' (p.192; see also Hall with Schwarz, 2017). As historian Wendy Webster has described in *There'll Always Be an England*, her study of how colonial wars and immigration have been represented in the British media in the post-war period, the image of the home as a fortress and of the white residents as vulnerable and embattled was already central to British media representations of colonial wars in Malaya and Kenya back in the 1950s (Webster, 2001, p.557).

It is tensions such as these that became visible at Broadmoor Lunatic Asylum (later renamed Broadmoor Special Hospital), where the ending of empire and the arrival of a relatively new population of non-white migrants seeking to settle in Britain and asserting their claims to be black and British were to have huge consequences for the institution. In the 1950s Broadmoor was already admitting a sizeable number of West Indian patients, and in 1960 the physician superintendent proposed that the 'repatriation' of such patients to the West Indies should be considered, in their best interests.[1] Needless to say, it did not occur to the authorities to ask the patients themselves what they might feel about this, and the potential consequences. Was this 'repatriation' or was it 'deportation'? In a controversial study of some 50 patients with severe mental illness who had been repatriated from Britain to Jamaica, British psychiatrist Aggrey Burke, himself of Jamaican origin, found that repatriation had a negative impact and was not in the best interests of the patients at all. As this was not the message that the authorities wanted to hear, the study was largely sidelined by the establishment (Burke, 1973, 1983, 2021).

In the tightly knit community of Broadmoor staff living on the neighbouring Broadmoor estate, there were households in which generations of the same family had worked at the hospital. Many were from ex-military backgrounds and most were members of the Prison Officers Association. As may be supposed, they formed a traditional institutional culture. It was 'a stratified, structured, very orderly community', writes Patrick McGrath (2012), whose father was the tenth and last medical superintendent of Broadmoor, and who grew up in the hospital in the 1950s and 1960s – a community that was not entirely well disposed towards these newcomers from outside, with their outlandish claims of belonging. Little surprise then that the situation generated a sense of 'defensive embattlement', and what Stuart Hall describes as 'the stubborn persistence of racial thinking as part of the deep, unconscious structures of British common sense, often crystallized in institutional cultures' (Hall, 1999, p.189).

This is the background against which, in the second chapter in this section, I shall explore the circumstances that led to the tragic death of the Jamaican-born Orville Blackwood in Broadmoor in 1992. As we shall see, there are marked and disturbing continuities between Broadmoor in the early 1990s and Kingston Lunatic Asylum in the 1850s, certainly as far as the 'treatment' offered in the so-called Special Care Unit at Broadmoor is concerned. I suggest that the names that have been given to the unit over the years, such as Norfolk and Oxford House, and more recently Cranfield and Stratford Ward, may serve as a deliberate blind to obscure a grim, and still darkening, reality by infusing it within an English pastoral imaginary (Levi & French, 2019, p.89).

---

1. See TNA: T 227/2460 (1960) in the list of Archives Consulted.

11

Winston Rose: Humanity violated

The shocking George Floyd video spread around the world like Covid-19. My immediate thought was of Winston Rose, a friend of mine who died in police custody in very similar circumstances in London in 1981... This has all connected me back into a world that I was deeply affected by when I lived in London. (Denzil Forrester, May 2020)[1]

Denzil Forrester and Winston Rose

Born in Grenada in 1956, artist Denzil Forrester moved to London with his family in 1967, where he was brought up in Stoke Newington. The Rose and Forrester families lived in the same house and he became a close friend of Winston Rose, who was two years older and had arrived from Jamaica in the same year. After studying at the Central School of Art, Forrester was excited to be accepted to pursue an MA at the Royal College of Art but, as he was embarking on his studies there in the summer of 1981, he was shocked to learn of the death of his friend in police custody, leading him to decide to research the circumstances leading to Winston's death for his thesis.

Forrester attended the inquest at Waltham Forest Magistrates Court and was acutely aware from the outset of the institutional assumption that Winston Rose was violent and that the use of police force was therefore justified and necessary. Forrester was greatly perplexed and perturbed because this was not the Winston Rose he had known and grown up with. In what follows, I will report the circumstances leading up to Winston Rose's tragic death by drawing on Denzil Forrester's dissertation (Forrester, 1982) as a poignant record of a sensitive and concerned observer. His account possesses an

---

1. https://c-a-s-t.org.uk/projects/artist-insights/denzil-forrester

immediacy, integrity and vitality that has not been contaminated by the subtle preconceptions and biases, in one direction or another, that a specialist mental health training or background frequently confers. The quotes, unless otherwise identified, are all from the dissertation.

WINSTON ROSE   DENZIL FORRESTER

Winston Rose was born in Jamaica on February the 28. 1954, and came to England in July 1967, with his younger brother Felix.
Winston attended Secondary School, but like a great deal of young West Indians, found it very difficult, their personalities and ways of learning about things had to undergo big changes Winston became a keen boxer and cricketer, he went boxing during the evenings and played cricket on weekends. He got married to Thora towards the end of the seventies, and had two children by her. Winston also had a child by another young lady before he married Thora, so he had three children. He was working
After leaving school Winston worked as an electrition for a co-operation. He was working in Liverpool Street at the start of his mental illness. It was on the twentieth of november that Thora received a phone call from the manager of Winston's work-place. The manager said Winston wouldn't get on with the work, and everything he said to Winston him, he would repeat the same statement back. He also stood still, absolutely still in one spot for a long length of time.
The manages was not going to take any chances, for Winston could easily blow-up and do something dangerous, like injury to the other workers, so he had to have Winston off the sight. Thora phoned Felix (Winston's younger brother), after the phone call from Winston's manager. Felix phoned their mother, and they all drove down to the sight in Liverpool Street.
    It's important to realized that the Police were on the sight before the Social Worker, Ambulance Service, and the family. There were eight Police officers in uniform, and two in Plain clothes. The whole sight was guarded and sealed off. Two Police officers were placed at the front of the gate to stop anyone from entering the sight. The two plain clothed officers were used to persuad Winston to come with them, while the inspector in charge with a Police constable in uniform stood close by. Winston's behavior was not violent in the presence of the Police force, he simply shyed away from them.
The Police arrived on the sight about twelve-fortyfive took control, and turned the whole work place upside down. Winston's family arrived after one, and his mother went down in the basement, where Winston was working, to try and talk to him. But by this time the Police had damaged whatever chances there were for the mother to influence the situation.
The inspector in-charge said he was expecting violence from Winston, so he had to have as much help as possible, yet all—

The first page of the draft of Denzil Forrester's MA dissertation on Winston Rose © and courtesy of Denzil Forrester MBE and the Cornubian Arts and Science Trust

As we shall see, this account of what has happened to Winston Rose and what was done to him touches on, and at points makes painfully palpable, a number of themes and concepts that I introduced earlier in this book. One such is the idea of 'living under occupation', where 'occupation' can variously mean constraints on, or around, a person's body or an insidious process that constitutes them as subjects and 'occupies' them at the same time – as, for instance, when police officers and other authorities descended unannounced on Rose in his house and garden, crowded around him, physically and also mentally, and inflicted on him – forced him to submit to – a stereotyped conception of himself that was wholly alien and repugnant to him. And, most abominable of all, here we have a re-enactment and a re-living, all over again, of Conrad's description of 'a n****r being beaten', and of being put, and then abandoned, 'in the hold', for, as Forrester reports, Winston Rose was held round the throat in an illegal neck-hold from which there was no return; it 'literally choked him to death'.

Winston Rose's first mental health crisis

In the late 1970s, Winston Rose was living with his wife Thora (they married in St Pancras in 1976) and their children in Leytonstone, and working as an electrician. He was also active as an amateur boxer. His first mental health crisis flared up in 1979, when he was at work on a building site in Liverpool Street, north London. His manager telephoned Thora to report that Winston 'wouldn't get on with the work… everything he said to him, he would repeat the same statement back' and he also 'stood still, absolutely still, in one spot for a length of time'. Thora and Felix (Winston's younger brother), together with Winston and Felix's mother, Miss Goody, hurried down to the site, but by the time they arrived there was already a presence of eight police officers in uniform and two in plain clothes. Miss Goody went down to the basement where Winston was working to try and talk to him, but 'by this time the police had damaged whatever chances there were for the mother to influence the situation'. The inspector in charge 'said he was expecting violence from Winston, so he had to have as much help as possible, yet all Winston was doing was refusing to talk to anyone, and if anyone made attempts to come close to him, he would simply shrug away'.

Initially, the police, a social worker and the family had some communication with Winston, and all acknowledged that he was not behaving violently. But such was the police expectation of violence that they turned the whole event into a 'bull-ring site'. The inspector sent one of his officers to the police station for a special stretcher for violent individuals. Miss Goody was persuaded by a female police officer to come upstairs for a cup of tea and, in her absence, the police rushed Winston, handcuffed him after a brief struggle, and then placed him in an ambulance in a straitjacket, with four police officers, a doctor and an ambulance service man in attendance.

Winston was taken to Claybury Hospital, the former Victorian asylum in Woodford Bridge, north London, where he came under the care of a Dr

Hughes. She, having been told that Winston had come into the hospital handcuffed and accompanied by four police officers, simply took it for granted that he must violent. Her first concern when visiting Winston, who had been placed in solitary seclusion, 'was one of protection for herself, for she was accompanied by eight male nurses to administer treatment'. Winston was heavily drugged for four weeks, becoming 'a cripple in a cage which made him a foreigner to everyone he knew and loved and also to himself'. The side effects of the drugs changed his physical appearance:

> His body was bloated-up all over, thus one can imagine the effect it had on his speech, for his tongue was swollen and heavy, so his speech was very slow.

He did, however, make a quick recovery during his stay in hospital, and on Christmas Day he was allowed to spend the whole day with his family. Forrester writes:

> Being at home with his children, his wife, mother and brother was probably the most comforting thing that happened to him since being in hospital.

Winston was finally discharged from Claybury in May 1981, but was made redundant because of his illness, so stayed at home, finding work to do around the house. Over the following weeks, Thora became increasingly concerned over his mental state. She:

> began to feel cut off, because no one really wanted to help. She could hardly sleep at night, because Winston would suddenly get out of bed, and start pacing up and down the room, reading a bible. She and Winston could no longer have a conversation together.

She resolved to seek support from social services, and phoned up all the people who were close to Winston, such as his sister, Joyce, and his mother, so that they could be there with him when the social services people came.

The events of Monday 13 July 1981

On Monday morning, 13 July 1981, Winston's GP (Dr V), received a phone call from the duty social worker, Karla A, to say that Winston had been very aggressive and violent towards his wife over the weekend. Writes Forrester:

The strange thing is, however, at the coroner's hearing there was not a single person, and this included Winston's wife, who admitted to Winston's behaviour as being violent and aggressive. In fact, on deeper questioning, Karla A's original statement weakened, and her original description of Winston seemed very exaggerated.

As Forrester stresses at this point, 'this reflects my general impression of the whole case'.

Around 12:00pm, Winston was sitting in his conservatory reading a book:

Suddenly his house was invaded with people, some of whom he had never seen before… Winston was surprised by the group visit, and even more surprised when his wife, Thora, explained the purpose of the group of visitors in their house… Doctor V decided to talk to Winston first, because she had some personal knowledge of his illness. Winston stood up as she moved towards him, the doctor asked him about his health, then Winston started questioning the doctor, asking him who was the gentleman standing behind her. She told him he was Mr W, a social worker. Mr W talked to Winston for about four minutes without any success. By now it was becoming impossible to hold any conversation with Winston. Winston's paranoid personality was gradually taking control of the real Winston, because a gentle caring approach was not adopted by the social workers and doctors. They surprised Winston, then they forcefully tried to convince him, within the space of eight minutes, that he should go into hospital.

Winston was further confused and upset when he came out of a back room in the house to see Karla A, the social worker, a stranger whom he had never seen before, using his phone, and the duty psychiatrist, Dr Cohen, standing near her:

Winston was very upset. He shouted out, 'Who are these people using my phone?' At this point Winston thought things were going too far, and he asked the intruders to leave, because he wished to sort it out with his wife alone. As the health officials were about to leave, the passage became very crowded with people. Winston held on to his wife's hands, trying to persuade her to stay, but she didn't want to stay. Mr W was standing in between Winston and Thora. At the Coroner's hearing, Mr W said he was accidentally caught in between the couple, and it was not a defensive move on his part to try and separate Winston from Thora, but it was at this very moment, in between the figures, that Mr W gave a sign to Karla A to call the police, yet another instance where things got out of hand and exaggerated. Karla A never stopped to remember the instruction given by Dr Kennedy, the person who understood Winston's illness, and who knew he was not violent, that the police should not be called into this case. She forgot that he should have been treated gently and she called the police. This decision was hasty and unprofessional.

Continues Forrester:

> Winston wanted to protect himself, his wife, and their home from intruders. He hadn't asked for anyone to visit him. He was not in a mentally paranoid state during the visit of the social services, but because he had a history of mental illness, his anger and normal fearful reactions, like the protection of his wife, were treated instead by the health services as a violent move towards his wife. Because he talked to them loudly and waved his arms, Dr V said that he was not in a normal state of mind. It was very difficult for Winston to trust these people, who certainly didn't trust him, because they had secretly surprised him in his house… The social workers made a mistake in thinking that Thora's reason for wanting to leave was in fearing Winston: she in fact was saying she would leave in order to make Winston co-operate. She was desperate for Winston to be cured.

When the police arrived, Winston was leaning on his front garden gate, with his mother holding a child beside him. He saw the police and said to his mother, 'Oh God, don't let them touch me!' and went inside his house, closing the door behind him. As the door was locked, the police went through the houses next door and at the back to gain access. The doctors and social workers had by this time all made their excuses and left, so the police were left to handle the situation completely, even though the health professionals must have realised the mental state Winston was in and that it was not a job for the police.

> There were ten police in the immediate area, some with riot shields… The London riots of June 1981 was at its peak, so the police behaviour was definitely predictable at the time.
>
> Winston was now hiding inside a shed in a state of shock. The surprise visit by complete strangers entering his house… trying to persuade him to go somewhere he didn't want to (i.e. hospital), the fact that they used his phone and the rushing of his house by the police, all

contributed to his running away and hiding… There were about six police spread out around the gardens. [One of the police] shouted out to Winston to come out with his hands above his head. Winston came out of the shed holding a bible in his hands, he looked around and saw he was surrounded by blue uniforms. None of the social workers ever entered the back garden… Winston asked about the welfare of his family, then he quickly ran and jumped over the fence into the next garden, he was speedily pursued by a couple of officers… Winston didn't want to fight with the police, he tried his best to keep away from them… However, the police were raving with riot fever, which prevailed all over London during that month of July '81, so feelings were running high and wild particularly in the police force.

As Winston struggled to free himself from the misguided actions of the blue uniforms, their attacks on his body grew worse. Winston fell on the ground… It was at this point that [one of the officers] applied pressure to the air passage of Winston's nose so he gradually weakened, and his hands and legs were held by four officers… [The officer] then decided to go for a headlock, which lasted for over two minutes. It was around this time some more police arrived to assist in holding Winston down…

Some of the police officers claimed that Winston was lying on his front while he was held down and struggling; others said he was on his back. However, concludes Forrester:

It's clear to me that at this stage Winston was unconscious, on his stomach, and had been placed in handcuffs without a key (which the police officers claimed they had not realised until later)… It was clear to the officers that Winston was not in a fit state to walk out to the van so it was decided to carry his body out. Two officers took hold of his arms , while another two carried his legs… When Winston was put in the back of the van he was flat on the floor with his hands handcuffed behind his back… none of the officers ever really knew what they were dealing with, because none of them made any attempt to find out. Some said he was a violent big black man who destroyed a room (totally untrue).

Once he was in the back of the van, it became clear that something was seriously wrong with Winston:

The officers knew it, because when they arrived at Elm Road [police station] no one got out of the back of the van… The social workers ignored all their responsibilities and didn't ask to see Winston when the van arrived on Elm Road. When Karla A got in the van, she said the police had their feet on Winston, using his body as a base for their feet. Winston's head was placed near Karla's seat, about a foot away. She said there was no sign of breathing or movement, so her first sight of Winston's body was of a totally lifeless body on the floor, yet she didn't ask the police if Winston was alright… On their way to the mental hospital the police claimed that they were constantly taking Winston's pulse… someone said he had no pulse.

They stopped a passing ambulance and the medics took Winston's pulse:

He didn't have any. One of the ambulance men said he was dead. Winston was placed in the ambulance with handcuffs on, because the officers didn't have the key. He was rushed to the nearest hospital to be officially pronounced dead. Mrs Rose, who had wanted to accompany Winston to the hospital, was not informed until the police van had left. The doctor said Winston choked on his own vomit without having been told what caused him to vomit in the first place.

Winston's funeral

Winston was buried on Tuesday 4 August at Manor Park Cemetery following a funeral service at the New Testament Church of God in Cricketfield Road, Hackney. This is Forrester's description of the funeral:

I arrived at the church about twelve noon, just to get a full account of what people's feelings were since the death of Winston, and it was my first attendance at a funeral service… There were some old folks standing on the pavement across the road facing the church and a few young personal friends of Winston's, including his first girlfriend, Merlene. Merlene was known as Miss X in the *West Indian World* newspaper and was the bearer of Winston's first child, Christopher. Merlene is a very intelligent sensitive young woman who always looks on the bright side of life, and is not easily frightened off by anyone… At the funeral service one felt Merlene's presence very strong, as if she was the true wife of Winston. It seems as if she was the only one truly on Winston's side, while his friends ignored her, by keeping a good distance. She obviously acknowledged what was happening and purposely said 'hallo' to her unfriendly friends… She carried three beautiful red roses.

Denzil Forrester's painting, 'Funeral of Winston Rose' (1981) (see p.161) depicts Winston Rose lying in a coffin in one of the Dub clubs where Forrester spent time drawing in that period, with a female figure placing a red rose on the body, surrounded by Rastafarians and others who had come to listen and dance. Also prompted by the death of his friend was Forrester's painting 'Three Wicked Men' (1982) (p.161), which takes its title from a Reggae George song of the same name. The painting shows a Rasta man being escorted by two policemen on the street at night; the song's refrain tellingly is about three men 'I don't trust in this world', three men who are 'a danger to me': Mister Slave Driver, Mister Exploiter and Mister Criticizer.

The Winston Rose Action Campaign

After the funeral, the Winston Rose Action Campaign (WRAC) was formed to call for a public inquiry into Winston's death in police custody. A report by an undercover Special Branch agent of a meeting of the WRAC held in London on 10 August 1981 has recently come to light as part of the ongoing Undercover Policing Inquiry. Attended by around 100 people, the 'mood of the meeting could be described as angry', the report says. 'Black separatists present, who advocated revenge attacks upon the police, while not gaining outright support, did provoke an amount of quiet sympathy from some of the audience'. Cecil Collier, Consul and First Secretary at the Jamaican High Commission, 'received a considerable amount of abuse and criticism from black members of the audience for hiding behind the skirts of protocol to justify doing nothing, as well as for trying to project the image of being a "good nigger"'. Cecil Gutzmore, of the Brixton Defence Campaign, 'an extremely articulate speaker, concentrated much of his speech on a Marxist view of social and capital relations in Britain, concluding that the only way for racism to be eliminated was to overthrow capitalism itself'. However, although his speech was reported to be very well received by the audience, overall, 'despite the angry atmosphere, it seemed apparent that most present would prefer to keep the campaign [of the WRAC] within legal bounds'. (WRAC, 1981).

The eight-day inquest into Winston Rose's death in October 1981 was the focus of wide-spread interest and concern. *The Times,* in its report on 13 October, stated that 'the public gallery was full of black people'. The inquest concluded that Winston Rose had been unlawfully killed, meaning, as the solicitor who acted for the Rose family put it, that 'the negligence of those concerned was so extreme that it could not be "lack of care"' (cited in Francis, 1989, pp.66–69). However, despite the verdict, the Director of Public Prosecutions determined in 1982 that none of the police officers involved in Rose's death were to be prosecuted. 'To the best of my knowledge,' the Rose family solicitor commented in 1986, 'nothing has ever happened to discipline those people who were involved in Winston Rose's death. One would include there the doctors and the local authority.' This last point is of signal importance since, as Denzil Forrester adroitly observed in his account, a largely misinformed, uninformed and untrained (for these purposes) police force was thrust into the position of handling the crisis around Winston Rose largely because the doctors and social workers connected with Rose's case failed to demonstrate, and assume, proper professional responsibility and leadership.

The Rose family began civil proceedings against the police and, in 1990, on the day the case was due to be heard in the High Court, eight and a half years after Winston's death, they received a settlement of £130,000 from the Metropolitan Police – without, however, any apology from the police, and nor has one ever been given (Yesufu, 2021, pp.36–37).

It was in 1981 that the State Brutality Group, a campaign organisation dedicated to challenging deaths in state custody, changed its name to 'Inquest (United Campaigns for Justice)'[2] and the violent and custodial deaths of black people became an increasing focus of its work. The first reported death of a black mental patient in custody was that of Richard 'Cartoon' Campbell in 1980. Campbell had a diagnosis of schizophrenia. According to the examining doctor at Ashford remand centre, he died as a result of dehydration (he had been on hunger strike) due to acute schizophrenia, and the doctor noted his 'ramblings about Jah, going to Africa, and helping the poor' (Scraton & Chadwick, 1987, pp.87–89). The doctors at the remand centre had tried to have Campbell transferred to Queen Mary's Hospital but the consultant psychiatrist said that the nursing staff there could not be expected to deal with Campbell's physical illness. Equally, it was known that the nursing staff at Ashford General Hospital had found it difficult to cope with the effects of his mental illness. So Campbell had to remain at the remand centre. At the inquest, the jury was pressured to return a verdict of 'death by self-neglect'. The jury foreman inquired if it was possible to return a verdict of 'negligence by the authorities', but was told, 'There is no such verdict as the one you are suggesting'. 'Was the fact that Campbell was a Rastafarian something that the authorities did not understand?' asked Tom Cox MP, in a House of Commons debate on 8 August, 1980 (Hansard, 1980). An unofficial inquiry chaired by Alf Dubs MP criticised the fact that Campbell's Rastafarianism was taken as an indication of a mental condition, concluding that he did not die of 'self-neglect'; rather, he was a 'helpless victim of a series of crucial failures by the authorities' (Scraton & Chadwick, 1987, pp.87–89; McIntosh, 2016, pp.111–112; Hansard, 1980).

---

2. www.inquest.org.uk

In an essay that attempted to open up the whole field of psychiatry as an area of political priority for black people, Errol Francis argues powerfully that the killing of Winston Rose was a 'typical over-reaction of psychiatry and social police to a supposed threat of black danger' (Francis, 1993, p.192). Francis describes psychiatry as a form of social police, and demands that it be recognised 'as a power to be reckoned with… as it affects individuals at the psychological level' (p. 204). He writes that the assessment of dangerousness is frequently much exaggerated and made over into a self-fulfilling prophecy. Legal concepts of social danger and medical concepts of mental pathology, generously spiced with racism and the supposed 'extra psychological danger of black madness', work on each other to produce a toxic brew that results in the administration of higher levels of coercion in the case of black patients, Francis argues. For black people, 'the difference between being criminalized by the police, courts and prisons, or medicalized by psychiatry, is merely a choice between two different forms of oppression', except that arguably psychiatric oppression may be worse in that, in the psychiatric report, 'all the fears in relation to the social, criminal and psychological risks posed by black people can be brought into play at once' (see also Keating et al., 2002 on 'breaking the circles of fear'). Here, we can hear echoes of the report on Alice Triggs as a moral imbecile that was produced by the alienist at Colney Hatch Asylum.

In July 2012 the campaign group Black Mental Health (UK) published a list of fatalities of mental health service users from the African Caribbean communities in the UK, starting with Winston Rose in 1981, and including Michael Martin (1984), Joseph Watts (1988), Orville Blackwood (1991), Jerome Scott, Munir Yusef Mojothi and Mark Fletcher (all in 1992), Rupert Marshall and Jonathan Weekes (both in 1994), Newton White, Ibrahim Sey and Veron Cowan (all in 1996), David Bennett (1998), Roger Sylvester (1999), Eugene Edigin (2001), Ertal Hussein, Mike Powell and Tema Kombe (all in 2003), Sean Rigg (2008), Godfrey Moyo (2009), Olaseni Lewis and Colin Holt (both in 2010) and Kingsley Burrell-Brown (2011).[3]

As Francis observes, the 'catalogue of black people dying at the hands of the psychiatric system is lengthening'. He adds to it the killing of Leon Briggs, a 39-year-old of mixed ethnic background. A father of two children and a lorry driver, who also taught computer skills to older people, Briggs was detained under the Mental Health Act and taken to Luton police station on 4 November 2013. He died about two hours later at Luton & Dunstable Hospital. Briggs was forcibly restrained and shackled, and transported face down on the floor in a police van. He died as a result of 'amphetamine intoxication in association with

3. See http://studymore.org.uk and https://irr.org.uk/article/black-deaths-in-custody

prone restraint and prolonged struggling', according to the coroner's report. The way in which police officers restrained him 'more than minimally' contributed to his death, a jury found by unanimous verdict in January 2021, concluding an inquest that had taken more than seven years to complete, compounding the grief and distress of Briggs' family over his loss (Taylor, 2021).

Opening a black British historical perspective on more than 50 years of police racial injustices and reviewing the deaths of black people in police custody in the UK, African criminologist Shaka Yesufu maintains that an equation of black people with sinfulness, barbarity and bestiality has persisted unchallenged for centuries. The intent, he argues, has been to relegate black people to the sub-human status that was used as a justification for slavery, colonialism and apartheid, and as a consequence black people are sometimes still treated with contempt, suspicion and hostility and denied access to the mainstream in Western societies. Yesufu points to the continuing relevance of Stuart Hall's argument from 1978 that 'few people have begun to understand the stress placed on [black people], or their complex needs and expectations, or their particular vulnerability' (Hall et al., 1978, p.425; Yesufu, 2021).

Winston Rose was wrestled to the ground by a police offer, 'held in headlock for several minutes until, in the words of one officer, his eyes were "bulging" and he had been "pacified". He was then carried unconscious, and with vomit in his mouth, to a police van and driven away,' writes Yesufu. This 'constitutes a callous murder as this author understands it'. Though the 'life of a black person is often portrayed as worthless by white folks', Yesufu continues:

> [one] black death in police custody is one life too many… No life must be wasted under the guise of policing. The right to life unarguably remains the most fundamental human right, which the state must protect at all times. Without the protection of life, all other fundamental human rights become meaningless and nugatory'. (2021, pp.33, 36–37, 43)

It is self-evident to me that there can be no closure to this narrative of the crisis and death of Winston Rose; it cannot be banished to the past, for it belongs, irredeemably, to the present, where it is very much alive – a continuing and essential focus of critical attention, care and concern.

12

Orville Blackwood: Humanity disavowed

Born in Jamaica in 1960, Orville Blackwood came to Britain with his family as a young child, becoming a naturalised British citizen in 1989. He struggled with literacy, had a difficult time at school and spent a short period in state care. Like a number of young men in the early 1980s, after he left school he found it difficult to find permanent work. His mental state began to deteriorate in his early 20s. He started to neglect his personal hygiene and was frequently aggressive, his moods fluctuating dramatically. His first contact with mental health services was in 1982, when he was described as 'acutely disturbed, dishevelled, angry and suspicious'.

In January 1986, he embarked on what turned out to be a tortured, circuitous and deeply frustrating relationship with penal and psychiatric services. By one account, he 'had a bit of a breakdown', took the tube to the end of the line at Walthamstow and held up a bookie's with a toy gun for some paltry sum, pausing before he left to write his name, 'Orville', on the board. Following this, he was arrested, assessed and subsequently sentenced to four years in prison for 'robbery and the possession of an imitation firearm with intent'. During his sentence, he was transferred to HM Prison Grendon, which has a longstanding reputation for operating on therapeutic community principles. However, for reasons that are unclear, Blackwood's stay there did not proceed at all well. In October 1987, after a short spell in a medium secure unit at the Bethlem Hospital, he was transferred to the Special Care Unit (SCU) at Broadmoor Special Hospital.

I have previously described Broadmoor's unfortunate history as a white institution that struggled to adjust to the influx of black people after the Second World War and whose staff were ill-disposed towards Afro-Caribbean migrant inmates asserting their claims to be black and British. Orville Blackwood was to die here in 1991, under very questionable circumstances in a seclusion room.

'No one really got to know Orville Blackwood'

In this chapter, I draw upon the report of the inquiry into Orville Blackwood's death led by Professor Herschel Prins (Prins et al., 1993), which is subtitled 'Big, Black and Dangerous?', with a very emphatic interrogative. Quotes hereafter come from the report, unless otherwise stated.

On 28 August 1991, a decision was made to seclude Blackwood when he refused to attend occupational therapy (OT). The inquiry team expressed concern over this, remarking:

> The course of action that was clearly not considered, given the evidence put before us, was that of *talking* to the patient. It seems not to have occurred to the nursing staff to ask Orville Blackwood why he did not want to go to OT. If it was because he found the occupational therapy provision within the Special Care Unit (SCU) to be extremely tedious – as we have been told that he did – his reluctance to attend was understandable, and discussing it could have led to an amicable resolution… Given that this was the '*Special Care* Unit' we are particularly concerned that no attempt was made to discuss this or to otherwise interact with the patient. (p.33; original emphases)

Clearly, something went very much awry with the care that Orville Blackwood was receiving, or failing to receive. What kind of care was it? Here is the account of a black patient, born in 1961, of their experience of special care at Broadmoor for black patients in the 1980s:

> Within my first hour of being in Broadmoor Hospital, any illusions I had of making a fresh start, and of not being racially abused, bullied or intimidated by those entrusted with caring for me, were shattered as I was put through the well-rehearsed admission process. This admission process was intended to dispossess me of any last vestige of hope or dignity that remained, and involved being stripped naked in front of six burly nurses and placed in a bath containing roughly four inches of yellowy orange water. Two of the nurses crowded in close and put their feet on the rim of the bath, leaning menacingly over me. They told me that they could deal with any 'hard nuts' that came from the prison system and if I stepped out of line I'd be dealt with. I was later to find out to my cost that this was no idle boast or threat… Largactil, the much feared and infamous 'liquid cosh', was often used in a punitive way with varying doses depending on your misdemeanour. I was placed on 200 milligrams of Largactil (forte suspension), four times a day, for telling

one member of staff to treat me with respect, after he had spoken to me in a manner which I found offensive. (Anon., 2000, pp.223–227)

Given this context, it is less surprising, though no less disturbing, to learn from the inquiry team that, 'it was clear to us that Orville Blackwood's primary nurse in the SCU had a very superficial knowledge of the patient. Indeed, we felt the nurse did not know the patient at all'. Moreover, the failing was not just that of the primary nurse:

> None of the staff in the SCU appear to have really got to know Orville Blackwood. Many of the pen-pictures of him provided by his carers verged on the patronising, and he was generally regarded by the staff to be of limited intellect. Yet we have noted earlier that psychological tests revealed his IQ to be higher than the average. (Prins et al., 1993, p.26)

They also noted:

> Prior to his admission to Broadmoor Hospital, Orville Blackwood was an enthusiastic painter. None of the SCU staff seemed to have been aware of this side to his nature, and the therapeutic value of this interest does not appear to have been recognised. (p.26)

In its disdain for the individualities, preferences and aptitudes of patients, the so-called 'special care' in this unit is again disturbingly reminiscent of the replacement of *Zorg* with *Zong*, where an official care sign (*Zorg*) has been painted over and all but erased – a situation in which, to borrow from the French sociologist Pierre Bourdieu's concept of the Left and Right hands of the state, the 'right hand' of disciplinary care or control has supplanted and suppressed the 'left hand' of therapeutic care (Bourdieu, 1992, 2014; Loyal, 2017). Indeed, as mental health policy specialist Ian Cummins has also commented, this description of the SCU reflects a more widespread trend in mental health services in which the contact of distressed clients with services is predominantly defined by 'risk' rather than by 'care' (Cummins, 2015). As we shall see, the stress on 'risk' at the expense of 'care' was very much part of the prevailing culture of the Broadmoor SCU.

The culture of the SCU

The inquiry team observed that there were similarities in the events leading up to the deaths of Orville Blackwood and two other patients, Joseph Watts and Michael Martin, notably in the use of seclusion:

Orville Blackwood refused to attend OT and as a result a Charge Nurse decided, for less than clear reasons, that he should be secluded. He went to a seclusion room voluntarily. He refused lunch and medication. When his room was unexpectedly entered by a doctor and between five and seven nurses, he became aggressive and, following a brief struggle, was restrained by nursing staff. He was then forcibly injected and stripped. Joseph Watts was involved in a violent altercation with another patient. He was restrained by nursing staff and escorted (possibly struggling, though this is not clear) to a seclusion room. No alternative to seclusion appeared to have been considered. A physically violent altercation with an unknown number of nursing staff took place in the seclusion room, followed later by a further struggle with between five and ten nursing staff. At some stage he was forcibly stripped. Michael Martin was said to have become verbally aggressive, to have threatened another patient and attempted to strike a student nurse. There was a violent struggle, he was eventually restrained and escorted, still struggling, to his bedroom where he was stripped.

According to the report into Martin's death by Shirley Ritchie QC cited by the Blackwood inquiry team, 'there was no practical reason why he should not have remained there', but in the event he 'was then removed forcibly (and still struggling) down two flights of stairs to the SCU seclusion room' (pp.49–50). All three of these men died after being placed in seclusion.

Dr Aggrey Burke related to the inquiry team an incident that had been described to him by Orville Blackwood three weeks after Joseph Watts' death. Blackwood was:

[in] a happy mood but staff allegedly told him to stop being cheerful. We were not told what his reaction was to this, but we were told that nursing staff restrained him, secluded him and stripped him. He later told Dr Burke that members of staff sat on him, and in his mind's eye he saw himself as Joseph Watts.

Orville Blackwood's mother, Clara Buckley, told the team that the staff in the hospital saw her son as 'a big monster' – in other words, as 'big, black, and dangerous' – a term that was used by several witnesses in describing him.

The inquiry team remarked that they would have expected to find a more intensely therapeutic regime in the so-called SCU, embracing counselling, psychotherapy and other non-physical interventions, but in actuality there was an almost exclusive reliance on high doses of medication, much in keeping with the trend among psychiatrists generally to adopt medication as the preferred treatment for Afro-Caribbean patients. This had the effect of instilling a climate of fear among Afro-Caribbean patients in the hospital that the authorities were 'killing them off', which was reported to the team by a number of witnesses (p.52). Still more troubling, perhaps, is the comment that, while the unit might have been regarded by staff as a 'special care' unit or an 'intensive care' unit, it was uniformly viewed by patients as a punishment block – 'a place they are sent to if they misbehave' (p.56). In their evidence, the representatives of the Mental Health Act Commission expressed concern at the extent of the use of stripping when patients were secluded in the unit, as if this was an integral part of the culture of the unit, or of the hospital as a whole, that 'it had always been done that way' (p.74).

The inquiry team considered that the decision to place Orville Blackwood in seclusion was 'an over-reaction to a patient unwilling to conform to a rigid, structured regime'. Staff, they believed, 'place too much emphasis on the potential for violence, almost to the extent that they make it more likely to happen':

> [The] sense of danger is exaggerated and may be 'hyped up' by some members of the nursing staff because it tends to reinforce the need for a more custodial rather than therapeutic regime. It promotes the macho culture that is still very much the norm on the SCU. (p.33)

The 'prevailing culture of the SCU is that staff must primarily deal with ever-present danger' (p.73). The first response to a management problem was to increase restrictions, and staff and patients alike expected seclusion to be used in this way, the inquiry report relates. It points out that the number of nursing staff on the SCU was double that on other wards in the hospital, and it should, therefore, have been possible to have reduced the need for seclusion by offering patients greater individual care and attention. However, this was not the case; the rates of seclusion on the SCU remained higher than elsewhere in the hospital (p.73). The heightened expectation of impending violence on the SCU 'inevitably results in custodial attitudes among staff', and 'the tension and sense of ever-present danger seemed to us to be as much a result of staff attitudes as due to the disturbed nature of the patients on the ward'. More than one member of the nursing staff told the team that they (the inquiry team) could not possibly know what it was like to care for such dangerous patients. In reply, the team simply pointed to their extensive experience and their qualifications to serve on the inquiry. They suggested that such comments revealed 'much about staff attitudes within the SCU', and their impression was that 'staff saw their role almost entirely as standing back from patients, observing behaviour and waiting for the next violent episode' (p.58).

Moreover, the therapies and activities on the unit appeared to the team to be biased towards 'white' expectations, indicating a lack of thought or concern for the needs and aspirations of patients from ethnic minorities. Black psychiatrist Suman Fernando and colleagues have also commented how, in their approach to managing a patient in mental health crisis, the Broadmoor staff took little or no account of who the patient actually was, or of his life situation, in terms of the conditioning and stresses exacerbated by an indifferent society (Fernando et al., 1998, pp.193–194). As the inquiry team discovered, Orville Blackwood 'did not believe that he should ever have been sent to Broadmoor. He did not believe that he should have been detained for as long as he had been, given the nature of his index offence.' He felt that he had been harshly and unfairly dealt with, and was being held in custody long after the expiry of his prison sentence, and 'his anger and frustration at this unfairness sometimes manifested themselves through aggression and violence' (p.22). Grievances of this sort were, however, treated by the staff as evidence of his continuing mental illness.

Institutional psychotherapy: Alienation and dis-alienation

It is worth pausing to stand back for a moment and interrogate what is happening here from the perspective of a radically different theoretical and practical tradition within psychiatry to the one that was on display at Broadmoor, and within the SCU in particular. A situation had arisen around Orville Blackwood, whose belief that he was the victim of a gross injustice was wholly at variance with that of the staff, who appeared to attribute all his grievances to his illness. I would argue that Blackwood's grievances reflected a condition of alienation that possesses both a psychic and a social dimension. It was exactly this relation between the 'psychic' and the 'social' that was the focal concern of the Catalan psychiatrist Francois Tosquelles (1912–1994) who, in the aftermath of the Second World War, together with Jean Oury (1924–2014) and other colleagues, pioneered an approach that they termed institutional psychotherapy at the Saint Alban Hospital in central France and its associated clinic of La Borde. The experience of *living under occupation* (variously, fascist, colonial or capitalist) became central to their interrogation of the meaning of alienation and to their critiques of madness. Robcis quotes the words of two members of the Saint Alban team:

> In the eyes of the dominant class, the mentally ill are the blacks, the natives, the Jews, the proletarians of the sick. Like them, they are victims of a number of prejudices and injustices… Only a new practice can demonstrate where we can travel in the transformation of psychiatric care or in the situation of the mentally ill person in society. (Robcis, 2021, p.40)

Tosquelles insisted, if madness is a social problem, it requires a social solution. 'Are these people really sick?' he asked. 'Does this notion of "sickness" exhaust all of the meanings of mental alienation?' Their goal at Saint Alban was to establish a new kind of practice founded on non-submission to the dominant clinical model in which the subject behind the symptom is erased (Robcis, 2021, p.37). For those living under such an occupation, it is not just a physical condition but also a state of mind, in which an insidious process – the result of multiple factors such as ideology or psychic colonialism, for example – constitutes them as subjects and at the same time 'occupies' them. 'Institutional psychotherapy is perhaps best defined,' wrote Jean Oury, 'as the attempt to fight, every day, against that which can turn the collective whole towards a concentrationist or segregationist structure' (Robcis, 2021, p.212). By 'concentrationism', he meant (roughly) totalitarianism. For Tosquelles, psychiatry and politics shared the goal of trying to bring about a form of true freedom through 'disoccupying' or 'disalienating' the minds of patients, and through the 'disoccupation' of the mind more widely.

As I have previously noted, following his training as a psychiatrist in France, Frantz Fanon worked with Tosquelles and his team for a period and, significantly, the original title for what eventually became *Black Skin, White Masks* (1952/2017) was *Essay for the Disalienation of the Black Man*. The 'true disalienation of the black man', Fanon asserted, was not just a psychic affair; it implied also 'a brutal awareness of the social and economic realities' (Robcis, 2021, p.55). After leaving Saint Alban, Fanon worked as a substitute doctor in a hospital in Pontorson, a small town in Normandy, where the patients spent their days locked up and treated like animals by a medical staff who appeared to be afraid of them. Determined to put into practice the theory of a psychiatry 'outside the walls' that he had been learning at Saint Alban, Fanon authorised 29 of the patients to go to the weekly morning market in the town, accompanied by some nurses. When the director of the hospital refused to sign the order, the patients at the hospital launched a general strike. Although Fanon was obliged to retreat, the patients themselves picked up the gauntlet he had thrown down.

These reflections, especially the notion of 'living under occupation', surely echo, and may help to illuminate, the experiences of black patients at Broadmoor. They also serve to underscore what was being neglected, and cruelly excised, within the Broadmoor SCU regime. It is likely that Orville Blackwood himself would have been receptive to some of these notions. Had he been permitted to join a conversation that validated his own sense of reality and acknowledged the injustice that had been shown to him, it might perhaps have seeded a process that, if tactfully negotiated on both sides, could have spared his life and opened a new horizon for him.

Big, black and dangerous?

In his book *Maybe I Don't Belong Here: A Memoir of race, identity, breakdown and recovery,* David Harewood writes:

> In my own records I'm often described as a 'large Black man' and it's also interesting to note the very large doses of drugs I received (Diazepam & Haloperidol), both at levels four times the current recommendations... Living in the UK where Black pain is denied, where your concerns aren't listened to, and where your self-worth is so non-existent that it seeps into the very fabric of your being... Can you imagine waking up in a hospital you don't recognise, surrounded by people who don't know you, full of antipsychotic drugs, and only being referred to as the 'large Black man'? (2021, p.196)

Although many Afro-Caribbean patients believed they were only sent to Broadmoor because they were 'big black men', the inquiry team were told that all the patients were there simply because they were mentally ill and that they often blamed their detention on other things 'because of *their lack of insight*' (p.17, original emphasis). The team did not invent the phrase 'big, black and dangerous'; it was openly used by the ICU nursing staff, and the team appropriated it as a shorthand for the ways in which Orville Blackwood and other black patients were perceived (Cummins, 2015). The assessment of dangerousness was frequently much exaggerated, as the case of Winston Rose also bears out. Michael Martin was sent to Broadmoor because he was, apparently, a 'highly dangerous and unpredictable individual', yet, as with Winston Rose (and in a different but distinctly related way with Alice Triggs), the accounts in the records that should authorise such descriptions are nowhere to be found (Francis, 1993, p.196). A post mortem revealed that Michael Martin's death was precipitated by, among other factors, the neck holds from the nurses' 'violent restraint' as he was 'pinned down on the floor by up to a dozen nurses' (Francis, 1993, p.195).

There was a pattern that was repeated over the course of Orville Blackwood's admission to Broadmoor that was in many respects only an exacerbation of his previous experience in the penal and mental health systems. Whenever he became more paranoid and aggressive, higher doses of medication would be prescribed, involving forcible interactions with large numbers of staff and leading to entrenched positions of hostility on both sides. In October 1987, just before his removal to Broadmoor, after he became very unsettled over a trivial incident, the police were called and reportedly 14 arrived, bringing with them 'riot shields and hats', because he was trying to break down the door of his seclusion room. Following his admission to Broadmoor, it is said that 12 nurses were required in order to administer his medication. In August 1991, while in seclusion, he damaged and rendered ineffective two seclusion rooms that had previously been considered impregnable. There were, however, some remarkable differences of perception. For instance, Clara Buckley, Orville Blackwood's mother, told the inquiry that her son was a caring person who was concerned about other people, not a hateful or selfish person. He had, however, been depressed by his experience of society in general, she said, and particularly by the harassment that he had frequently received from the police (p.16). It should not be too difficult to appreciate that this could indeed be the case. Orville Blackwood himself 'appeared to have concerns about the standard of care he was receiving at Broadmoor. He said the staff brought out the worst in him. He told Dr Burke that when his nephew was murdered, staff gave him no help or support' (p.26).

Psychiatry, race and Broadmoor

Psychiatry, as the inquiry team noted, is a 'white, middle-class profession', and when psychiatrists diagnose psychotic patients from poor, black African-Caribbean communities, the 'social perspective' is frequently wanting (p.52). Suman Fernando and colleagues remark:

> The labels those charged with delivering care and treatment to Orville Blackwood applied to him, and the expectations they held of him, were underpinned by a variety of pre-conceptions that set in motion the series of events which led to his eventual death. That labelling process involves racism. (Fernando et al., 1998, pp.193–194)

The 'history of psychiatry and mental health services,' observes Ian Cummins in a commentary on the circumstances leading to the death of Orville Blackwood, 'is scarred by racism… Psychiatry, along with the agencies of the criminal justice system, has played a key role in creating the racist stereotype of the psychically aggressive violent black male' (Cummins, 2015, p.19). Though patients were quite aware that racism existed, 'because the staff and management at the hospital do not recognise the subtle way in which racism can operate, they do not see it as a problem and there is a dissonance of viewpoint,' the inquiry team noted:

> Broadmoor is a white middle class institution in rural Berkshire. The majority of members of staff are white. Many have a working-class rural background. A significant number have a history of military service.

All these factors play a part in determining the value-judgements of the nursing community at the hospital… African-Caribbean patients from poor inner city areas therefore find themselves in an alien environment. The closed, in-bred community of nurses, some from a military-type background, has little understanding of the needs and cultural differences of ethnic minority patients. It is not good enough to maintain that all patients are treated the same regardless of colour or ethnic background… This implies that all patients are treated as white European men.[1] (p.55)

The inquiry report also highlighted the conflicting assessments of Orville Blackwood by black and white psychiatrists. So, for example, the (white) Director of Medical Services (DMS) at Broadmoor declared that Orville Blackwood 'suffered from delusions' and most of the time had 'no insight into his illness', whereas Dr Aggrey Burke, an independent black psychiatrist who came to know Blackwood well over a number of years and to gain his trust, described how the first time he saw him they discussed conceptual issues in psychiatry and other topics together, leading Burke to the conclusions 'that he was *not* a man without insight, rather he was a man with *profound* insight' (original emphasis). The DMS was satisfied that Blackwood suffered from a 'chronic schizophrenic condition', or a 'process psychotic disorder'. One may elect either to compliment the white DMS on his professional acumen and rectitude or deplore his stupefying ineptitude in the face of Orville Blackwood's humanity. For his part, Burke could not accept that Blackwood suffered from schizophrenia or from a process psychotic disorder. In his opinion, Blackwood displayed a stress-related acute psychotic disorder or a schizo-affective psychosis. Burke compared him to other insecure and sensitive inner-city Afro-Caribbean young men, who could be seen as paranoid because of their tendency to project a lot and to blame others, but were in Burke's words 'turbo-jetting' or letting off steam (p.18).

An indefatigable champion of racial justice for more than 50 years, and the first Black Caribbean consultant psychiatrist in Britain, Aggrey Burke has consistently spoken out on behalf of a beleaguered minority whose circumstances have left them as 'non-persons', and who must strive all their lives 'to be a person'. He has done so even at the cost of marginalising himself from the psychiatric mainstream and depriving himself of the professional recognition that is certainly his due (Burke, 2021, pp.6–7).

As Ian Cummins brings out in an insightful discussion, Aggrey Burke was arguing very much from his experience of the Afro-Caribbean young

---

1. On the history of the former Broadmoor Criminal Lunatic Asylum, see especially Shepherd (2013, 2016), also Winchester (1998).

men he met in the course of his work, who were often insecure as a result of the wider problems they faced. However, these insecurities were frequently hidden behind challenging behaviours that could be interpreted by the authorities as a form of paranoia, or mental illness. In Ian Cummins's account, therefore, the whole process of diagnosis in this racialised setting is an out-and-out expression of racism, as is also the whole atmosphere and culture of 'emergency' and incipient violence that the Broadmoor SCU exemplified (Cummins, 2015).

Aggrey Burke's opinion was not, of course, shared on the SCU at Broadmoor, but it was endorsed by Orville Blackwood's family. As reported by the inquiry team, Blackwood's sister said Orville 'would compare himself to other people in the hospital and ask himself why he was there', so 'he decided to play along and he said he accepted he was mentally ill'. But, she added, his doctor then told the family that this only proved that he *must* be mentally ill (p.17).

The way in which seclusion was routinely threatened and deployed at the SCU is, of course, strongly reminiscent of the use of 'tanking' as a punishment at the Kingston asylum in Jamaica in the 1850s. So too is the compulsory bathing described by the anonymous Black patient on admission to the hospital. These experiences also involved a rather similar concentration of agitated, intrusive and hectoring attendants around the body of the 'offending' patient. It is as if, despite differences in time and place, these sets of practices were the progenies of a cognate perverse racial imaginary. In the SCU, 'there appeared to be no perception of the patient's individuality or empathy with him or his situation' (p.33). Leading up to Blackwood's death in a seclusion room, 'we are left with a picture of a large group of men unexpectedly entering the room of a calm patient' (p.30). He was injected with promazine at three times the maximum recommended dose and with twice the recommended dose of fluphenazine, and he died almost immediately. The pathologist gave as the cause of death 'cardiac failure associated with the administration of phenothiazine drugs'.

A racist collective imaginary

All considered, the report of the Prins Inquiry is an iconic cultural document that, even after the passage of almost 30 years, possesses the capacity to shock, and all the more so perhaps because it is consistently scrupulous and under-stated in its choice of words, yet recounts a deeply disturbed, and disturbing, state of affairs from which no one in the Broadmoor Hospital staff emerges at all well, or displays any integrity, from the ICU nursing staff up to the Director of Medical Services. Nor, most worrying of all, do they show any insight into the racial nexus in which they were all entangled, and which they were reproducing daily, hour by hour, through their prejudices, reflexes and actions. In a discussion about opportunities for developing a completely new therapeutic environment, the inquiry team reports, 'We were particularly concerned that many of our witnesses appeared unable to comprehend the concept of a totally new regime' (p.57). Apart from Orville Blackwood's immediate family, the only person whose insight and compassion is convincing and persuasive is Dr Aggrey Burke.

The inquiry team alludes to a want of opportunities for counselling and psychotherapy, by which they mean to point to periods of time in which Orville Blackwood and a mental health professional might have been alone in a room together, on a regular basis, for therapeutic encounters. However, it is exactly this simple notion of just one person sitting, listening and talking with another, on an equal human level, that seems quite unattainable, almost unimaginable, in this setting. Instead, it is crowded out by groups of policemen or nurses armed with riot shields and syringes, routinely descending on the scene. It is as though, in distancing themselves from Orville Blackwood's humanity, the staff absented themselves from the resources of their own humanity. When they speak about 'danger', they frequently appear to be talking not so much about what is real as about what has been stirred up by their racist collective imaginary. Disability studies scholar Michelle Jarman asks how the system should change:

> to allow for the need to occasionally protect people in mental distress through involuntary holds while remaining equally committed to respecting and protecting their personhood... The result of dismissing the words, feelings and testimonies of people in states of mental distress is ultimately to rob them of personal signification, and to force their understanding of their own lives into an involuntary hold of its own. (Jarman, 2012, p.25)

The names that have been given to the Broadmoor SCU over the years, such as Norfolk or Oxford House, and more recently Cranfield and Stratford Ward, appear to entertain the fantasy that fearsome black bodies and minds may be tamed and tranquillized by infusing them within an English pastoral imaginary.

After their inquiry was completed and the report was published, the team offered to return to the hospital to monitor the implementation of their recommendations. The offer was, not altogether surprisingly, firmly rejected. Professor Herschel Prins later reported that, somewhat ironically, in 1998 he was invited to return to Broadmoor to participate in a seminar examining how successful the hospital had been in developing its anti-racist policies, only to discover that there were still no black members of senior management and apparently even fewer black staff working on the wards than at the time of the inquiry. 'All institutions are notoriously impervious to change', he concluded; 'the only way to bring about such change is to make them more openly accountable. Sadly, we still have a long way to go' (Prins, 1998).

Mrs Clara Buckley holding a photograph of her son, Orville Blackwood

After Orville Blackwood's death

After her son's death, Clara Buckley remained determined to seek justice for him. 'Godfearing Clara', as she has been described, 'an elder in her congregation, gained the confidence to fear no man when she stood up and told people about her son Orville, and how he died, and asked people to sign her petition for justice'. She 'could make a bunch of raucous passing youth stop, shut up, and listen to her story.'[2] In November 2011, at a community meeting calling for action against black deaths in custody, youth pastor Nathan John introduced himself as the son of Orville Blackwood, revealing that he was seven years old when his father died in psychiatric custody and that he grew up worrying whether he would have mental health issues. 'What was taken away from me is something that I think every child should have,' he told the meeting. 'It doesn't matter who my father was, whether he was a good man or a bad man, I should have access to him' (Ojieto, 2011).

In actuality, some small (though faltering) changes were being introduced at Broadmoor in the late 1990s. Thanks to the determination of a group of

2. https://randompottins.blogspot.com/2005/10/for-orville-and-others.html

staff members who formed the Equal Opportunities Working Group and who recognised the pressing need for the employment of a black therapist, Stan Grant (aka Arike) was appointed. However, his appointment was clearly tentative, experimental and uncertain, if not to say equivocal, as his opening words to his account of his work make clear:

> I am not writing from a neutral and detached position – I am being deliberately subjective. I am writing as a black man born into this country fifty years ago, in a white supremacist society. I am writing as a man whose father was diagnosed as schizophrenic by the mental health system, taken from him and never seen again. (Grant, 2000, pp.135–147)

The seemingly insuperable challenge that Grant was facing in confronting the powerlessness of inmates and the loss of credibility they suffered – true of all patients at Broadmoor certainly, but much aggravated for black patients – are conveyed in the words of a black patient at Broadmoor in 1997:

> You can't trust these people – they are a law unto themselves –they get away with murder here. If for any reason you cross them, they don't like you, or they see you as a problem, all they've got to do is put it down on paper and it's on your record. It doesn't matter that it's not true, when another colleague reads it, then to them it is true, and so on it goes. It's only your word against theirs and you know who is going to be believed. (cited in Grant, 2000, pp.135–147)

Ironically, it has been suggested that the fallout from the Blackwood and related inquiries may have hastened an increasingly restrictive ideological trend in government legislation towards implementing a more punitive and controlling criminal justice system to protect the public (Fernando et al., 1998, p.197). As a consequence, and aping developments in the United States where the prison world has become a battlefield and the prisoners, to use the words of Vivien Stern when Secretary General of Penal Reform International, 'are prisoners of war – people of another country or another ethnic group, nothing to do with us' (Fernando et al., 1998, p.200), the culture in the Intensive Care Unit at Broadmoor has reportedly become increasingly adversarial. In 2019, the atmosphere there was described as 'consistently tense', and when a patient needed to be moved, reportedly six staff had to be present, often wearing riot gear, before the door to their room was unlocked (Levi & French, 2019, p.89).

PART 5

After

Part 5 – Prologue

The word 'After' may signify many things – a relief, a prospect opened, a heavy weight lifted, or a combination of these – a time of hope, maybe, but not infrequently also a time of grievous disenchantment. In the early 21st century, we cannot fail to be forcibly struck by the eerie familiarity of many of the events and circumstances that we routinely encounter taking place around us – by disturbing continuities in political struggles over the black body and psyche especially, as we shall explore in the next chapter; specifically, and just to take one example, between the *Zong* episode in the 1780s and the recent case of Jimmy Mubenga, who died at the hands of security guards while being forcibly deported from the UK; also between Lord Mansfield in 1783 and Judge Robin Spencer in 2014, and, more generally and pervasively, between Jamaica in the 19th century and the struggles of families where a family member has died in police custody in Britain today, in the aftermath of empire.

In the final chapter, I draw on a recent study by the black scholar Nicola Rollock that shows how racism is hard-wired into the fabric of a modern society like Britain – an analysis that is of considerable import when we turn to consider how British psychiatry now situates itself in relation to the racialised terrain in which it originated and, to some extent, still exists. It is striking, for example, that while the Royal College of Psychiatrists has issued strong statements on racism and mental health, to a large extent it fails to interrogate, or even to acknowledge, the culture of whiteness in which it is situated and that informs its most basic day-to-day reflexes. Seemingly, in the mind of the Royal College, racism in contemporary Britain, so far as it still exists, is a problem 'out there', not inside the fabric of its own house. As I show, a rather more revealing perspective on the hegemony of whiteness in mental health and psychiatry is to be gained from the experiences and reflections of two black survivors, advocates and teachers, Doreen Joseph and Colin King.

Finally, I engage with the challenge of afropessimism – a controversial topic that is identified especially with the outlook of the Afro-American scholar Frank Wilderson III in his thought-provoking book by that title (2020), which is at once a philosophical and a mental health memoir in the spirit of Frantz Fanon, told in part from, and around, a gurney in a psychiatric ward. The subject area of afropessimism, not least Wilderson's own slant on it, is inevitably open to multiple interpretations but I distill from it an unflagging commitment to a thorough-going revaluation of pathology – of all that the whole tradition of scientific naturalism in psychiatry reviles as abject or defective. It endorses, and strengthens, many of the questions and discoveries we have encountered in the journey of this book and, without taking refuge in any form of neat conclusion, may nonetheless help to expose a horizon and path of hope.

13

Disturbing continuities

From Lord Mansfield in 1783 to Judge Robin Spencer in 2014

In March 2023, three decades on from the murder of Stephen Lawrence and almost 25 years after the landmark Macpherson Report (1999), Baroness Louise Casey produced an excoriating review of the standards of behaviour and internal culture of the Metropolitan Police. Her conclusion was that policing by consent in London was 'broken', with the black community over-policed and under-protected and more likely to be tasered, handcuffed and stopped and searched than white residents. After all these years, the Met was still, in that stark but enduringly controversial phrase, 'institutionally racist' (Casey, 2023). As Imran Khan, the lawyer for the Lawrence family, has remarked, when the Macpherson Report was published in 1999 'many chief police officers robotically accepted the notion of institutional racism', but with hindsight it is clear that this was 'simply an outward sign of penitence for public consumption'. The real driver for the Met was always protect its own, Khan acidly concludes, and it has never really changed. Racism is still rife in British society 'whether it is the alarming rate of deaths of Black men in custody, or the differential treatment of Black mothers-to-be in the health system' (Khan, 2023).

Yet, as if this was not enough, not so long ago we were also witness to a reprise of an episode that happened almost two and a half centuries earlier at the hearing of the *Zong* case in Lord Chief Justice Mansfield's court in Westminster Hall in 1783, where the humanity of enslaved Africans – were they actually persons, or were they just goods and items of trade? – was being hotly contested. On 12 October 2010, Jimmy Mubenga, a healthy 46-year-old African man who had been living in Britain with his family for eight years, died under restraint on British Airways flight 77 to Luanda, while being deported to Angola. The evidence of the racist views of two of the three G4S security guards involved that was revealed at the inquest into his death in 2013 led the coroner to observe that 'the potential impact on detainees of a racist culture is that detainees and deportees are not "personalised". This might, she continued, 'self-evidently, result in a lack of empathy and respect for their dignity and humanity, potentially putting their safety at risk, especially if force is used against them' (Monaghan, 2013).

These are precisely the kinds of concerns that Granville Sharp was adducing in 1783 in referencing the racist culture of Lord Mansfield's court as intent upon distancing itself from questions about slave humanity and personhood (Walvin, 2011, pp.153, 158). There followed, in the case of Jimmy Mubenga, further developments that were to make the comparison between 1783 and the present even sharper. Over a period of eight weeks, the inquest jury had heard evidence that Mubenga was 'pushed or held down by one or more of the guards causing his breathing to be impeded', most likely using an illegal hold called 'carpet karaoke', which involved 'forcing an individual's face down towards the carpet with such force that they were only able to scream inarticulately like a bad karaoke singer' (Amnesty International, 2011). The security firm G4S was paid by 'results': failed deportations were bad for their profit margins. The security guards (who were on zero-hours contracts) were also paid extra for a successful removal. Hence both the company and its operatives were strongly incentivised by economic imperatives to 'get the job away' (Chatterjee, 2013).

The coroner was disconcerted that 'Mr Mubenga died in front of a number of people without anyone stepping in to see if he could be helped', even though witnesses heard him repeatedly cry out for help, saying that he couldn't breathe. Disbelief may have inhibited any display of concern, the coroner intimated, prompted by a racist supposition that black people are inclined to fake their suffering (Monaghan, 2013). Jimmy Mubenga seemingly died in a *Zong*-like situation in which indifference or disbelief prevailed above, or even occluded, any declarations or demonstrations of human solidarity or care by any of the other participants, or bystanders, in the scene. A passenger sitting across the aisle from Mubenga could hear him 'moaning and groaning' and watched as the three security guards restrained him with what he believed, he said, was excessive force. Mubenga complained repeatedly, 'I can't breathe, I can't breathe', for about 10 minutes before he lost consciousness (Lewis & Taylor, 2010). Only after an appeal for information by the *Guardian* newspaper was such passenger testimony brought to light, contradicting the official story that Mubenga had simply fallen ill on the plane (Sambrook, 2013).

Extreme racist texts that had been circulated to friends and colleagues were found on two of the guards' phones. Although the guards all denied hearing Mubenga's cries, nevertheless, by a majority of nine to one, the inquest jury returned a verdict of unlawful killing, ruling that they were using unreasonable force and acting in an unlawful manner. Initially, the Crown Prosecution Service (CPS) had refused to bring criminal charges against the security guards, claiming there was 'insufficient evidence' – their usual 'default position when it comes to deaths in custody', according to Frances Webber, ex-barrister and vice-chair of the Institute of Race Relations. However, in the wake of the inquest verdict, they were obliged to arraign the three men on charges of manslaughter by gross negligence. There followed a six-week trial at the Old Bailey presided over by the Hon. Mr Justice Robin Spencer, and it is at this point that the comparison with the *Zong* trial of 1783 becomes directly visible, for Judge Spencer, using restrictive powers, ordered at the outset that the racist texts from the guards' phones and the inquest verdict, together with the coroner's report, were all to be withheld from the jury and made inadmissible in the trial.

As Frances Webber points out, a very high standard of proof is required to sustain an unlawful killing verdict at an inquest, and it might have been supposed that a prosecution in a criminal trial would therefore succeed. However, the judge's manipulation of the *mise-en-scène,* through his decision to exclude significant evidence, meant that the case lacked a large part of its context, thus preventing the jury from properly weighing and contextualising the information that was brought before them. Judge Spencer evidently meant to restrict (though no doubt Granville Sharpe would have put it more strongly) the scope of the Mubenga case, and to disable the jury from learning what was humanly actually at stake here, much in the way that Lord Justice Mansfield had meant to exclude questions about slave humanity and personhood from the *Zong* case. By doing this, he effectively set it up so that Jimmy Mubenga's cries literally could no longer be heard.

And so it turned out when it came to the verdict. Ignorant of the substance of much of what had been going on, the jury was persuaded to acquiesce with the defence suggestions, drawing yet again on the racist stereotype of the black offender ('big, black, and dangerous'), that Mubenga was to a large extent the author of his own demise, and the three security guards were acquitted of the charges against them.

Contested though it properly still is by organisations such as Inquest, the Institute of Race Relations (IRR), and the London-based All African Women's Group, whose members include people affected by deportations, the shocking outcome of this trial demonstrates that a black man can so easily be done away with and disposed of, both in the actual event and subsequently in the process of the law, because he counts for so little and does not really matter in the gaze of the state. As Frances Webber has helpfully explained, in the Stephen Lawrence case there was a strong state incentive to make the prosecution succeed in order to demonstrate the capacity of the legal system to deliver justice for the victim of a racist attack, but with Jimmy Mubenga there was no such incentive – he was just 'a foreign national offender, convicted of an assault in a club – someone as far down the social pecking order as it is possible to be'. Moreover, 'in all the dozens of deaths in custody involving undue force researched by the IRR over the last 25 years, no one has ever been convicted of homicide' (Webber, 2014). All told, this was an affront to justice that, in terms of its ethical weight and significance, put the life and death of Jimmy Mubenga and the role of Judge Spencer in the trial of those accused of his killing in 2014 on a par with the infamous *Zong* massacre and the role of Lord Mansfield in the trial that followed in 1783. Even though, or arguably exactly because, it only involved one victim who could not breathe, Jimmy Mubenga's death stands wholly representative and emblematic of a larger state of affairs that is somatic, existential, structural and political all at once.

Lesser beings or even socially dead

The Jamaican-born poet Claudia Rankine writes:

> Not long ago you are in a room where someone asks the philosopher Judith Butler what makes language hurtful. You can feel everyone lean in. Our very being exposes us to the address of another, she answers. We suffer from the condition of being addressable. Our emotional openness, she adds, is carried by our addressability. Language navigates this. For so long you thought the ambition of racist language was to denigrate and erase you as a person. After considering Judith Butler's remarks, you begin to understand yourself as rendered hyper-visible in the face of such language acts. Language that feels hurtful is intended to exploit all the ways that you are present. Your alertness, your openness, your desire to engage, actually demand your presence, your looking up, your talking back as insane as it is, saying please. (Rankine, 2015, p.49)

As the campaign and support group Inquest discovered in the course of researching their report *'I Can't Breathe': Race, Death and British Policing* (2023), bereaved families uniformly divulge how, in their experience, black people appear less deserving of care and concern in the eyes of the police:

> The way the police – and in some cases the health service – neglected to respond or treat their relatives' condition as a medical emergency

when they struggled to breathe or became unconscious was profoundly shocking to the families. It suggested their loved one's life had little value in the minds of the police or emergency services.' In several cases, officers spoke of the men as 'faking' the gravity of their state as they lay dying. 'He was a piece of shit to them', one family member said. (Inquest, 2023, p.59)

The independent inquiry into the death of David 'Rocky' Bennett, the 38-year-old African Caribbean and Rastafarian man with a history of schizophrenia, heard from his sister, Dr Joanna Bennett, that she had been informed by her brother that it was not unusual for him to be racially abused and physically attacked by other patients. 'When you are mentally ill and isolated from your family in a predominantly white area,' she told the panel, 'when you feel oppressed and are experiencing racial abuse, you think that you are a lesser being' (Bennett Inquiry, 2003, pp.23). The panel formed 'the strong impression' that, on the evening on which David Bennett died after being held face-down on the floor by at least four nurses:

he was not treated by the nurses as if he were capable of being talked to like a rational human being, but was treated as if he was 'a lesser being', to use Dr Bennett's phrase, who should be ordered about and not be given a chance to put his own views about the situation before a decision was made. (p.25)

The staff appeared unaware of the 'corrosive and cumulative effect of racial abuse upon a black patient' (p.27).

The inquiry concluded that people from the black and minority ethnic communities were not getting the kind of service they were entitled to. The panel called this omission a 'festering abscess' and a 'blot upon the good name of the NHS' (p.58). One of the most serious allegations in the report was that lessons had not been learnt from previous deaths, referring specifically to the Prins inquiry (Prins et al., 1993) into the deaths of Orville Blackwood, Michael Mann and Joseph Watts that we discussed in the previous section .

Underlying these experiences is a sombre acknowledgement that racism is not merely, or perhaps even primarily, about words but also about the *value* that society places on different groups of people, and the incontrovertible truth that black people – notably, black men with mental health issues – are accorded very little at all (Inquest, 2023, p.18). The families who spoke to Inquest for its review sensed the existence of an implicit hierarchy that placed being black and in a mental health crisis lower down the social scale. In analogous terms, the black psychotherapist Aileen Alleyne has called attention to 'the chokehold of historical enmeshment' that 'speaks to the entangled relationship between the black race and the white race that creates psychic burdens which continue to weigh on black lives in the present' (Alleyne, 2022, p.155).

The political philosopher Judith Butler charges that 'part of the very problem of contemporary political life is that not everyone counts as a subject'. Some groups or populations 'are considered from the start very much alive and others more questionably alive, perhaps even socially dead' (Butler, 2009, pp.41–42). Liberal racism operates within the logic of nominally colourblind but in actuality racist ideologies that perceive some people within racialised groups as more worthy, and hence more grievable, than others (Younis, 2021a, p.1833). As the educationist Diane Reay and her team discovered:

> value lies at the heart of white middle-class identity. In a class-ridden, racist society, to embody both whiteness and middle classness is to be a person of value. It is also to be a person who makes value judgments that carry symbolic power; a valuer of others. (Reay et al., 2007, p.1042)

By contrast, a majority of both the white and the black working classes, and those who are perceived not to share white middle-class values, are residualised and positioned as excessive or even dispensable. Symbolically, they come to represent the abject 'other' of no value (Reay et al., 2007). As David Gillborn describes, the 'White poor have long existed on the boundaries of Whiteness, what Ricky Lee Allen (2009, p.214) terms: "White but not quite"' (Gillborn, 2010, p.14). Though the white working class may be beneficiaries of whiteness, they are also 'at times in a liminal position where they can be demonised when necessary or useful… they provide a buffer, a safety zone that protects the White middle classes' (Gillborn, 2010, p.22). And the intersection of race and psychiatric diagnosis may trump class in the assignation of human value for, as Frantz Fanon described, the 'fact of blackness' still haunts the black person, irrespective of their class status (Fanon, 1952/2017, pp.88–89; see also Rollock, 2022, p.227).

Prominent among the less grievable population groups who do not count for very much are the mad poor. The harsh and disturbing truth is that, in the eyes of the state, mad lives today do not much matter either, and mortality statistics strongly suggest that they may count for even less than they did in the past. The life-expectancy gap between people with mental illness and the general population has widened over the last 30 years, and the average reduction in life expectancy for people with a diagnosis of schizophrenia, for instance, is now 10–20 years. Moreover, studies have shown that after one year of treatment, patients with a diagnosis of schizophrenia are 10 times more likely to be dead than they were 100 years ago, rising to 11 times more likely after five years of treatment (Healy et al., 2012). Mental disorder bears an ineluctable stigma and in consequence people who are 'unreasonable' are made to join a 'surplus' or dispensable population. The significance of imperialism has changed, the critic John Berger proposed some years ago, for today it demands a mankind that counts for nothing, thus validating the idea even of a 'surplus' population (Berger, 2013, p.7) Though the mental health survivor today is not the mental patient, nor even the ex-mental patient, of yesteryear, even so, frequently the reflexes of psychiatric officialdom and the mainstream mental health system emit the message that nothing has really changed at all, and they are still dealing with the same 'inferior', substandard 'natives' who have long resided at the racialised heart of the psychiatric imaginary (Barham, 1992/2020, pp.6–26).

Political struggles over the black body and psyche

Madness and blackness have been far more entangled at the end of empire than is commonly supposed. Based on extensive research in the British national archives, *The Afterlife of Empire* is a remarkable study by Jordanna Bailkin (2012), an American historian of Britain and empire, that explores this and related themes, demonstrating how the post-imperial played a singular part in the making of the post-war. She demonstrates how the distinctive forms of welfare that emerged in Britain in the 1950s and 1960s were shaped by decolonisation and its perceived demands, and how the disciplines of psychology and psychiatry played vital parts in securing a basis for governance (Bailkin, 2012, pp.2, 37). The end of empire produced a 'complex intermingling of power and pathology', argues Bailkin, focusing especially on the 'stereotype of the "mad" West Indian migrant', the culmination of 'a long history of treating the black psyche as the site of political struggle' – or more accurately, the black body and psyche – plentiful examples of which we saw earlier in the chapters concerning Jamaica (Bailkin, 2012, pp.37, 43, 124).

In Britain today, it is in the dramatic increase in recent years in the recourse to coercion and constraint in the delivery of mental health care that the political struggle over the black body and psyche and the continuing racialisation of mental patient destinies turn out to be most visible (Keating, 2016). The number of people detained involuntarily in mental hospitals in England and Wales rose from 21,897 in 1988 to 58,399 in 2015. Nearly 50% of inpatients are now detained on an order under the Mental Health Act, reports Szmukler (2018). And, strikingly, it is people from ethnic minorities who are disproportionately sectioned under the Act. In the year to March 2022, black people were almost five times as likely as a white people to be detained under the Mental Health Act – 342 black detentions compared with 72 white for every 100,000 people. Detention under the Act means that patients can be held on a secure ward and treated against their will. Out of all ethnic groups, the black 'other' ethnic group have the highest rate of detention – 760 detentions for every 100,000 people compared with 69 detentions for every 100,000 people among the white British population (HM Government, 2023). Moreover, even when discharged from hospital, black patients are subjected to community treatment orders requiring them to maintain strict medication and assessment schedules and even certain living arrangements at nearly 10 times the rate of white patients (Barham, 1992/2020).

The families that Inquest has engaged with know full well at first hand what is involved when the state treats the black body and psyche as the site of political struggle. The concentration of state-sanctioned violence that may accrue here is graphically and distressingly illustrated by what happened to Darren Cumberbatch in 2017. A 32-year-old, qualified black electrician, Cumberbatch died in hospital nine days after the use of force by police officers while he was experiencing a mental health crisis at McIntyre House, the bail hostel in Nuneaton where he was living at the time. He had a history of depression and anxiety and, on this particular day, after becoming agitated, fearful and paranoid, sought shelter in a toilet cubicle, provoking concern among the hostel staff, who resorted to calling the police. As soon as they arrived on site, without any further ado:

> seven police officers entered the cubicle and, over the course of the next ten minutes, Darren was punched 10–15 times; struck with batons; kicked, stamped on; tasered 3 times; sprayed with PAVA incapacitant; handcuffed, and restrained on the ground in the prone position. (Inquest, 2023, p.93)

Officers then pulled Darren out of the cubicle and further restrained him in the corridor, before lifting and dragging him to the police van in which he was driven to the hospital. As he entered the hospital, he was hyperventilating, sweating and his heart rate and temperature were high. Further restraints were applied to his thighs and ankles before he was placed on a trolley on his back and made to lie on his handcuffed hands.

In 2022, five years after her brother's death, Darren's elder sister Carla was still waiting for a final report from the Independent Office for Police Conduct (IOPC), and by this time she had lost all faith in the police watchdog. Bereaved families are 'pushed from pillar to post' by the authorities, she said, 'we are disrespected and treated with disdain'. Later that year, however, the IOPC admitted that its inquiry had been 'flawed', and that it was commencing a re-investigation into the officers' entry into the toilet cubicle at McIntyre House where Darren had retreated and their subsequent use of force. Up until George Floyd's murder, Carla said, she did not have the confidence to speak out about how she understood Darren's death: 'I couldn't find the words.' But when the protests in Britain seemed to her to be focusing largely on the situation in the US, to the exclusion of the picture in Britain, she found her voice and she has endeavoured to become an expert on the law:

> I've got something to live for. I've got life – something Darren hasn't got. I've stopped saying 'rest in peace'. He's got to rest in power. They took his power away from it, but they can't take his voice away from him. Because that's me. (Inquest, 2023: pp.96–99)

Carla contributed to the IOPC's review of the police's use of taser stun guns, published in 2021, which found that the police use them too often, with black people much more likely to be given shocks lasting more than five seconds (60% of black cases reviewed, compared with 29% of white cases). This review also found that mental health played a key role, concluding that the intersectionality of race and mental health can increase the risk of higher levels of use of force (Inquest, 2023, p.94). In a review of cases in the United States, Canadian-Jamaican legal scholar Camille Nelson also concluded that 'people of colour who are mentally ill, or whose mental situation is unstable, are at greater risk of being subjected to police brutality' (Nelson, 2010, p.7).

Families and their struggles for racial justice

'How does it feel to be a problem?' asked the legendary Afro-American scholar and civil rights activist W.E.B. Du Bois (1868–1963), addressing black folk primarily, but also a wider circle of marginalised groups – slaves, untouchables, mad people, women… the list lengthens – all of whom could discover a common bond and solidarity in the fact that they had been framed as 'a problem' in the gaze of some official agency and so were subject to the scrutiny and control of white officialdom. One consequence of living life as 'a problem', Du Bois observed, was that one lived with a 'double consciousness', two souls in one body:

> It is a peculiar sensation, this double-consciousness, this sense of always looking at one's self through the eyes of others, of measuring one's soul by the tape of a world that looks on in amused contempt and pity. (Du Bois, 1903/1969, pp.43–45; see also Pandey, 1995, p.230)

From Henrietta Dawson and Ann Pratt through to Winston Rose and Orville Blackwood, the families with whom Inquest has engaged and countless more, there is a long line of 'devalued others' – black people mainly but also 'poor whites' – branded and unremittingly hectored as 'problems', who have found the strengths, from within themselves and from each other, to talk back to the agents of white hegemony.

As Carla Cumberbatch bears witness, it is frequently female members of the family who emerge as the most forceful and determined advocates and spokespersons. Olaseni Lewis, a 23-year-old IT graduate, died in 2010 after he was held down on the floor for more than 45 minutes in successive episodes of prolonged restraint by 11 Metropolitan Police officers following an episode of mental ill health for which he had voluntarily been admitted, in the company of his parents, to the Bethlem Royal Hospital in south-east London. 'This was the first and only episode he'd ever had,' said his mother, Mrs Ajibola Lewis, a retired lawyer and former teacher. 'It was our first dealing with an institution. We thought that we were doing the best thing as parents, not knowing we were taking him to his death' (Yates, 2017). The police treated Olaseni as if he were an animal rather than human, she said:

> They treated him in such an appalling way. No empathy. No thought.
> And the same language that comes up at inquests where Black people are concerned. They spew out the same thing, 'big, black and dangerous'.

She is certain that racism played a part in her son's death. 'Of course! We're a Black family. You cannot live in our skin and not know. This is our reality.' As Nicola Rollock frames it: 'The Black British mother knows from the moment he is conceived that her son is in danger' (Rollock, 2022, p.185).

At Olaseni Lewis' inquest, seven years after his death, the family wanted to question the officers involved about the extent to which their actions were shaped by their perception of their son as a young black man, and about the guidance and training they had received about racial stereotypes and bias. The coroner refused, on the basis that there was no evidence that race had played a part in their son's death, only to refer to race a few days later as 'the elephant in the room'. The apparent contradiction failed to surprise Aji Lewis:

> It confirmed what we already knew, that there is no accountability. They know. It's staring them in the face, but they just don't acknowledge it. They just can't acknowledge it. They don't have the guts. They don't have the honesty to acknowledge it. (Inquest, 2023, pp.76-77)

What made her most incredulous was the way the state resisted being held accountable for these deaths:

> It beggars belief. I'm dumbfounded that they can go on thinking that to ignore, or bury it, is going to solve the problem. It doesn't. But who am I? Just an ordinary citizen who has lost her son. (Inquest, 2023, pp.76–77)

Following years of tenacious campaigning by Aji Lewis and her family, supported by Inquest and their MP Steve Reed, Seni's Law, restricting the use of dangerous restraint practices in mental health units, came into force on 31 March 2022, four years after it was passed. Aiming to improve transparency and accountability, it requires every mental health unit to publish its policy on the use of restraint, keep a record of occasions on which it is used, and designate one person who is responsible for implementing the policy. There was no police body-worn camera footage of Seni's restraint but police officers who attend mental health settings now have to wear, and operate, body cameras (Inquest, 2023, p.74).

Marcia Rigg, sister of Sean Rigg, a 40-year-old musician and music producer with a mental health history who died after being taken into police custody at Brixton police station in 2008, has campaigned indefatigably for several years to achieve justice for her brother. In 2018, the IOPC directed the Metropolitan Police to bring gross misconduct charges against five officers involved in Sean Rigg's death. All were accused of failing in their responsibility to ensure Rigg's safety; four of them of lying to investigators, and to an inquest jury, to hide the truth, and three of them of using excessive force. In March 2019, after six weeks of hearings, the misconduct panel dismissed all the charges on the grounds that 'none of the allegations are proved'. However, Marcia Rigg remains undeterred. She is now 'absolutely, categorically certain' of the role racism plays in the deaths of black men following police use of force and she is at the same time acutely aware of the systemic patterns of cover-up and denial that are implicated in any such investigations. She does not believe, however, that the police will ever acknowledge it. 'Because it's embarrassing for them. The British establishment does not like embarrassment. They'd rather lie'. In 2022 she addressed the UN Human Rights Council about police violence and systemic racism: 'I'm talking about race now. Because I was always going to. At the end' (Inquest, 2023, p.71).

In their inquiry, Inquest established that, in the aftermath of a death, families frequently experience 'the police seeking to deflect from and minimise their possible wrongdoing by demonising their loved ones and drawing on racist stereotypes of Black men that "vilified" them' (Inquest, 2023, p.16). There is a moment in Nicola Rollock's account (2022) that abuts very graphically on the experiences of the racialised mentally ill and their families when they are caught up in such adversarial ideologies:

> the complainant becomes dehumanized, that is, treated not as a sensing or hurt human being but as an inconvenience or threat to be resolved or eliminated. The complainant as opposed to the issues they raised becomes the problem. (Rollock, 2022, p.165)

Although Black people are seven times more likely than white people to die following police restraint, the role of racism in these deaths is not substantially scrutinised, reflecting a 'chronic inability to see racism being pertinent to the situation in which a Black person has died in police custody despite a wealth of evidence to suggest it is' (Inquest, 2023, pp.11–12; see also Angiolini Review, 2017). Deaths tend to be treated as isolated incidents, with no connections made between them that might point to racism being structural. Overall, 'the question of racism is a problem the state would rather not discuss; it is neither identified in the investigation process nor in inquests or other legal processes' (Inquest, 2023, p.28). The issue of race is thus absent from the official narrative of what happened to their loved ones, resulting in a gulf between the way in which the state describes these deaths and how they are understood by families themselves.

As the Inquest report incisively states:

> The idea that racism exists beyond explicit bigotry is not accounted for in the current bureaucratic and political structures. These are failing to recognise that racism exists in a much deeper way in society that has roots in its power structures. (2023, p.12)

At the level of day-to-day living, this has the consequence that families, keenly aware of the negative attitudes towards naming racism that exist in British society, feel uneasy, or reluctant, to raise concerns about racism for fear that it will be used against them and 'hinder their prospects of unearthing the truth about how their family member died' (Inquest, 2023, p.16). 'I didn't want the perception of the public, "oh they've got a chip on their shoulder because he's Black"... I knew it was there, I just didn't highlight it,' stated Marcia Rigg. Truth was patently in short supply, for families felt that neither the investigation by the IOPC nor the inquest 'adequately addressed their questions about why their loved one met with force, not care; why they were treated as a threat rather than in need of help; and why force was escalated when their relative was asking for assistance' (Inquest, 2023, p.16).

Although George Floyd's murder has undoubtedly led to a heightened awareness of systemic racism among the wider British public, forcing the police to acknowledge that there is a wider issue that has not been adequately dealt with, for families of black people who died following police contact in the UK, what happened in Minneapolis was neither a surprise nor a shock; the phrase 'I can't breathe' had been a refrain among their loved ones for many years before George Floyd's dying words propelled them into a wider public awareness. Even so, the public outrage over Floyd's murder has undoubtedly hastened a sea-change in how racist text messages on the phones of police officers and other responsible parties are viewed, and it may not be unduly sanguine to suppose that it might be indelicate for a Judge Spencer, or similar, to contemplate an equivalent stunt in withholding such evidence from a jury in a criminal trial today.

To strengthen the context of this discussion, it is worth underlining that the crisis of care, and the erosion of the conditions for care, in the contemporary British polity has recently been forefronted as a cardinal cause for concern (Bunting, 2022; Butler, 2023; Dowling, 2022). On the same theme, in her account of what she terms 'cannibal capitalism', the social justice theorist Nancy Fraser shows how capitalism devours care, entwining with racism in creating a hierarchical order of lesser beings and dependent subjects of expropriation (Fraser, 2022).[1]

The Canadian-Jamaican legal scholar Camille Nelson (2010, 2016) has also produced thought-provoking theoretical treatments of the race–mental health nexus, revealing that, among the cases reviewed, for people 'who are negatively racialized, that is people who are perceived as being non-white, and for whom mental illness is either known or assumed, interaction with the police is precarious and potentially dangerous' (Nelson, 2010, p.4).

Younis and Jadhav (2019) have documented the fear and racialised self-censorship produced by the government's PREVENT anti-terrorism training programme for public sector staff, placing additional pressure on Muslims to appear as 'good Muslims', conforming and obedient to state policy, in an initiative that was perceived by some participants as largely racist in targeting

---

1. Unfortunately, space prohibits any closer analysis, but for discussions about recent treatments of race and mental health, particularly concerning the intersections between race and other identities, between mental health and punitive violence, and the psychologisation of counter-extremism strategies in the government's counter-radicalisation policy PREVENT, see Bhatia & Bruce-Jones (2021); Bruce-Jones (2015 & 2021); Goldberg et al., (2017); Thompson (2021); Younis (2021a, 2021b). An important and historically well-grounded study of black resistance to British policing is Elliott-Cooper (2021). See also an older study by the Black Health Workers and Patients Group (1983), *Psychiatry and the Corporate State*.

Muslim populations first and foremost and adding Western extremism only as an afterthought. The authors hypothesise that the PREVENT policy may be productive of moral distress among healthcare staff – a state of mind defined by the British Medical Association as 'the feeling of unease stemming from situations where institutionally required behaviour does not align with moral principles' (BMA, 2021). Last, as the activist and scholar Frank Wilderson underlines in a discussion we shall turn to shortly, it is important to think about Whiteness in relation to the police. 'White people *are* the police,' writes Wilderson, for policing is 'woven into the fabric of their subjectivity', even among those who 'at the level of consciousness may reject this birthright deputation', and this is perhaps 'the most constitutive element of Whiteness' (Wilderson, 2020, p.208).

14

Burn the ship! Escape the hold!

The racial code and intersectionality

It is highly germane to mention here a book that appeared quite late on during the time I have been working on this text but bears very directly on the themes and concerns we have been discussing and in numerous ways complements and strengthens the arguments about racism advanced in its pages. *The Racial Code: Tales of resistance and survival*, by the black scholar and professor of social policy and race Nicola Rollock (2022), above all sets out to demonstrate and explore how racism works – how it maintains and renews its power, and how it is hard-wired into the fabric of British society through deep historical roots and in different ways to that of other Western societies. Mainstream perceptions of racism, argues Rollock, have been unduly preoccupied with overt or extreme expressions of racism on the fringes of society and have ignored the existence of more subtle forms of racism that in actuality 'saturate everyday life and shape interactions between (and sometimes within) different racialized groups' and where racism 'sits below the thin surface of most interactions with whites' (Rollock, 2022, pp.9, 163). These interactions:

> help determine who is seen to belong, who is included and excluded
> from different social spaces and roles, and, crucially, help maintain a
> racial status quo where white people remain at the top of the hierarchy
> and people of colour are at the bottom. This racism makes itself known
> through racial microaggressions, stereotyping and policies that proclaim
> an adherence to equalities but which instead embed and even rationalize
> worse outcomes and poorer experiences for Black and minority ethnic
> groups. (Rollock, 2022, pp.9–10; see also Rollock, 2006).

Rollock invokes the notion of a racial code to specify a structure or scaffold, or 'a rulebook that documents the rules that govern our lives', as useful analogies to help us see and understand 'the connections between what might appear to be isolated incidents but which, in reality, are deeply rooted and historically intertwined' in structures of society that are intrinsically racist and help to expose 'the commonalities between the assumptions and behaviours white people hold and enact about race' and the stubborn endurance of structures of white dominance (2022, pp.9, 200).

Racial power resides unblushingly with Whiteness and determines the ability to shape the racial status quo and dictate which norm will be given a platform and who is seen as normal, 'one of us', or aberrant, different, odd or inferior (pp.11, 109). Rollock draws on the tools of critical race theory (CRT) such as counternarrative to lay bare 'the casual, pervasive nature of everyday racism' and above all 'the effort, the emotional cost and the fortitude required to navigate and survive in a society shaped by race and racism'. She alludes at one point to 'the existential pain' she feels in her core at 'having borne witness, yet again, to the indignities of having to negotiate society when Black' (Rollock, 2022, pp.13, 200, 170; for more on CRT, see especially Rollock & Gillborn, 2011; also Gillborn, 2005).

Rollock refers on occasions (Rollock, 2012) to the intersections between different categories of oppression such as race, class, disability and gender, and in doing so references the concept of 'intersectionality' that originated from the legal scholar and activist Kimberlé Crenshaw (1991). This idea has, in recent years, become extremely topical and been applied across multiple fields and disciplines. Crenshaw's original purpose was to flag up the way in which the legal system tended to treat black women purely as women *or* purely as black and thus to sideline, or disregard, the challenges or burdens that were specific to being a *black woman*, relegating the identity of women of colour, in Crenshaw's apt phrase, to 'a location that resists telling' (Crenshaw, 1991, p.1242). Intersectionality thus became a prism to cast light on, or to identify, dynamics that were mostly ignored by the courts. Thereafter, as David Gillborn phrases it, it has become a method for examining how 'multiple dimensions of oppression (such as race, gender, class, sexuality and disability) work relationally, sometimes in union, sometimes in conflict, sometimes in uncertain and unpredictable ways' (Gillborn, 2010, p.4). 'We might frame the contemporary climate', disability studies scholar Dan Goodley has written, 'as one of working in an age of intersectionality' (Goodley, 2018; see also Davis, 2002).

Indisputably, this book discloses a complex, and conflict-ridden, intersectional terrain, replete with multiple entanglements among identities in locations that mostly resist untangling. However, I have held back from invoking 'intersectionality' as a term of art and claiming this work directly as an intersectional study, largely because I incline to view it as an exploratory or provisional study that requires closer, and more exacting, scrutiny. Nevertheless, in many respects, what Nicola Rollock articulates in teasing out the historicity of systemic racism and advancing the case for an all-embracing racial code chimes with, and strengthens, the arguments I have been making about the intertwining of madness, Blackness and class in a terrain that has been dominated by White reason. Thus, after reading Rollock, it is now startlingly obvious to me that the credibility predicaments to which 'mentally ill' people are liable or subject, that we discussed earlier, are an expression, or consequence, of just the kind of rulebook or racial code that Rollock so astutely discerns and analyses.

The legacies of empire

I have been trying in this book to explore different facets of the colonial legacies in which Black lives and Mad lives in Britain are still entangled under the sway of White reason and of the politics of Whiteness as 'an occupying force in the mind' (Eddo-Lodge, 2017, p.170). Entanglement is an apt term, I believe, for what I have been assaying, which may be seen to complement, though on a greatly reduced scale, what Saidiya Hartman is doing in setting out 'to detail the entanglement of humanity and violence, liberal philosophy and racial reason, the human and its devalued others' in the afterlife of slavery (Hartman, 2022). As has been revealed by recent incidents involving the discovery of a number of 'dirty' files that had been intended for destruction and whose existence had been denied, the legacies of empire are inevitably interwoven with the intrigues of officialdom in curating, and not infrequently in dissembling, what is to be remembered across the whole period of decolonisation through to the present day. Files intended for retention were known as 'legacy' papers, and labelled as 'clean', and the remainder, intended for destruction, were identified as 'dirty'. The 'dirty' files that have come to light are, it appears only a small proportion of a much larger body of material that has either been incinerated or dumped at sea (Anderson, 2012, 2015; Elkins, 2011; Sato, 2017).

As we have been exploring, the historical legacy of psychiatry is inevitably implicated in these largely under-explored and unavowed questions of what has been hidden, denied, dumped, forgotten or remembered. So how does contemporary British psychiatry now see itself in relation to the racialised terrain in which it originated, and that has provided the conditions for, and to a considerable extent manufactured, its being and in which it still lives and moves? Formally, the answer must be quite encouraging, since the Royal College of Psychiatrists has issued a strong statement on racism and mental health and also a robust riposte to the report by the government's Commission on Race and Ethnic Disparities (CRED), which had concluded that structural racism does not exist here in the UK. The Royal College of Psychiatrists (2021) stressed that the CRED report 'failed to take notice of the compelling evidence that racial disparities in health, and particularly in mental health, are driven in large part by social factors which are structurally determined'. At more informal levels, however, the impression is that, in time-honoured British and colonial fashion, the profession does its level best to ignore discomfiting realities, or engages with them only in a rather perfunctory and selective fashion, remaining silent on what it means to be white, for example.

Recently there has appeared a quasi-official social history of psychiatry and mental health in Britain from 1960 to 2010, published on behalf of the Royal College of Psychiatrists under the title *Mind, State and Society* and edited by two distinguished psychiatrists, George Ikkos and Nick Bouras (Ikkos & Bouras, 2021). It is a magnificent volume in many ways, but has some striking absences and distortions. Perhaps most disquieting is that, with the exception of a single chapter, the editors, and the volume as a whole, are largely silent about the legacies of empire. For the most part, the unsettling history of post-war psychiatry in Britain that Jordanna Bailkin relates does not figure here.

Joanna Bourke, a cultural and social historian of great distinction, contributes a keynote presentation of historical perspectives on mental health and psychiatry that is, for the most part, adroitly done, though a few of her judgements are rather off beam (Bourke, 2021). 'There is no consensus', she declares, 'about whether deinstitutionalisation has been a good or bad thing' – it is as though the old guard might step back in at any time and resume control. Whose 'consensus' is this, in any case? Has Bourke gone out and canvassed opinion among the beneficiaries of mental health services? I scarcely think so. Maybe this is, indeed, what Bourke's imagined audience want to hear but, in actuality, the social and cultural reality of 'madness' has changed out of all recognition in recent decades and, though much may still be unresolved, and without question many struggles lie ahead, there is really no mileage in hankering after, or attempting to reinvent, the *ancien regime* in the administration of mad lives.

The more telling stricture, however, is that Bourke's chapter itself, and the way in which the volume as a whole has been curated, are steeped in an unacknowledged whiteness that informs the selection of contributors and of material, the emphases that are made, what is said and, above all, what is left unsaid. You could come away from Bourke's chapter without being aware that Britain ever had an empire or that the history of post-war mental health and psychiatry is deeply riven by the impact and consequences of decolonisation, for British society and for its institutions. Needless to say, Bourke never refers to Bailkin's work. Perhaps it has escaped her attention? I do not find this in the least credible and I am willing to wager that Joanna Bourke knows her Bailkin as least as well as I do. More likely, she has elected to exclude Bailkin from consideration so as to be able to curate a historical account that will align convincingly with the storyline that she believes the psychiatric hierarchy at the Royal College will want to hear. For the same reason, Errol Francis's (1993) landmark essay, 'Psychiatric racism and social police: black people and the psychiatric services', does not merit a mention in Bourke's chapter – an astonishing omission in an account of the social history of mental health in Britain over this period. The contributors to this collection are, without exception, a distinguished bunch but there are some notable absences, such as Kehinde Andrews, Aggrey Bourke, Suman Fernando, Errol Francis, Jayasree Kalathil, Colin King (more of him later), Sashi Sashidharan and Hari Sewell – all of whom, in different ways, at different times, and to varying degrees, have disturbed the complacency of white British psychiatry.

Black history only figures on the margin in this volume. Tucked away at slot 35 is a chapter on 'Race, State and Mind', in which Doreen Joseph – born in Southall, West London, in 1959, a British African Caribbean woman, a mother and a grandmother, a qualified teacher with a higher degree in ethnicity, culture and globalisation, who identifies as a Black survivor and mental health trainer – collaborates with Kam Bhui, a distinguished psychiatrist from a Punjabi Sikh background, born in Kenya but educated in Britain and imbued from an early age with a strong commitment to challenging prejudice and social injustice. Together they elaborate a narrative that resolutely rescues the experiences of black and minority ethnic communities from the margins, locating them firmly in the foreground of any mindful account of the state of the nation in Britain over the past half century. The main part of the chapter is called 'Doreen's narrative and the research evidence' and it beggars belief that it requires the determination of a black woman of enormous resolve, with many years of contact with psychiatric services, who has been given ECT and diagnosed with schizophrenia 'I don't know how many times but quite a few times',[1] to break with the crimping and cramping conventions and assumptions of hegemonic whiteness and open a window on an alternative reality that is also an alternative view, or reading, of British history over this period, and of the part that psychiatry has played in it.

---

1. Quoted from 'Unmasking the Black-White Mirror to save black lives in the mental health system', with Doreen Joseph and Colin King. In 'Racism and Mental Health: How to be an anti-racist mental health researcher', 9 March 2021. https://livpsych.wordpress.com/how-to-be-an-anti-racist-mental-health-researcher

Locating her concerns against the background of a legacy of slavery and colonialism that is perpetuated through racist policies and legislation, Doreen Joseph speaks her mind on the meaning of what has been happening in the period 1960–2010 that would not otherwise be accessible to the reader of the Ikkos and Bouras tome. And in doing so, she shows how the official mind of the state has mostly trampled roughshod over the sensibilities, concerns and needs of black and minority ethnic communities, and of children and young people especially. Though 'modern commentators still resort to cultural and racial pathology, proposing that black people need to take care of their addictions, mental illnesses, and propensities to join gangs', she insists that historical, economic and political factors, manifesting in pockets of clustered disadvantage, are more significant drivers of black discontent, or malaise, than individual 'bad' choices or bad behaviour. Black people are considered by the white majority to be too 'visible' in British society, she argues. She describes how the existence of a widespread, suppressed desire to make them less visible struck her forcibly when she learnt that in Brazil there was a tradition of painting pictures of Black people without defining features – faces that lacked eyes, nose or mouth – thus dehumanising or 'invisibilising' them.

As Joseph and Bhui observe in conclusion, historical injustices are mostly silenced in contemporary debate, just as the promises generated by crises are soon forgotten when the political and public gaze shifts (p.357). Although attention has been drawn to the injustice of mental health care becoming more coercive and less therapeutic for black and minority ethnic groups, 'even this, despite decades of evidence, will still be disputed by some commentators whose location of problems is not in race, ethnicity or culture, but in *individual* risk behaviours', they write. Though Doreen Joseph and Kam Bhui's contribution succeeds in lending a critical edge in challenging racial injustice that might otherwise have left the editors open to a charge of complacency, nevertheless, because of the way in which the volume has been curated and choreographed, it is White Joanna, not Black Doreen at slot 35, who steals the show, and I am reminded of black actor David Harewood's observation, in his imaginary dialogue with the slave master from whom he is descended, that 'You barely notice I'm there, even though I've lived here all my life' (Harewood, 2021, p.232). Of course, this is how 'racism and its counterparts of white privilege and power continue to be kept alive', by skilfully marginalising and, above all, ignoring other positions and outlooks through 'concerted attempts at denial' with 'corresponding sleights of the hand' (Rollock, 2022, p.69). And to help challenge some of this, we may benefit from the critical armoury and vision of Colin King.

Speaking back to whiteness in psychiatry

There are several possible descriptions of Colin King, all equally plausible, and even if he frequently identifies as a mental health survivor, activist or researcher, it should also be said that he is more, much more, than this. Describing himself aptly as a survivor of European misconceptions, and a constant source of arresting, sometimes startling and always challenging ideas, King has emerged as a formidable analyst and critic of social and racial injustices, and notably of the hegemony of whiteness in mental health and psychiatry. The daunting task that he assigns to himself is to demonstrate that much of what the majority white culture takes to be 'true' or 'natural' is actually deeply ideological, and thus to attempt to disambiguate from within an obdurate, and sometimes hostile, dominant 'reality' or regime of 'truth' that he is, all the while, living in and having to contend with daily. It is a project that bears comparison with the critical analysis by the French philosopher Louis Althusser of the ideological nature of everyday reality, and of ideology as a 'representation of the imaginary relationship of individuals to their real conditions of existence' (Althusser, 2008).

All along the road, King seeks to situate himself, and the experience of black people like him, historically, especially as regards the echoes of slavery in the biography of the disordered patient. He wants to know 'if there was a relationship between what happened 400 years ago when black men like me were chained, lynched and brutalized' and 'the way I was overtly medicated, locked up and injected by white men who replaced their white sheets with medical coats'. The ward round 'represents evidence of my resistance in the court of whiteness'; 'the injection of haloperidol is the slave master's whip, wielded by the white male psychiatrist, distant from the emotion of this intrusion, leaving me dazed, mortified and controlled' (King, 2016, pp.75–76). All the theories and studies that he has read have never come near to explaining, or understanding, what it means to be diagnosed, or misdiagnosed, as a black man in English society (King, 2007). Interrogated by an audience of practitioners to see if he meets their job specification of madness, his status as 'mentally ill' is complete. Restrained for outbursts on a number of occasions, 'the echo of slavery became more acute, locked up, forced into menial jobs, and threatened not with the whip but with a deadly needle-full of medication. White staff in their falseness tried to converse to… pass the time'. In a 40-year career, he has become 'a risk to white norms', and been sectioned on four occasions (King, 2007).

Crossing over to the other side, where he trained as a social worker, and going 'back stage', where the psychiatric patient or client is constructed in their absence, gave him compelling insights into whiteness as a process, how it is put together and enacted as a performance. But inevitably it also took its toll on him personally, such that the 'white mask' used during his journey into hospital now became a 'collusive and submissive mask, failing to speak out against the injustice witnessed'. Finding himself lost in the system into which he was again sectioned, he determined that these episodes had come to a head:

> No longer do I want to go into the homes of black men, as a researcher or a practitioner, and understand their lives through tools that bear no resemblance to their world.

Through the use of his 'white mask', he came to realise that no matter 'how I demonstrated I could be white to be accepted as normal, I could not change or alter the static minds of those who assess through their polluted notions of whiteness' (King, 2007). From the conversations that King then went on to have, outside of his role as an approved social worker, with people who had been sectioned, he realised that the next step was to challenge the processes that had destroyed these lives, to redress the theories that had pathologised them, and to produce a black perspective on research and diagnosis – 'a theory that sees British society as the wider psychiatric ward in which black men are stereotyped' (see also King, 2018).

Among his influences, King mentions Frantz Fanon (1952/2017), especially for his theory of the 'white mask', Michel Foucault, Paul Gilroy's (1993) idea of 'double consciousness' (which in turn is adapted from W.E.B. Du Bois (1903/1969) and also Erving Goffman (1956/1971, 1961), whose work instructed King in the outcomes of being defined as mad. Unwittingly, King observes, Goffman makes apparent the 'arrogance of whiteness as a set of negative beliefs about the other' that enable 'the white researcher, unmonitored, to make *implicit* forms of knowledge about mental illness that had profound implications for my life as a black patient' (King, 2007). Elsewhere, King complains about the power exercised by 'an implicit whiteness, an implicit white privilege', such that 'race as a priority is invisible' and absent from the research agenda (King, 2021a). Post-colonial racism in mental health, argues King, manifests as a lack of awareness of whiteness. The invisibility of whiteness and its unconscious performance within psychiatry mean that the influence of whiteness is also invisible in European psychiatry's construction of mental illness in African men and so it cannot be held to account for its impact on them. King wants to throw light on the mismatch between the language of white psychiatry and the reality of African men (King, 2016):

> During my career as a schizophrenic, I never had the power to challenge the interpretation of symptoms that represented the delusions of whiteness that diagnosed me. My life has been controlled by ideas

constructed by whiteness about how I should think and behave that led to becoming a diagnosis. (2016, p.73)

White male psychiatrists 'do not question their own cultural symptoms, which allows them to distance themselves from the phenomenon they construct; they fail to see what Renato Rosaldo (1993) calls the "culture of their truth"' (2016, p.73).

In a commentary on the 2021 Mental Health Act White Paper, King and Tamar Jeynes ask:

'Has White psychiatry really moved on from the mid-19th century when US physician Samuel Cartwright proposed that Black slaves attempted to escape their captivity because of a mental illness he termed drapetomania?' (King & Jeynes, 2021; Cartwright, 1851/2004). They argue that aspects of Cartwright's thinking are re-enacted within the White Paper, which set out proposals for the most recent reform of the Mental Health Act. The parallels with drapetomania are still apparent in the diagnosis of African men like him with schizophrenia, King claims, arguing that the denial of the validity of African men's perception of reality in relation to the diagnosis of schizophrenia in today's mental health wards reflects how black men's resistance to slavery was presented by slave masters as a mental disorder rather than a reasoned desire to flee an unbearable situation (King, 2016). There is a general reluctance in the mental health system to decolonise the hegemonic power of whiteness, King and Jeynes assert. It is in this 'incuriosity and adherence to the norms of Whiteness that the legacy of drapetomania lives on, in the form of legal control over the Black body and mind.' This is not only a White Paper but a paper 'characterised by Whiteness, as retained in its political power' (King & Jeynes, 2021). It portends, King averred in a workshop in March 2021, 'the most dangerous legislation implemented in English society in the past 200 years' (King et al., 2021b; King, 2021b).[2]

King now places his hopes in coproduction, widely touted as a modality of service development and delivery in the health, economic and social arenas (Realpe & Wallace, 2010; Smith et al., 2022; Pettican et al., 2023; www.coproductionworks.co.uk). 'Current medical practise', he provocatively asserts, 'might be seen as a colonial biomedical knee analogous to that which killed George Floyd, because it fails to see how it denies the life of Black people.' Wholly essential, therefore, is a challenge of equity between white psychiatry and the black community so as to bring about the transition 'from the

---

2. Workshop on 'Unmasking the Black-White Mirror to save black lives in the mental health system', with Doreen Joseph and Colin King. 'Racism and Mental Health: How to be an anti-racist mental health researcher', 9 March 2021. https://livpsych.wordpress.com/how-to-be-an-anti-racist-mental-health-researcher

preproduction stage of disempowerment and slavery to the empowerment of Black communities in the coproduction stage, involving meaningful collaboration with the medical profession' (King et al., 2021a; see also King & Gillard, 2019; King, 2022).

The challenge of afropessimism

Finally, we must engage briefly with the challenge of afropessimism (sometimes termed afro-pessimism), which is grounded in an outlook on the structural roots of racism as hard-wired into the fabric of Western modernity and the denial of value in Black lives. This is close to what Nicola Rollock and Colin King are arguing, but Frank Wilderson III, to whom we shall turn shortly, raises these critiques to a whole new level. Afropessimism is the name not so much for a philosophy or a movement as for what one of its leading contributors or adherents, Jared Sexton, describes as a 'gathering', as in 'gathering momentum' or a 'gathering storm', or what I might be inclined to describe as a convergence or mingling of disparate voices around basic questions about the understanding of post-emancipation society. Crucially, it answers the challenges posed by Saidiya Hartman's influential notion of the 'afterlife of slavery' to describe the structural hold of racial slavery, or the continuing 'hold of slavery' through into the present (Hartman, 2022). How do we reflect upon 'the tragic continuity between slavery and freedom' and 'the incomplete nature of emancipation?' Hartman asks (2022). As Sexton observes, over the past decade there have been thousands of online conversations 'across Africa, the Americas, Asia and Europe… adjudicating the relative merits of Afro-Pessimism' (Sexton 2016), testifying to a compelling sense of a historical moment in which the project of Black liberation seems to be lamentably incomplete or unfinished, together with the resonance of the idea that anti-black violence is the essential antagonism that undergirds civil society.

'Black lives,' Hartman wrote some years ago:

> are still imperilled and devalued by a racial calculus and a political arithmetic that was entrenched centuries ago. This is the afterlife of slavery – skewed life chances, limited access to health and education, premature death, incarceration, and impoverishment. I, too, am the afterlife of slavery. (Hartman, 2008)

With the advent of emancipation:

> only the most restricted and narrow vision of freedom was deemed plausible… The gulf between blacks, marked and targeted as not human or as lesser humans and social inferiors, and white citizens only widened.

Hartman realised how 'formative and enduring the hold of slavery continued to be', for the 'liberal conception of freedom had been built on the bedrock of slavery' (Hartman, 2022).

For Frank Wilderson III, and for other exponents of afropessimism such as Jared Sexton, Hartman's ruminations on the continuing afterlife of slavery have been a powerful influence in propelling them towards a political ontology that divides the Slave from the world of the Human in a constitutive way, concluding that 'black life represents an ontological shift in the human' and that racial slavery is 'a foundational event that, far from being over, is endlessly repeating' (Sexton 2012, 2016; Marriott, 2016, p.40). However, Sexton's writings seem quite moderate and tentative, by comparison, for nothing quite prepares us for Frank B. Wilderson III's extraordinary *Afropessimism* (2020), a mixed-genre creation, part critical theory, part manifesto, part memoir, by an author with a varied and distinguished career – a writer and dramatist but also an activist and former member of the armed wing, Umkhonto we Sizwe, or 'The Spear of the Nation', of the African National Congress, and now a university professor of African American studies. It is a summation of where Wilderson's critical reflections on racial slavery have led him that seeks to capture the moral high ground, delivering a no-holds-barred statement on how things stand, humanly and otherwise, with Black people. In earlier life, Wilderson saw himself as an African American, 'a degraded human' on a level footing with other groups of oppressed people. Gradually, however, he came to see that there was something essential about the suffering of Black people that could not be reconciled with the suffering of other people:

> Black suffering is of a different order than the suffering of other oppressed people. We cannot analogize Black suffering with the suffering of other oppressed beings. (Wilderson 2020, p.200, 14)

At the same time, he adds: 'Black suffering is the life force of the world' (p.200).

'Anyone who thinks that 19th century slave narratives are reports on the past isn't paying attention,' Wilderson admonishes. Indeed, as Jesse McCarthy, Professor of African and American Studies at Harvard, remarks in a long review of *Afropessimism*, 'There is a complicated sense in which Wilderson has written a slave narrative in the present, insofar as it is his contention that he actually is a slave right now' (McCarthy, 2020). As Wilderson describes, 'Afropessimism is premised on a comprehensive and iconoclastic claim: that Blackness is coterminous with Slaveness: Blackness is social death' (2020, p.101). Blacks are not human subjects; rather, they are 'structurally inert props, implements for the execution of White and non-Black fantasies and sadomasochistic pleasures'.

They do not function as political subjects; instead, their 'flesh and energies are instrumentalized for postcolonial, immigrant, feminist, LGBTQ, transgender, and workers' agendas' (p.15). Where *Humans* suffer through an 'economy of disposability', *Blacks* suffer by way of '*social death*' (p.16, original emphases). As a paradigmatic position, antithetical to humans, Blackness is elaborated through slavery (p.102).

At the same time, as Wilderson adumbrates, 'through the lens of Afropessimism, slavery is essentially a relational dynamic, rather than a historical era or an ensemble of empirical practices (like whips and chains)' (p.229). It is essential to maintain this relation since 'if Black people were recognized and incorporated as Human beings, Humanity would cease to exist'. Having lost its baseline 'other', Humanity would in consequence lose its conceptual coherence, and find itself standing in the abyss of an epistemological void: 'The Black is needed to mark the border of Human subjectivity' (p.164).

There is something to celebrate here, Wilderson believes:

> Afropessimism is Black people at their best. 'Mad at the world' is Black folks at their best. Afropessimism gives us the freedom to say out loud what we would otherwise whisper or deny: that no Blacks are in the world, but, by the same token, there is no world without Blacks. The violence perpetrated against us is not a form of discrimination; it is a necessary violence; a health tonic for everyone who is not Black. (p. 40)

Wilderson's thinking on these questions may only have peaked fairly recently but it has obviously been germinating a long time. Already as an adolescent, the young Frank discovered a sympathetic spirit in his Grandmother Jules, and together they were able to let their 'rage speak its truth':

> Human life is dependent on Black death for its existence and coherence. Blackness and Slaveness are inextricably bound in such a way that whereas Slaveness can be separated from Blackness, Blackness cannot exist as other than Slaveness. There is no world without Blacks, yet there are no Blacks who are in the world. (p.42)

How to read this book? If in one respect it is a narrative of a major epistemological breakthrough, in another it is a narrative of a psychotic breakdown and of a constant sense of emotional and psychological discordance. *Afropessimism* actually commences on a gurney in a psychiatric ward where Wilderson, as a graduate student, has been taken in a state of psychotic distress, most likely brought on, as he describes, by the stakes, the implications, of where his thinking was taking him – of what it all meant for the dissertation he was writing and, beyond that, for Black life. He revisits this formative episode later on, and it is somehow always lurking below the surface in the text, which, despite its aspirations and its moments of high seriousness, never quite succeeds in shaking off, or discarding, its psychiatric ward cladding and some of the time reads like a psychiatric memoir. He confides:

> This realization that I am a sentient being who can't use words like 'being' or 'person' to describe myself without the scare quotes and the threat of raised eyebrows from anyone within earshot was crippling. (p.15)

It all happened quite suddenly, as he recalled. 'One day I was attending seminars and political rallies, the next day I was groaning on a gurney in the student health psych ward' (p.310). They sent him home from the clinic with SSRIs (selective serotonin reuptake inhibitors), uppers for depression and chlordiazepoxide for panic attacks, and for several weeks after he left the clinic he sought out Black therapists, who reminded him of his parents, in the belief that they could help him best. 'They cared like none of the White therapists I had sampled cared,' he discovered (p. 312).

Afropessimism is throughout punctuated by mental health as a recurring theme and preoccupation. This has troubled critics such as Jesse McCarthy (2020), for whom the text is sometimes 'even alarming in its confessions, which begin in the opening sentences and essentially never let up'. McCarthy likens to talk therapy Wilderson's approach to the narration of his journey into the bondage of his worldview. Indeed, *Afropessimism* 'wades into what sometimes feels like the very frightened quagmires of an extremely intelligent and also deeply unsettled psychological state of mind', McCarthy writes. McCarthy wishes that Wilderson had delivered his philosophy straight rather than mixing it in a psychological memoir. Certainly, he has a point, but this is, perhaps, to misunderstand what Wilderson is doing, and trying to achieve, in this text in interweaving the psychological or the psychiatric with the political. The gurney in the psychiatric ward is scarcely an unfortunate, or adventitious, interruption of what otherwise might have been a 'pure' philosophical memoir; it is actually integral to it. Wilderson's model here may well be Frantz Fanon, whom he greatly admires.

'In our anti-black world, blacks are pathology,' avers Lewis Gordon (Gordon, 2000, p.87). Gordon's comment, and Wilderson's experience of psychotic distress in an anti-Black world, speak loudly to the experience of the redoubtable poet, playwright and activist, Jamaican-born Una Marson (1905–1965). Marson, a friend of George Orwell, was the first Black producer and broadcaster at the BBC, appointed during the Second World War, who gave voice to numerous Caribbean writers and intellectuals. Worn down by the war and her years of lonely struggle with bitter experiences of racism in the motherland, which she unflinchingly narrated in her poem 'N****r' (1933), Marson returned to Jamaica in 1945, and was admitted shortly afterwards to Bellevue Mental Hospital in Kingston with what seems to have been a major depressive breakdown with psychotic dimensions, from which she never fully recovered (Jarrett-Macauley, 1998; Campbell & Russell, 2022).

Yet, as Gordon underlines and Jared Sexton elaborates, in the idea of black people as pathology we may re-discover the value and insight of Frantz Fanon, for Fanon 'fully accepts the definition of himself as pathological as it is imposed by a world that knows itself through that imposition'. The affirmation of blackness as an affirmation of pathological meaning demonstrates:

> [a] willingness to pay whatever social costs accrue to being black, to inhabiting blackness, to living a black social life under the shadow of social death. (Sexton, 2012)

This is not an accommodation to the dictates of the anti-black world, for in a world structured by a negative categorical imperative – 'above all, don't be black' (Gordon, 1997, p.63) – the refusal to distance oneself from blackness and a turn towards 'the shame, as it were, that resides in the idea that "I am thought of as less than human"' (Nyong'o, 2002, p.389), may hasten 'a transvaluation of pathology itself, something like an embrace of pathology without pathos' (Sexton, 2012). Afropessimism, declares Jared Sexton, is both an epistemological and an ethical project that, in the words of Christina Sharpe, 'insistently speaks what is being constituted as the unspeakable and enacts an ethical embrace of what is constituted as (affirmatively) unembraceable' (Sexton, 2016; see also Sharpe 2012). Sharpe draws on the meditation by the Trinidadian Canadian lesbian poet and activist Dionne Brand on the real and mythical door of no return as 'an optic and haunting that continues to construct and position black people in the "new world"'. For Brand, the door is the 'modality of exploring the various and varied black lives lived under occupation… of black (social) life lived in, as, under, in spite of black (social) death' in which she 'embraces "without pathos" that which is constructed and defined as pathology' (Sharpe, 2012).

Mental health is, in any case, very much part of Frank Wilderson's own background. Both his parents were psychologists and, in addition to their day jobs, maintained a private practice as psychotherapists, also contributing to grassroots initiatives such as mental health programmes for people without means (Wilderson, 2020, pp.41–42). In his adolescence, his mother might emerge on the back porch to ask 'in her mental health voice' if he was all right (p.50). Although he gives the impression early on that he, like other Black people, cannot escape a state of bondage, it turns out that Wilderson can allow that it is not necessary for Black people to resign themselves to the inevitability of social death since, 'like class and gender, which are also constructs, not divine designations, social death can be destroyed' (p.103). However:

> the first step toward the destruction is to assume one's position (*assume,* not *celebrate* or *disavow*), and then burn the ship or the plantation, in its past and present incarnations, from the inside out. (2020, p.103, original italics)

However, he evinces some scepticism as to whether many Black people are psychically able and willing to assume this position. His mother especially pulls no punches in expressing her misgivings about afropessimism:

> We were down to brass tacks, my mother and I.
>
> She said, 'What's the use of afropessimism? What *practical* use does it have?'
>
> I said, 'It's not a tractor, it can't mow your lawn… But it makes us worthy of our suffering.'
>
> She said: 'How's suffering going to make me a good citizen?'
>
> I said, 'I can't believe you're a Black psychologist who's read Fanon.' (p.328)

'Ultimately', concludes Afro American literary scholar Selamawit Terrefe, *Afropessimism* 'places into relief the consequences of one's understanding that madness, death and the "hold of the ship" are the here, now, and heretofore all at once, until the world we understand within this current symbolic order ceases to exist' (Terrefe, 2020).

Eventually, Wilderson seems to tire of his tablets, his 'two best friends in orange-brown bottles', and resolves to flush them down the toilet:

> I was committing to make madness my refuge; to face the fact that my death makes the world a decent place to live; to embrace my abjection and the antagonism that made me Humanity's foil. I would make my home in the hold of the ship and burn it from inside out. (Wilderson, 2020, p.323)

Here, perhaps, is the nub of it: through a willing embrace of abjection, and abjected forms of humanity, afropessimism comprises a gathering discourse, or convergence of voices, that enjoins a deep and dedicated revaluation of pathology, and of the hegemony of scientific naturalism that casts madness as dysfunction or as defects in reason. As we have learnt in the journey of this book, the scourge of this hegemony forms a 'mesh that girdles our thought so tightly that it has become nearly impossible to see it as a tradition' (Garson, 2022a), depriving mad people of their worth and legitimating their treatment as objects (Smith, 2023, pp.17–21; Barham, 1984/1993, pp.vii-xii; Barham, 2023).

The story of the racialised origins, and passage, of psychiatry through modernity can be told in a number of ways but, as we have discovered, any telling that is to lay a credible claim to historical truth must highlight the racially charged historical terrain, dominated by the power house of whiteness, in which Black lives and Mad lives, and especially Mad Black lives, have long been, and are still, entangled, provoking questions about humanity, and the limits of the human, at every twist and turn (Mignolo, 2015). Going forward, we must return madness to the 'communal world of life, meaning and philosophy' (Kusters, 2020) and risk sharing in 'the entanglement of philosophy and madness' (Kusters, 2021). By rescuing madness from the isolating discourse of mental illness and exposing a horizon that enjoins relational theories of what it means to be 'human' (Ingold, 2011/2022; Laplanche, 1998; McKittrick, 2015; Smith, 2023), we may succeed in spurring forms of collaboration and co-production that coalesce in new methodologies of hope and renewal, to which the discipline of 'mad studies' are already beating a path (Beresford & Russo, 2022; Rose, 2022).

There are affinities here with African philosophies and cosmologies, and with the radical school of Black psychology (Ade-Serrano & Gordon, 2021; Cokley & Garba, 2018; Nobles, 2013, 2015), with roots in the African worldview, embracing the notion that everything in the universe is interconnected and that, as in the philosophy of Ubuntu, 'a person is a person through other persons' (Ngomane, 2019). All this is in the spirit, perhaps, of another of Denzil Forrester's paintings, which is reproduced on the cover of this book. The exuberant 'All Hands on Deck' is both an invitation to participate in and celebrate a plurality of ways of being human on multiple dispersed dance floors, and equally a rallying cry to rise to the myriad challenges of social protection and welfare, and above all of social and racial injustice, in a world constantly on the move (Cokley, 2021; Harper, 2016; Kinouani, 2021, pp.157–158; Levitt et al., 2023).

References

Achebe, C. (1977). An image of Africa: Racism in Conrad's 'Heart of Darkness'. *Massachusetts Review*, 18.

Ade-Serrano, Y. & Gordon, L. (2021, March 1). Black psychology and African spirituality: The origin of therapeutic practice. *The Psychologist*. www.bps.org.uk/psychologist/black-psychology-and-african-spirituality-origin-therapeutic-practice

Akala. (2018). *Natives: Race and class in the ruins of empire*. Two Roads Books.

Akyeampong, E., Hill, A.G. & Kleinman, A. (Eds.). (2015). *The culture of mental illness and psychiatric practice in Africa*. Indiana University Press.

Allen, R.L. (2009). What about poor white people? In W. Ayers., T. Quinn & D. Stovall, *Routledge handbook of social justice in education* (pp. 209–230). Routledge.

Alleyne, A. (2022). *The burden of heritage: Hauntings of generational trauma on black lives*. Karnac Books.

Althusser, L. (2008). *On ideology*. Verso Books. (First published by New Left Books in 1971).

Altink, H. (2001). Slavery by another name: Apprenticed women in Jamaican workhouses in the period 1834–8. *Social History*, 26(1), 40–59.

Altink, H. (2012). Modernity, race and mental health care in Jamaica, 1918–44. *Journal of the Department of Behavioural Sciences*, 2(1), 1–19.

Amnesty International. (2011). *Out of control: The case for a complete overhaul of enforced removals by private contractors*. Amnesty International UK.

Anderson, D. (2012). British abuse and torture in Kenya's counter-insurgency, 1952–1960. *Small Wars & Insurgencies*, 23(4–5), 700–719.

Anderson, D. (2015). Guilty secrets: Deceit, denial and the discovery of Kenya's 'migrated archive'. *History Workshop Journal*, 80, 142–160.

Andrews, J. (1999). Raising the tone of asylumdom: Maintaining and expelling pauper lunatics at the Glasgow Royal Asylum in the nineteenth century. In J. Melling & B. Forsythe (Eds.), *Insanity, institutions & society: A social history of madness in comparative perspective* (pp.200–222). Routledge.

Angiolini Review. (2017). *The report of the independent review of deaths and serious incidents in police custody*. Dame Elish Angiolini. www.gov.uk/government/publications/deaths-and-serious-incidents-in-police-custody

Anon. (1916). The native states in India. *The Round Table: The Commonwealth Journal of International Affairs*, 7(25), 91–113.

Anon. (2000). The experience of being a black patient. In C. Kaye & T. Lingiah (Eds.), *Race, culture and ethnicity in secure psychiatric care: Working with difference* (pp.223–227). Jessica Kingsley.

Arlidge, J. (1859). *On the state of lunacy and the legal provision for the insane.* John Churchill.

Armstrong, T. (2005). Slavery, insurance, and sacrifice in the Black Atlantic. In B. Klein & G. Mackenthun (Eds.), *Sea changes: Historicizing the ocean* (pp.167–185). Routledge.

Armstrong, T. (2007). Catastrophe and trauma: A response to Anita Rupprecht. *Journal of Legal History, 28*(3), 347–356.

Bailkin, J. (2012). *The afterlife of Empire.* University of California Press.

Bakhtin, M. (1965/1984). *Rabelais and his world.* Indiana University Press.

Barfoot, M. & Beveridge, A. (1990). Madness at the crossroads: John Home's letters from the Royal Edinburgh Asylum, 1886–87. *Psychological Medicine, 20*(2), 263–284.

Barham, P. (1984/1993). *Schizophrenia and human value* (2nd ed.). Free Association Books.

Barham, P. (2004). *Forgotten lunatics of the Great War.* Yale University Press.

Barham, P. (1992/2020). *Closing the asylum: The mental patient in modern society.* Process Press. (First published by Penguin Books 1992).

Barham, P. (2020). 'Eating at Joe's': The shared fate of Mad lives and Black lives. *Asylum,* 27(4), 17–18.

Barham, P. (2023). Schizophrenia in history: Outsiders, innovators and race. In K. Jacobsen & R. Hinshelwood (Eds.), *Psychoanalysis, science and power: Essays in honour of Robert Maxwell Young* (pp.184–201). Routledge.

Bateson, G. (1968). Conscious purpose versus nature. In D. Cooper (Ed.), *The dialectics of liberation* (pp.34–49). Penguin Books.

Baucom, I. (2005). *Specters of the Atlantic: Finance capital, slavery, and the philosophy of history.* Duke University Press.

Beckert, S. (2014). *Empire of cotton.* Alfred A. Knopf.

Bell, C. (2006). Introducing white disability studies: A modest proposal. In L.J. Davis (Ed.), *The disability studies reader* (pp.275–282). Routledge.

Bell, C. (Ed). (2012). *Blackness and disability: Critical examinations and cultural interventions.* Michigan State University Press.

Bennett Inquiry. (2003). *Independent inquiry into the death of David Bennett.* Norfolk, Suffolk & Cambridgeshire Health Authority.

Beresford, P. (2002). Thinking about 'mental health': Towards a social model. *Journal of Mental Health,* 11(6), 581–584.

Beresford, P. & Russo, J. (Eds.). (2022). *Routledge international handbook of mad studies.* Routledge.

Berger, J. (2013). Image of imperialism. In G. Dwyer (Ed.). *Understanding a photograph: John Berger* (pp.10–21). Penguin Books.

Berrios, G.E. & Markova, I.S. (2015). Towards a new epistemology of psychiatry. In L.J. Kirmayer, R. Lemelson & C.A. Cummings (Eds.), *Re-visioning psychiatry* (pp.41–64). Cambridge University Press.

Berrios, G.E. & Markova, I.S. (2017). The epistemology and classification of 'madness' since the eighteenth century. In G. Eghigian (Ed.), *The Routledge history of madness and mental health* (pp. 115–134). Routledge.

Beveridge, A. (1997). Voices of the mad: Patients' letters from the Royal Edinburgh Asylum, 1873–1908. *Psychological Medicine, 27*(4), 899–908.

Bhatia, M. & Bruce-Jones, E. (2021). Introduction. Special issue on race, mental health and state violence. *Race & Class, 62*(3), 3–6.

Black Health Workers & Patients Group. (1983). Psychiatry and the corporate state. *Race & Class, 25*(2), 49–64.

Bland, L. (2021). *Britain's 'brown babies': The stories of children born to black GIs and white women in the Second World War.* Manchester University Press.

BMA. (2021). *Moral distress and moral injury: Recognising and tackling it for UK doctors.* British Medical Association. www.bma.org.uk/media/4209/bma-moral-distress-injury-survey-report-june-2021.pdf

Bogues, A. (2018). Liberalism, colonial power, subjectivities, and the technologies of pastoral coloniality: The Jamaican case. In T. Barringer & W. Modest (Eds.), *Victorian Jamaica* (pp.156–173). Duke University Press.

Bonnett, A. (1998). How the British working class became white: The symbolic (re)formation of racialized capitalism. *Journal of Historical Sociology, 11*(3), 316–340.

Bonnett, A. (2000). *White identities: Historical and international perspectives.* Routledge.

Bott, E. (1976). Hospital and society. *British Journal of Medical Psychology, 49*(2), 97–140.

Bourdieu, P. (1992, January 14). The left hand and the right hand of the state. Interview with R.P. Droit & T. Ferenczi. *Le Monde.*

Bourdieu, P. (2014). *On the state: Lectures at the College de France, 1989–1992.* Polity Press.

Bourke, J. (2021). Historical perspectives on mental health and psychiatry. In G. Ikkos & N. Bouras (Eds.), *Mind, state and society: Social history of psychiatry and mental health in Britain 1960–2010* (pp.3–12). Cambridge University Press.

Brown, V. (2003). Spiritual terror and sacred authority in Jamaican slave society. *Slavery & Abolition, 24*(1), 24–53.

Brown, V. (2009). Social death and political life in the study of slavery. *American Historical Review, 114*(5), 1231–1249.

Brown, V. (2020). *Tacky's revolt: The story of an Atlantic slave war.* Harvard University Press.

Bruce, L.M.J. (2021). *How to go mad without losing your mind: Madness and radical black creativity.* Duke University Press.

Bruce-Jones, E. (2015). German policing at the intersection: Race, gender, migrant status and mental health. *Race & Class, 56*(3), 36–49.

Bruce-Jones, E. (2021). Mental health and death in custody: The Angiolini review. *Race & Class, 62*(3), 7–17.

Bunting, M. (2022). *Labours of love: The crisis of care.* Granta Books.

Burke, A.W. (1973). The consequences of unplanned repatriation. *British Journal of Psychiatry, 123*(572), 109–111.

Burke, A.W. (1983). Outcome of mental illness following repatriation: A predictive study. *International Journal of Social Psychiatry, 29*(1), 3–11.

Burke, A.W. (2021). A costly struggle for racial justice. *RCPsych Insight, 15*(Spring), 6–7. www.rcpsych.ac.uk/docs/default-source/members/rcpsych-insight-magazine/rcpsych-insight-15---spring-2021.pdf

Burnard, T. (2004). *Mastery, tyranny and desire: Thomas Thistlewood and his slaves in the Anglo-Jamaican World*. University of North Carolina Press.

Burnard, T. (2015). Slaves and slavery in Kingston, 1770–1815. *International Review of Social History, 65*(s28), 39–65.

Burnard, T. (2019). A new look at the *Zong* case of 1783. *Revue de la Société d'Etudes Anglo-Americaines des XV11e et XVIIIe Siècles, 79*. https://doi.org/10.4000/1718.1808 http://journals.openedition.org/1718/1808

Burnard, T. (2020). *Jamaica in the age of revolution*. University of Pennsylvania Press.

Butler, J. (2009). *Frames of war: When is life grievable?* Verso.

Butler, J. (2023, March 2). This concerns everyone. *London Review of Books, 45*(5).

Callaway, H. (2004). Sylvia Hope Leith-Ross, 1884–1980. *Oxford Dictionary of National Biography*. www.oxforddnb.com

Campbell, P. (1989). Peter Campbell's story. In A. Brackx & C. Grimshaw (Eds.), *Mental health care in crisis* (pp.11–20). Pluto Press.

Campbell, P. (2022). Speaking for ourselves: An early UK survivor activist's account. In P. Beresford & J. Russo (Eds.), *Routledge international handbook of mad studies* (pp.57–59). Routledge.

Campbell T. & Russell A. (Dirs.). (2022). *Una Marson: Our lost Caribbean voice*. [Documentary film]. Douglas Road Productions.

Carby, H.V. (2019). *Imperial intimacies: A tale of two islands*. Verso.

Carlyle, T. (1849, December). Discourses on the n****r question. *Fraser's Magazine for Town & Country*. (Revised and reprinted as *Occasional discourse on the n****r question* (Thomas Bosworth, 1853).)

Cartwright, S. (1851/2004). Report on the diseases and peculiarities of the negro race. In A. Caplan, J.J. McCartney & D.A. Sisti (Eds.), *Health, disease, and illness: Concepts in medicine* (pp.28–39). Georgetown University Press.

Casey, L., Baroness of Blackstock DBE, CB. (2023). *Baroness Casey review: An independent review into the standards of behaviour and internal culture of the Metropolitan Police Service: Final report*. Baroness Casey Review.

Chatterjee, P. (1994). *The nation and its fragments: Colonial & post-colonial histories*. Princeton University Press.

Chatterjee, P. (2013, July 10). Family sues G4S for killing Angolan deportee. *CorpWatch*. www.corpwatch.org/article/family-sues-g4s-killing-angolan-deportee

Chevannes, B. (2000). *Betwixt and between: Explorations in an African-Caribbean mindscape*. Ian Randle.

Clarkson, T. (1788). *Essay on the slavery and commerce of the human species*. J. Phillips.

Cleall, E. (2022). *Colonising disability: Impairment and otherness across Britain and its Empire*. Cambridge University Press.

Cobbett, W. (1821, August 4). *Cobbett's weekly political register* (p.147).

Cokley, K. (Ed.). (2021). *Making black lives matter: Confronting anti-black racism*. Cognella Publishing.

Cokley, K. & Garba, R. (2018). Speaking truth to power: How Black/African psychology changed the discipline of psychology. *Journal of Black Psychology, 44*(8), 695–721.

Comaroff, J. & Comaroff, J.L. (1992). Home-made hegemony: Modernity, domesticity and colonialism in South Africa. In K. Hansen (Ed.), *African encounters with domesticity* (pp.37–74). Rutgers University Press.

Conrad, J. (1899/2017). *Heart of darkness*. W.W. Norton & Co.

Copland, I. (1997). *The Princes of India in the endgame of Empire, 1917–1947*. Cambridge University Press.

Cox, P. (2007). Compulsion, voluntarism and venereal disease: Governing sexual health in England after the Contagious Diseases Acts. *Journal of British Studies, 46*(1), 91–115.

Crenshaw, K. (1991). Mapping the margins: Intersectionality, identity politics and violence against women of color. *Stanford Law Review, 43*(6), 1241–1299.

Croce, B. (1949). *Filosofica e storiografica*. Laterza.

Cummins, I. (2015). Discussing race, racism, and mental health: Two mental health inquiries reconsidered. *International Journal of Human Rights Healthcare, 8*(3), 160–172.

Davis, L. (2002). *Bending over backwards: Disability, dismodernism and other difficult positions*. New York Universities Press.

Dayan, J. (2002). Held in the body of the state: Prisons and the law. In A. Sarat & T.R. Kearns (Eds.), *History, memory and the law* (pp.183–248). University of Michigan Press.

Delap, L. (2011). *Knowing their place: Domestic service in twentieth century Britain*. Oxford University Press.

Derrida, J. (1967/2016). *Of grammatology*. John Hopkins University Press.

Dowling, E. (2022). *The care crisis: What caused it and how can we end it?* Verso.

Du Bois, W.E.B. (1903/1969). *The souls of black folk*. Signet.

Dunkley, D.A. (2012). Leonard Howell's leadership of the Rastafari movement and his 'missing years'. *Caribbean Quarterly, 58*(4), 1–24.

Dunkley, D.A. (2013). The suppression of Leonard Howell in late colonial Jamaica, 1932–1954. *New West Indian Guide, 87*(1–2), 62–93.

Eddo-Lodge, R. (2017). *Why I'm no longer talking to white people about race*. Bloomsbury Publishing.

Edmonds, E.B. (2003). *Rastafari: From outcasts to culture bearers*. Oxford University Press.

Eley, G. (2014, June 27). No need to choose: History from above, history from below. *Viewpoint Magazine*.

Elkins, C. (2011). Alchemy of evidence: Mau Mau, the British Empire, and the High Court of Justice. *The Journal of Imperial and Commonwealth History*, 39(5), 731–748.

Elliott-Cooper, A. (2021). *Black resistance to British policing: Racism, resistance and social change*. Manchester University Press.

Epstein, S. (1996). *Impure science: AIDS, activism and the politics of knowledge*. University of California Press.

Ernst, W. (1997). Idioms of madness and colonial boundaries: The case of the European and 'native' mentally ill in early nineteenth-century British India. *Comparative Studies in Society & History*, 39(1).

Evans, C. (2016). 'At Her Majesty's Pleasure': Criminal insanity in 19th century Britain. *History Compass, 14*(10), 457–532.

Evans, C. (2021). *Unsound Empire: Civilization and madness in late Victorian law*. Yale University Press.

Fabian, J. (2000). *Out of our minds: Reason and madness in the exploration of Central Africa*. University of California Press.

Fanon F. (1952/2017). *Black skin, white masks.* Pluto Press.

Fanon, F. (1961/2001). *The wretched of the earth.* Penguin Books.

Faubert, M. (2018). *Granville Sharp's uncovered letter and the Zong massacre.* Palgrave Pivot.

Fernando, S. (2012). Race and culture issues in mental health and some thoughts on ethnic identity. *Counselling Psychology Quarterly, 25*(2), 113–123.

Fernando, S. (2017). *Institutional racism in psychiatry and clinical psychology: Race matters in mental health.* Palgrave Macmillan.

Fernando, S., Ndegwa, D. & Wilson, M. (1998). *Forensic psychiatry, race and culture.* Routledge.

Fischer-Tiné, H. (2012). Reclaiming savages in 'Darkest England' and 'Darkest India': The Salvation Army as transnational agent of the civilizing mission. In C. Watt & M. Mann (Eds.), *Civilizing missions in colonial and postcolonial South Asia: From improvement to development* (pp.125–164). Cambridge University Press.

Forrester, D. (1982). *Dissertation on Winston Rose.* CAST. https://c-a-s-t.org.uk/projects/artist-insights/denzil-forrester

Foucault, M. (1961/2006). *History of madness.* Routledge.

Foucault, M. (1966/1970). *The order of things: An archaeology of the human sciences.* Tavistock.

Foucault, M. (1994). *Ethics: Subjectivity and truth.* (P. Rabinow (Ed.)). Free Press.

Francis, E. (1989). Black people, 'dangerousness' and psychiatric compulsion. In A. Brackx & C. Grimshaw (Eds.), *Mental health care in crisis* (pp.62–78). Pluto Press.

Francis, E. (1993). Psychiatric racism and social police: Black people and the psychiatric services. In W. James & C. Harris (Eds.), *Inside Babylon: The Caribbean diaspora in Britain* (pp.179–206). Verso.

Fraser, N. (2022). *Cannibal capitalism: How our system is devouring democracy, care and the planet.* Verso.

Fricker, M. (2006). Powerlessness and social interpretation. *Episteme: A Journal of Social Epistemology, 3*(1–2), 96–108.

Fricker, M. (2007). *Epistemic injustice: Power and the ethics of knowing.* Oxford University Press.

Fryar, C.D. (2016). Imperfect models: The Kingston Lunatic Asylum scandal and the problem of postemancipation imperialism. *Journal of British Studies, 55*(4), 709–727.

Fryar, C.D. (2018). The narrative of Ann Pratt: Life-writing, genre, and bureaucracy in a postemancipation scandal. *History Workshop Journal, 85,* 265–279.

Furedi, F. (2001). How sociology imagined 'mixed race'. In D. Parker & M. Song (Eds.), *Rethinking 'mixed race'* (pp.42–65). Pluto Press.

Garson, J. (2022a). *Madness: A philosophical exploration.* Oxford University Press.

Garson, J. (2022b, September 7). Review of Wouter Kusters' 'A philosophy of madness: The experience of psychotic thinking'. *Notre Dame Philosophical Reviews.*

Gilbert, H. (2005). *Power writers and the struggle against slavery.* Hansib Publications.

Gillborn, D. (2005). Education policy as an act of white supremacy: Whiteness, critical race theory and education reform. *Journal of Education Policy, 20*(4), 485–505.

Gillborn, D. (2010). The white working class, racism and respectability: Victims, degenerates and interest-convergence. *British Journal of Educational Studies, 58*(1), 3–25.

Gillett, G. (2015). When the mirror cracks: Well-being, moral responsibility, and the postcolonial soul. *Studies in Sociology of Science, 6*(2), 1–7.

Gilroy, P. (1993). *The Black Atlantic: Modernity and double consciousness.* Verso.

Godwin, W. (1797). Of servants: Essay IV. In W. Godwin, *The enquirer: Reflections on education, manners and literature*. G.G. & J. Robinson.

Goffman, E. (1956/1971). *The presentation of self in everyday life*. Pelican Books.

Goffman, E. (1961). *Asylums*. Penguin Books.

Goldberg, D.T. (2002). *The racial state*. Blackwell.

Goldberg, D., Jadhav, S. & Younis, T. (2017). Prevent: What is pre-criminal space? *BJPsych Bulletin, 41*(4): 208–211.

Goodfellow, M. (2020). *Hostile environment: How immigrants became scapegoats*. Verso.

Goodley, D. (2018). The dis/ability complex. *Journal of Diversity and Gender Studies, 5*(1), 5–22.

Gordon, L. (1997). *Her Majesty's other children: Sketches of racism from a neocolonial age*. Rowman & Littlefield.

Gordon, L. (2000). *Existentia Africana: Understanding Africana existential thought*. Routledge.

Gosselin, A. (2022). *Mental patient: Psychiatric ethics from a patient's perspective*. MIT Press.

Grant, S. (2000). Black men in Broadmoor. In C. Kaye & T. Lingiah (Eds.), *Race, culture and ethnicity in secure psychiatric care: Working with difference* (pp.135–146). Jessica Kingsley.

Granville, J.M. (1877). *The care and cure of the insane: Reports of the Lancet Commission on lunatic asylums 1875–1877*. Hardwicke & Bogue.

Guillaumin, C. (1995). *Racism, sexism, power and ideology*. Routledge.

Hall, C. (2002). *Civilizing subjects: Metropole and colony in the English imagination 1830–1867*. Polity.

Hall, C. (2009). Macaulay's nation. *Victorian Studies, 51*(3), 505–523.

Hall, S. (1991/2018). Old and new identities, old and new ethnicities. In S. Hall, *Essential Essays* (Vol. 2). Duke University Press.

Hall, S. (1999). From Scarman to Stephen Lawrence. *History Workshop Journal, 48*, 187–197.

Hall, S. with Schwarz, B. (2017). *Familiar stranger: A life between two islands*. Allen Lane.

Hall, S., Cricher, C., Jefferson, T., Clarke, J., & Roberts, B. (1978). *Policing the crisis: Mugging, the state, and law and order*. Palgrave.

Haller, J.S. (1971). *Outcasts from evolution: Scientific attitudes of racial inferiority, 1859–1900*. Southern Illinois University Press.

Hanley, R. (2016). Slavery and the birth of working-class racism in England, 1814–1833. *Transactions of the Royal Historical Society, 26*, 103–123.

Hansard. (1980, August 8). *Richard Campbell (death in custody)*. UK Parliament. https://hansard.parliament.uk/Commons/1980-08-08/debates/48279ab9-c881-4b7c-88e8-a893c1aeeb1b/RichardCampbell(DeathInCustody)

Harewood, D. (2021). *Maybe I don't belong here: A memoir of race, identity, breakdown and recovery*. Bluebird Books.

Harper, M. (2016). *Migration and mental health: Past and present*. Palgrave.

Harris, J. (1993). *Private lives, public spirit: Britain 1870–1914*. Oxford University Press.

Hartman, S.V. (1997). *Scenes of subjection: Terror, slavery and self-making in nineteenth century America*. Oxford University Press.

Hartman, S. (2008). Venus in two acts. *Small Axe, 12*(2), 1–14.

Hartman, S. (2019). *Wayward lives, beautiful experiments: Intimate histories of social upheaval*. Serpent's Tail.

Hartman, S. (2022, October 24). The hold of slavery. *New York Review of Books*.

Healy, D., Le Noury, J., Harris, M., Butt, M., Linden, S., Whitaker, C., Zou, L. & Roberts, A.P. (2012). Mortality in schizophrenia and related psychoses: Data from two cohorts, 1875–1924 and 1994-2010. *British Medical Journal Open, 2*(5).

Hesse, B. (2007). Racialized modernity: An analytics of white mythologies. *Ethnic & Racial Studies, 30*(4), 643–663.

Heuman, G. (2018). Victorian Jamaica: The view from the Colonial Office. In T. Barringer & W. Modest (Eds.), *Victorian Jamaica* (pp.139–155). Duke University Press.

Heuring, D.H. (2011). 'In the cheapest way possible...': Responsibility and the failure of improvement at Kingston Lunatic Asylum, 1914–1945. *Journal of Colonialism and Colonial History, 12*(3).

Hickling, F. & Gibson, R.C. (2005). Philosophy and epistemology of Caribbean Psychiatry. In F. Hickling & E. Sorel (Eds.), *Images of psychiatry: The Caribbean* (pp.75–108). Department of Community Health and Psychiatry, University of the West Indies.

Hill, R. (2001). *Dread history: Leonard P. Howell and millenarian visions in the early Rastafarian religion*. Frontline Distribution International.

Hilton, C. (2017). *Improving psychiatric care for older people: Barbara Robb's Campaign 1965–1975*. Palgrave Macmillan.

Himmelfarb, G. (1991). *Poverty and compassion: The moral imagination of the late Victorians*. Alfred Knopf.

Hirsch, A. (2018). *Brit(ish): On race, identity and belonging*. Jonathan Cape.

HM Government. (2023, May 26). Detentions under the Mental Health Act. gov.uk. www.ethnicity-facts-figures.service.gov.uk/health/mental-health/detentions-under-the-mental-health-act/latest

Hobbs, A. (2014). *A chosen exile: A history of racial passing in American life*. Harvard University Press.

Hochschild, A. (2005). *Bury the chains: The British struggle to abolish slavery*. Macmillan.

Hoenisch, M. (1988). Symbolic politics: Perceptions of the early Rastafari movement. *The Massachusetts Review, 29*(3), 432–449.

Hokkanen, M. (2019). 'Madness', emotions and loss of control in a colonial frontier: Methodological challenges of crises of mind. In T. Laine-Frigren, J. Eilolo & M. Hokkanen (Eds.), *Encountering crises of the mind* (pp.277–296). Brill.

Holt, T (1992). *The problem of freedom: Race, labour & politics in Jamaica & Britain, 1832-1938*. John Hopkins University Press.

hooks b. (2020). Feminism is for everybody. In T. Ball, R. Dagger & D.I. O'Neill. *Ideals and ideologies: A reader* (11th ed.). Taylor & Francis.

Houghton, B. (1921). *The psychology of empire*. The Cambridge Press.

Houghton, B. (1922/2018). *The mind of the Indian Government*. Forgotten Books.

Hurren, E.T. (2011). 'Abnormalities and deformities': The dissection and interment of the insane poor, 1832-1939. *History of Psychiatry, 23*(1), 65–77.

Hutton, C.A., Barnett, M.A., Dunkley, D.A. & Jahlani, A.H. (2015). *Leonard Percival Howell and the genesis of Rastafari*. University of West Indies Press.

Ikkos, G. & Bouras, N. (Eds.). (2021). *Mind, state and society: Social history of psychiatry and mental health in Britain 1960-2010*. Cambridge University Press.

Ingold, T. (2011/2022). *Being alive: Essays on movement, knowledge and description.* Routledge.

Inquest. (2023). *'I can't breathe': Race, death and British policing.* Inquest. www.inquest.org.uk

Ishiguro, K. (1995). *The unconsoled.* Faber & Faber.

Jackson, W. (2013). *Madness and marginality: The lives of Kenya's white insane.* Manchester University Press.

Jarman, M. (2012). Coming up from underground: Uneasy dialogues at the intersections of race, mental illness, and disability studies. In C. Bell (Ed.), *Blackness and disability: Critical examinations & cultural interventions* (pp.9–30). Michigan State University Press.

Jarrett-Macauley, D. (1998). *The life of Una Marson 1905–65.* Manchester University Press.

Johnston, J. (1903). *Jamaica: The new Riviera.* Cassel.

Jones, G.S. (1971). *Outcast London: A study in the relationship between classes in Victorian society.* Oxford University Press.

Jones, M. (2008). The most cruel and revolting crimes: The treatment of the mentally ill in mid-nineteenth-century Jamaica. *Journal of Caribbean History, 42*(2), 290–309.

Jones, M. (2013). *Public health in Jamaica, 1850–1940: Neglect, philanthropy & development.* University of the West Indies Press.

Joseph, D. & Bhui, K. (2021). Race, state and mind. In G. Ikkos & N. Bouras, N. (Eds.), *Mind, state and society: Social history of psychiatry and mental health in Britain 1960–2010* (pp.348–360). Cambridge University Press

Kant, I. (1764/2011). Essay on the maladies of the head. In P. Frierson & P. Guyer (Eds. & trans.), *Kant: Observations on the feeling of the beautiful and sublime and other writings* (pp.203–218). Cambridge University Press.

Kapila, S. (2002). *The making of colonial psychiatry: Bombay presidency, 1849–1940.* Unpublished PhD thesis. University of London, School of Oriental & African Studies.

Kapila, S. (2005). Masculinity and madness: Princely personhood and colonial sciences of mind in Western India, 1871–1940. *Past & Present, 187,* 121–156.

Kapila, S. (2007). The 'Godless' Freud and his Indian friends: An Indian agenda for psychoanalysis. In S. Mahone & M. Vaughan (Eds.), *Psychiatry and empire* (pp.124–152). Palgrave Macmillan.

Keating, F. (2016). Racialized communities, producing madness and dangerousness. *Intersectionalities, 5*(3), 173–185.

Keating, F., Robertson, D., McCulloch, A. & Francis, E. (2002). *Breaking the circles of fear: A review of the relationship between mental health services and African and Caribbean communities.* Sainsbury Centre for Mental Health.

Keats, J. (1817/1958). In H.E. Rollins (Ed.), *The letters of John Keats* (pp.193–194). Cambridge University Press.

Khan, I. (2023, April 19). From Stephen Lawrence to Sarah Everard: The awful price of 30 years of police failure. *The Guardian.* www.theguardian.com/commentisfree/2023/apr/19/stephen-lawrence-sarah-everard-30-years-police-failure-reform

Kiernan, V. (1969/2015). *The lords of human kind: European attitudes to other cultures in the Imperial Age.* Zed Books.

Kincheloe, J. (1999). The struggle to define and reinvent whiteness: A pedagogical analysis. *College Literature, 26*(3), 162–194.

King, C.B. (2007). 'They diagnosed me a schizophrenic when I was just a Gemini': The other side of madness. In M.C. Chung, B. Fulford & G. Graham (Eds.), *Reconceiving schizophrenia* (pp.11–28). Oxford University Press.

King, C.B. (2016). Whiteness in psychiatry: The madness of European misdiagnoses. In J. Russo & A. Sweeney (Eds.), *Searching for a rose garden: Challenging psychiatry, fostering mad studies* (pp.69–76). PCCS Books.

King, C.B. (2018, April 5). *My experiences on both sides of the Mental Health Act.* [Blog.] Mind. www.mind.org.uk/information-support/your-stories/my-experiences-on-both-sides-of-the-mental-health-act

King, C.B. (2021a, May 9). Unmasking race in mental health. *Journal of Mental Health.* doi: 10.1080/09638237.2021.1898561

King, C.B. (2021b, March 8). *Let me die, before I am killed: A black male schizophrenic pleas in relation to the Mental Health Act White Paper.* [Blog.] NSUN. www.nsun.org.uk/let-me-die-before-i-am-killed/

King, C.B. (2022). 'Madness' as a term of division, or rejection. In P. Beresford & J. Russo (Eds.), *Routledge international handbook of Mad Studies* (pp.351–362). Routledge.

King, C.B. & Gillard, S. (2019). Bringing together coproduction & community participatory research approaches: Using first person reflective narrative to explore coproduction and community involvement in mental health research. *Health Expectations, 22*(4), 701–708.

King, C.B. & Jeynes, T. (2021). Whiteness, madness and reform of the Mental Health Act. *Lancet Psychiatry, 8*(6), 460–461.

King, C.B., Bennett, M., Fulford, K.W.M., Clarke, S., Gillard, S., Bergqvist, A. & Richardson, J. (2021a). From preproduction to coproduction: COVID-19, whiteness, and making black mental health matter. *Lancet Psychiatry, 8*(2), 93–95.

King, C.B., Clarke, S., Gillard, S. & Fulford, B. (2021b). Beyond the color bar: sharing narratives in order to promote a clearer understanding of mental health issues across cultural and racial boundaries. In D. Stoyanov, B. Fulford, G. Stanghelli, W. van Staden & M.T.H. Wong (Eds.), *International perspectives in values-based mental health practice* (pp.403–410). Springer.

Kinouani, G. (2021). *Living while Black: The essential guide to overcoming racial trauma.* Ebury Press.

Kolsky, E. (2015). The colonial rule of law & the legal regime of exception: Frontier 'fanaticism' and state violence in British India. *American Historical Review, 120*(4), 1218–1246.

Kristeva, J. (1980/1984). *Powers of horror: An essay on abjection.* Columbia University Press. (First published in France in 1980).

Kusters, W. (2016). Philosophy and madness. Radical turns in the natural attitude to life. *Philosophy, Psychiatry & Psychology, 23*(2), 129–146.

Kusters, W. (2020). *A philosophy of madness: The experience of psychotic thinking.* MIT Press.

Kusters, W. (2021, April 12). Philosophy and madness: A discussion. Interview with James Barnes. *Mad in the UK.* www.madintheuk.com/2021/04/philosophy-madness-a-discussion-with-wouter-kusters/

Laplanche, J. (1998). *Essays in otherness.* Routledge.

Laqueur, T. (1989). Bodies, details and the humanitarian narrative. In L. Hunt (Ed.), *The new cultural history* (pp.176–204). University of California Press.

Larson, E.J. (1991). The rhetoric of eugenics: Expert authority and the Mental Deficiency Bill. *British Journal for the History of Science, 24*(1), 45–60.

Laurance, J. (2003). *Pure madness: How fear drives the mental health system*. Routledge.

Lawrence, C. & Weisz, G. (Eds.). (1998). *Greater than the parts: Holism in biomedicine 1920–1950*. Oxford University Press.

Lee, H. (1999/2003). *The first Rasta: Leonard Howell and the rise of Rastafarianism*. Lawrence Hill Books.

Levi, J. & French, E. (2019). *Inside Broadmoor*. Blink Publishing.

Levitt, P., Dobbs, E., Sun, K. & Paul, R. (2023). *Transnational social protection: Changing social welfare in a world on the move*. Oxford University Press

Lewis, G., Croft-Jeffreys, C. & David, A. (1990). Are British psychiatrists racist? *British Journal of Psychiatry, 157*(3), 410–415.

Lewis, P. & Taylor, M. (2010, October 14). Security guards accused over death of man being deported to Angola. *The Guardian*. www.theguardian.com/uk/2010/oct/14/security-guards-accused-jimmy-mubenga-death

Lewis, R. (1987). Garvey's forerunner: Love and Bedward. *Race & Class, 28*(3), 29–40.

Light, A. (2007). *Mrs Woolf and the servants: An intimate history of domestic life in Bloomsbury*. Penguin Books.

Linstrum, E. (2012). The politics of psychology in the British Empire, 1898–1960. *Past & Present, 215*(215), 195–233.

Linstrum, E. (2016). *Ruling minds: Psychology in the British Empire*. Harvard University Press.

Littlewood, R. (1993). Ideology, camouflage or contingency? Racism in British psychiatry. *Transcultural Psychiatry, 30*(3), 243–290.

Littlewood, R. & Lipsedge, M. (2014). *Aliens and alienists: Ethnic minorities and psychiatry* (3rd ed.). Routledge.

Lorimer, D. (2013). *Science, race relations and resistance: A study of late Victorian and Edwardian racism*. Manchester University Press.

Low, D.A. (2009). *Fabrication of Empire: The British and the Uganda kingdoms 1890–1902*. Cambridge University Press.

Lowe, L. (2015a). History hesitant. *Social Text 125, 33*(4), 85–107.

Lowe, L. (2015b). *The intimacies of four continents*. Duke University Press.

Loyal, S. (2017). *Bourdieu's theory of the state: A critical introduction*. Palgrave.

Macaulay, T.B. (1833, July 10). Government of India: A speech delivered in the House of Commons. *Miscellaneous Writings & Speeches* (Vol. 4). Outlook Verlag.

Macnicol, J. (1983). Eugenics, medicine and mental deficiency: An introduction. *Oxford Review of Education, 9*(3), 177–180.

Macpherson, W. (1999). *The Stephen Lawrence inquiry: Report of an inquiry by Sir William Macpherson of Cluny*. HMSO. https://assets.publishing.service.gov.uk/government/uploads/system/uploads/attachment_data/file/277111/4262.pdf

Maragh, G.G. (1935/2014). The promised key: The sublime essence of Rastafari. CreateSpace.

Markova, I.S. & Berrios, G.E. (2012). Epistemology of psychiatry. *Psychopathology, 45*(4), 220–227.

Marriott, D. (2016). Corpsing; or, the matter of black life. *Cultural Critique 94*, 32–64.

Marson, U. (1933, July). N****r. *The Keys*, 8–9.

Mbembe, A. (2017). *Critique of black reason*. Duke University Press.

McCarthy, J. (2020, July 20). On 'Afropessimism'. *Los Angeles Review of Books*. https://lareviewofbooks.org/article/on-afropessimism/

McCarthy, T. (2009). *Race, empire and the idea of human development*. Cambridge University Press.

McClintock, A. (2001). *Double crossings: Madness, sexuality & imperialism*. Ronsdale Press.

McCulloch, J. (1995). *Colonial psychiatry and 'the African mind'*. Cambridge University Press.

McGrath, P. (2012, August 21). A boy's own Broadmoor. *The Economist*.

McIntosh, S. (2016). *Open justice and investigations into deaths at the hands of the police, or in police or prison custody*. Unpublished PhD thesis. City, University of London.

McKittrick, K. (Ed.). (2015). *Sylvia Wynter: On being human as praxis*. Duke University Press.

McWhorter, L. (2005). Where do white people come from? A Foucaultian critique of whiteness studies. *Philosophy & Social Criticism, 31*(5/6), 533–556.

Mignolo, W. (2015). Sylvia Wynter: What does it mean to be human? In K. McKittrick (Ed.), *Sylvia Wynter: On being human as praxis* (pp.106–123). Duke University Press.

Miles, R. (1988). Beyond the 'race' concept: The reproduction of racism in England. *Sydney Studies in Society & Culture, 4*, 7–31.

Miles, R. (1993). *Racism after 'race relations'*. Routledge.

Miles, R. (2000). Apropos the idea of 'race'… again. In L. Back & J. Solomos (Eds.), *Theories of race and racism: A reader* (pp.125–143). Routledge.

Mill, J.S. (1861). *Considerations on representative government* (2nd ed.). London.

Mills, C.W. (1997/2022). *The racial contract*. Cornell University Press.

Mills, C.W. (2008). Racial liberalism. *Publications of the Modern Language Associations of America, 123*(5), 1380–1397.

Mills, C. (2018). The mad are like savages and the savages are mad: Psychopolitics and the coloniality of the psy. In B.M.Z. Cohen (Ed.), *Routledge international handbook of critical mental health* (pp.205–212). Routledge.

Monaghan, K. (2013). *Inquest into the death of Jimmy Kelenda Mubenga: Report by the Assistant Deputy Coroner, Karon Monaghan QC under the Coroner's Rules 1984, Rule 43*. 42 Bedford Row. www.42br.com/_files/content/42br-Mubenga.pdf

Moore, B. & Johnson, M. (2004). *Neither led, nor driven: Contesting British cultural imperialism in Jamaica 1865–1920*. University of the West Indies Press.

National Museum Jamaica. (2013). *Rastafari: Unconquerable!* Exhibition catalogue. The Institute of Jamaica.

National Museum Jamaica. (2015). *Uprising: Morant Bay, 1865 and its afterlives*. Exhibition catalogue. The Institute of Jamaica.

Nayak, A. (2009). Beyond the pale: Chavs, youth and social class. In K.P. Sveinsson (Ed.), *Who cares about the white working class?* (pp.28–35). The Runnymede Trust.

Nelson, C. (2010). Racializing disability, disabling race: Policing race and mental status. *Berkeley Journal of Criminal Law, 15*(1).

Nelson, C. (2016). Frontlines: Policing at the nexus of race and mental health. *Fordham Urban Law Journal, 43*(3).

Nettleford, R. (1997). The continuing battle for space – the Caribbean challenge. *Caribbean Quarterly, 43*(1/2), 90–95.

Ngomane, N.M. (2019). *Everyday Ubuntu: Living better together the African way*. Bantam Press.

Niaah, J. & MacLeod, E. (Eds.). (2013). *Let us start with Africa: Foundations of Rastafari scholarship*. University of the West Indies Press.

Nobles, W.W. (2013). Fundamental task and challenge of black psychology. *Journal of Black Psychology, 39*(3), 293–299.

Nobles, W.W. (2015). From black psychology to *Sakhu Djaer*: Implications for the further development of a Pan African black psychology. *Journal of Black Psychology, 41*(5), 399–414.

Nyong'o, T. (2002). Racist kitsch and black performance. *Yale Journal of Criticism, 15*(2), 371–391.

O'Connell, A. (2009). The pauper, slave and aboriginal subject: British parliamentary investigations and the promotion of civilized conduct (1830s). *Canadian Social Work Review, 26*(2), 171–193.

Ojieto, C. (2011, November 8–14). Community leaders call for action against black deaths in custody. *AfroNews, 25,* 3.

Oliver, R. (1957). *Sir Harry Johnston and the scramble for Africa*. St Martin's Press.

Oliver, R. (2004). Sir Henry Hamilton ('Harry') Johnston. *Oxford Dictionary of National Biography*.

Olusoga, D. (2016). *Black and British: A forgotten history*. Macmillan.

Olusoga, D. (2021). Foreword. In D. Harewood. *Maybe I don't belong here*. Bluebird Books.

Owen, D.S. (2007). Towards a critical theory of whiteness. *Philosophy & Social Criticism, 33*(2), 203–222.

Pandey, G. (1995). Voices from the edge: The struggle to write subaltern histories. *Ethnos, 60*(3/4), 223–242.

Pankhurst, C. (1913). *The great scourge and how to end it*. E. Pankhurst. https://wellcomecollection.org/works/sshusq9a/items?canvas=6

Parker, D. & Song, M. (Eds.). (2001). *Rethinking 'mixed race'*. Pluto Press.

Paton, D. (2009). Obeah acts: Producing and policing the boundaries of religion in the Caribbean. *Small Axe 28,* 1–18.

Paton, D. (2018). State formation in Victorian Jamaica. In T. Barringer & W. Modest (Eds.), *Victorian Jamaica* (pp.125–138). Duke University Press.

Paton, D. & Forde, M. (Eds.). (2012). *Obeah and other powers: The politics of Caribbean religion and healing*. Duke University Press.

Patterson, O. (1990). *Slavery and social death: A comparative study*. Harvard University Press.

Perry, K.H. (2015). *London is the place for me: Black Britons, citizenship and the politics of race*. Oxford University Press.

Pettican, A., Goodman, B., Bryant, W., Beresford, P., Freeman, P., Gladwell, V., Kilbride, C. & Speed, E. (2023). Doing together: Reflections on facilitating the co-production of participatory action research with marginalised populations. *Qualitative Research in Sport, Exercise and Health, 15*(2), 202–219.

Philip, M.N. (2008). *Zong!* Wesleyan University Press.

Pickens, T.A. (2019). *Black madness: Mad blackness*. Duke University Press.

Pilgrim, D. & Tomasini, F. (2012). On being unreasonable in modern society: Are mental health problems special? *Disability & Society 27*(5), 631–646.

Portelli, A. (1991). *The death of Luigi Trastulli and other stories: Forms and meanings in oral history*. State University of New York Press.

Porter, D. (1991). 'Enemies of the race': Biologism, environmentalism, and public health in Edwardian England. *Victorian Studies, 34*(2), 159–178.

Porter, R. (2001). *The enlightenment*. Palgrave.

Porter, R. (2003a). *Flesh in the age of reason*. Allen Lane

Porter, R. (2003b). Introduction. In R. Porter & D. Wright (Eds.), *The confinement of the insane: International perspectives, 1800–1965* (pp.1–19). Cambridge University Press.

Post, K. (1978). *Arise ye starvelings: The Jamaican labour rebellion of 1938 and its aftermath*. Springer.

Pratt, A. (1860). *Seven months in the Kingston lunatic asylum and what I saw there*. George Henderson, Savage & Co.

Price, C. (2009). *Becoming Rasta: Origins of Rastafari identity in Jamaica*. New York University Press.

Prince, R. (1970). The Ras Tafari of Jamaica: A study of group beliefs and social stress & Delusions, dogma and mental health. *Transcultural Psychiatric Research, 7*(1), 58–62.

Prins, H. (1998, August 6). Rooted racism. Letter to the editor. *The Independent*.

Prins, H., Backer-Holst, T., Francis, E. & Keitch, I. (1993). *Report of the Committee of Inquiry into the death in Broadmoor Hospital of Orville Blackwood and a review of the deaths of two other African-Caribbean Patients: 'Big, black and dangerous?'* Special Hospitals Service Authority.

Rankine, C. (2015). *Citizen: An American lyric*. Penguin Books.

Razanajao, C.L., Postel, J. & Allen, D.F. (1996). The life and psychiatric work of Frantz Fanon. *History of Psychiatry, 7*, 499–524.

Realpe, A. & Wallace, L. (2010). *What is co-production?* The Health Foundation.

Reay, D., Hollingworth, S., Williams, K., Crozier, G., Jamieson, F., James, D. & Beedell, P. (2007). 'A darker shade of pale?' Whiteness, the middle classes and multi-ethnic inner-city schooling. *Sociology, 41*(6), 1041–1060.

Richards, G. (1997). *'Race', racism and psychology: Towards a reflexive history*. Routledge.

Robcis, C. (2016). Francois Tosquelles and the psychiatric revolution in postwar France. *Constellations, 23*(2), 212–222.

Robcis, C. (2021). *Disalienation: Politics, philosophy, and radical psychiatry in postwar France*. University of Chicago Press.

Rollock, N. (2006). Beyond the status quo? Challenging normative assumptions about race. *British Journal of Sociology of Education, 27*(5), 673–677.

Rollock, N. (2012). The invisibility of race: intersectional reflections on the liminal space of alterity. *Race, Ethnicity and Education, 15*(1), 65–84.

Rollock, N. (2022). *The racial code: Tales of resistance and survival*. Allen Lane.

Rollock, N. & Gillborn, D. (2011). *Critical race theory (CRT)*. British Educational Research Association (BERA). www.bera.ac.uk/publication/critical-race-theory-crt

Rosaldo, R. (1993). *Culture and truth: The remaking of social analysis*. Routledge.

Rose, D. (2018). Renewing epistemologies and service-user knowledge. In P. Beresford & S. Carr (Eds.), *Social policy first hand: An international introduction to participatory social welfare* (pp.132–141). Policy Press.

Rose, D.S. (2022). *Mad knowledges and user-led research*. Palgrave Macmillan.

Rupprecht, A. (2007). A very uncommon case: Representations of the *Zong* and the British campaign to abolish the slave trade. *Journal of Legal History, 28*(3), 329–346.

Saha, J. (2013). Madness and the making of a colonial order in Burma. *Modern Asian Studies, 47*, 406–435.

Sambrook, C. (2013, October 12). Jimmy Mubenga and the shame of British Airways. [Blog.] *OpenDemocracy.* www.opendemocracy.net/en/shine-a-light/jimmy-mubenga-and-shame-of-british-airways

Samuels, E. (2014). *Fantasies of identification: Disability, gender and race.* New York Universities Press.

Sanghera, S. (2021). *Empireland: How imperialism has shaped modern Britain.* Penguin Books.

Sashidharan, S. (2001). Institutional racism in British psychiatry. *Psychiatric Bulletin, 25*, 244–247.

Sato, S. (2017). 'Operation Legacy': Britain's destruction and concealment of colonial records worldwide. *The Journal of Imperial and Commonwealth History, 45*(4), 697–719.

Schoffeleers, J. M. (1975). The interaction of the Mbona cult and Christianity. In T.O. Ranger & J.C. Weller (Eds.), *Themes in the Christian history of Central Africa,* (pp.14–29). University of California Press.

Schoffeleers, J.M. (1987). Mbona. *Encyclopedia.com.* www.encyclopedia.com/environment/encyclopedias-almanacs-transcripts-and-maps/mbona

Schoffeleers, J. M. (1992). *River of blood: Genesis of a martyr cult in Southern Malawi circa AD 1600.* University of Wisconsin Press.

Schuler, M. (1979). Myalism and the African religious tradition. In M.E. Crahan & F.W. Knight (Eds.), *Africa and the Caribbean: 'The legacies of a link* (pp.65–79). John Hopkins University Press.

Schuler, M. (1980*). 'Alas, Kongo': A social history of indentured African immigration into Jamaica 1841–65.* University of John Hopkins Press.

Schwarz, B. (2013). *The white man's world: Memories of empire, volume 1.* Oxford University Press.

Scraton, P. & Chadwick, K. (1987). *In the arms of the law: Coroners' inquests and deaths in custody.* Pluto Press.

Semmel, B. (1962). *The Governor Eyre controversy.* MacGibbon & Kee.

Seshagiri, U. (2010). *Race and the modernist imagination.* Cornell University Press.

Sexton, J. (2012). Ante-anti-blackness: Afterthoughts. *Lateral, 1.*

Sexton, J. (2016). Afro-pessimism: The unclear word. *Rhizomes: Cultural Studies in Emerging Knowledge, 29.* https://doi.org/10.20415/rhiz/029.e02

Shapin, S. (1995). Cordelia's love: Credibility and the social studies of science. *Perspectives on Science, 3*(3), 255–275.

Shapin, S. (2010). *Never pure: Historical studies of science as if it was produced by people with bodies, situated in time, space, culture, and society, and struggling for credibility and authority.* John Hopkins University Press.

Sharpe, C. (2012). Response to Jared Sexton's 'Ante-anti-blackness: Afterthoughts'. *Lateral, 1.*

Sharpe, C . (2016). *In the wake: On blackness and being.* Duke University Press.

Shaw, G.B. (1903/2006). Man and superman. Echo Library.

Sheller, M. (2003). *Consuming the Caribbean: From Arawaks to zombies.* Routledge.

Sheller, M. (2011). Hidden textures of race and historical memory: The rediscovery of photographs relating to Jamaica's Morant Bay rebellion of 1865. *The Princeton University Library Chronicle, 72*(2), 533–567.

Shepherd, J. (2013). *Victorian madmen: Broadmoor, masculinity and the experiences of the criminally insane, 1863–1900.* PhD thesis. Queen Mary, University of London.

Shepherd, J. (2016). 'I am very glad and cheered when I hear the flute': The treatment of criminal lunatics in late Victorian Broadmoor. *Medical History, 60,* 473–491.

Shilliam, R. (2018). *Race and the undeserving poor: From abolition to Brexit.* Agenda Publishing.

Shohat, E. & Stam, R. (2014). *Unthinking Eurocentrism: Multiculturalism and the media* (2nd ed.). Routledge.

Simpson, G.E. (1955). The Ras Tafari movement in Jamaica: A study in race and class conflict. *Social Forces, 34*(2), 168–170.

Simpson, G.E. (1962a). The Ras Tafari movement in Jamaica in its millennial aspect. In S. Thrupp (Ed.). *Millennial dreams in action: Essays in comparative study* (pp.160–165). Mouton & Co.

Simpson, G.E. (1962b). Social stratification in the Caribbean. *Phylon, 23*(1), 29–46.

Simpson, G.E. (1985). Religion and justice: Some reflections on the Rastafari movement. *Phylon, 46*(4), 286–291.

Sinha, M. (1995). *Colonial masculinity: The 'manly Englishman' and the 'effeminate Bengali' in the late nineteenth century.* Manchester University Press.

Smith, B., Williams, O., Bone L. & the Moving Social Work Coproduction Collective. (2022). Co-production: A resource to guide co-producing research in the sport, exercise and health sciences. *Qualitative Research in Sport, Exercise and Health.* DOI: 10.1080/2159676X.2022.2052946

Smith, L. (2014). *Insanity, race and colonialism: Managing mental disorder in the post-emancipation British Caribbean, 1834–1914.* Palgrave Macmillan.

Smith, R. (2023). Relations: History of science and the thought of the therapist. In K. Jacobsen & D. Hinshelwood (Eds.), *Psychoanalysis, science and power: Essays in honour of Robert Maxwell Young* (pp.15–32). Routledge.

Spandler, H., Anderson, J. & Sapey, B (Eds.). (2015). *Madness, distress and the politics of disablement.* Policy Press.

Spandler, H. & Poursanidou, D. (2019). Who is included in the Mad Studies project? *Journal of Ethics in Mental Health, 10.* https://clok.uclan.ac.uk/23384/8/23384%20JEMH%20 Inclusion%20iii.pdf

Stam, R. (2001). Cultural studies and race. In T. Miller (Ed.), *A companion to cultural studies* (pp.471–489). Blackwell.

Steedman, C. (2007). *Master and servant: Love and labour in the English industrial age.* Cambridge University Press.

Steinhart, E. (1977/2019). *Conflict and collaboration: The kingdoms of Western Uganda, 1890–1907.* Princeton University Press.

Stewart, D. (2018). Kumina: A spiritual vocabulary of nationhood in Victorian Jamaica. In T. Barringer & W. Modest (Eds.), *Victorian Jamaica* (pp.602–621). Duke University Press.

Stoler, A.L. (1992). In cold blood: Hierarchies of credibility and the politics of colonial narratives. *Representations, 37,* 151–189.

Stoler, A.L. (1995). *Race and the education of desire: Foucault's history of sexuality and the colonial order of things.* Duke University Press.

Stoler, A. (2013). Reason aside: Reflections on enlightenment and empire. In G. Huggan (Ed.), *The Oxford handbook of postcolonial studies* (pp.39–66). Oxford University Press.

Stubblefield, A. (2007). 'Beyond the pale': Tainted whiteness, cognitive disability and eugenic sterilization. *Hypatia, 22*(2), 162–181.

Suzuki, A. (2007). Lunacy and labouring men: Narratives of male vulnerability in mid-Victorian London. In R. Bivans & J. Pickstone (Ed.), *Medicine, madness and social history* (pp.118–128). Palgrave Macmillan.

Swartz, S. (2010). The regulation of British colonial lunatic asylums and the origins of colonial psychiatry, 1860–1864. *History of Psychology, 13*(2), 160–177.

Szmukler, G. (2018). *Men in white coats: Treatment under coercion.* Oxford University Press.

Tavan, G. (2005). *The long slow death of white Australia.* Scribe Publications.

Taylor, D. (2021, March 12). Police restraint contributed to Leon Briggs' death, jury finds. *The Guardian.* www.theguardian.com/uk-news/2021/mar/12/police-restraint-contributed-leon-briggs-death-inquest-jury

Taylor, M. (2020). *The Interest: How the British establishment resisted the abolition of slavery.* Vintage.

Terrefe, S. (2020, Winter). On *Afropessimism* by Frank Wilderson III. *The Georgia Review.* https://thegeorgiareview.com/posts/on-afropessimism-by-frank-b-wilderson-iii

Thomas, A. & Sillen, S. (1972). *Racism and psychiatry.* Citadel Press.

Thompson, K. (2007). *An eye for the tropics: Tourism, photography and framing the Caribbean picturesque.* Duke University Press.

Thompson, V.E. (2021). Policing in Europe: Disability justice and abolitionist intersectional care. *Race & Class, 62*(3), 61–76.

Thomson, M. (1999). 'Savage civilization': Race, culture and mind in Britain, 1898–1939. In W. Ernst & B. Harris (Eds.), *Race, Science & Medicine, 1700–1960* (pp.235–258). Routledge.

Todd, S. (2009). Domestic service and class relations in Britain, 1900–1950. *Past & Present, 203*, 181–204.

Tosh, J. (2005). *Manliness and masculinities in nineteenth-century Britain.* Pearson Longman.

Tredgold, A.F. (1921). Moral imbecility. *Proceedings of the Royal Society of Medicine, 14*, 13–22.

Van Dijk, F.J. (1995). Sociological means: Colonial reactions to the radicalization of Rastafari in Jamaica, 1956–1959. *New West Indian Guide, 69*(1/2), 67–101.

Vaughan, M. (1983). Idioms of madness: Zomba Lunatic Asylum, Nyasaland, in the colonial period. *Journal of Southern African Studies, 9*(2), 218–238.

Vaughan, M. (1993). Madness and colonialism, colonialism as madness. Re-reading Fanon, colonial discourse and the psychopathology of colonialism. *Paideuma, 39*, 45–55.

Waldstreicher, D. (1999). Reading the runaways: Self-fashioning, print culture, and confidence in slavery in the eighteenth-century Mid-Atlantic. *The William and Mary Quarterly, 56*(2), 243–272.

Walker, K. (2014, February 1). Leonard Howell and the struggles that he fought. *Jamaica Observer.*

Walmsley, J. (2000). Women and the Mental Deficiency Act of 1913: Citizenship, sexuality and regulation. *British Journal of Learning Disabilities, 28*, 65–70.

Walvin, J. (2011). *The Zong: A massacre, the law, and the end of slavery.* Yale University Press.

Webber, F. (2014). *Justice blindfolded? The case of Jimmy Mubenga.* Institute of Race Relations.

Webster, J. (2007). The Zong in the context of the eighteenth-century slave trade. *Journal of Legal History, 28*(3), 285–298.

Webster, W. (2001). 'There'll always be an England': Representations of colonial wars and immigration, 1948–1968. *Journal of British Studies, 40*(4), 557–584.

Wedenoja, W. (1983). Overview: Jamaican psychiatry. *Transcultural Psychiatric Research Review, 20*, 233–258.

Wedenoja, W. & Anderson, C. (2014). Revival: An indigenous religion and spiritual healing practice in Jamaica. In P. Sutherland, R. Moodley & R. Chevannes (Eds.), *Caribbean healing traditions: Implications for health and mental health* (pp.128–139). Routledge.

Wilderson, F. (2020). *Afropessimism*. Liveright Publishing Corporation.

Williams, E. (1944). *Capitalism and slavery*. University of North Carolina Press.

Winchester, S. (1998). *The surgeon of Crowthorne: A tale of murder, madness and the Oxford Dictionary*. Penguin Books.

Winston Rose Action Campaign. (1981, August 18). *Special Branch report on a public meeting called by the Winston Rose Action Campaign to discuss calling for a public inquiry into Rose's death in custody*. UCPI0000015540. WRAC.

Winter, S. (2012). On the Morant Bay rebellion in Jamaica and the Governor Eyre-George William Gordon Controversy, 1865–70. [Online.] *BRANCH*. https://branchcollective. org/?ps_articles=sarah-winter-on-the-morant-bay-rebellion-in-jamaica-and-the-governor-eyre-george-william-gordon-controversy-1865-70

Wohl, A. (1977/2017). *The eternal slum: Housing and social policy in Victorian London*. Routledge.

Wood, M. (2000). *Blind memory: Visual representations of slavery in England and America, 1780–1865*. Manchester University Press

Wrench, G. (1908/2010). *The grammar of life*. Nabu Press.

Wrench, G.T. (1911). *The mastery of life*. M. Kennerley.

Wrench, G. (1913/2018). *The healthy marriage*. Forgotten Books.

Wrench, G. (1938/2009). *The wheel of health: A study of the Hunza*. Distant Mirror.

Wrench, G.T. (1947). *Land and motherland: Eighteen talks on the Indian question*. Faber.

Wynter, S. (2003). Unsettling the coloniality of being/power/truth/freedom: Towards the human, after man, its overrepresentation – an argument. *The New Centennial Review, 3*(3), 257–337.

Yates, K. (2017, August 25). The state continuously fails BME mental health patients. *Vice*. www.vice.com/en/article/j55d74/the-uk-must-stop-marginalising-bme-mental-health-patients,

Yawney, C. (1978). *Lions in Babylon: The Rastafarians of Jamaica as a visionary movement*. PhD thesis. McGill University, Montreal.

Yesufu, S. (2021). Deaths of blacks in police custody: A black British perspective of over 50 years of police racial injustices in the United Kingdom. *Eureka: Social Humanities, 4*, 33–45.

Young, A. (1982). The anthropologies of illness and sickness. *Annual Review of Anthropology, 11*, 257–285.

Younis, T. (2021a). The muddle of institutional racism in mental health. *Sociology of Health & Illness, 43*, 1831–1839.

Younis, T. (2021b). The psychologisation of counter-extremism: Unpacking PREVENT. *Race & Class, 62*(3), 37–60.

Younis, T. & Jadhav, S. (2019). 'Keeping our mouths shut': The fear and racialized self-censorship of British healthcare professionals in PREVENT training. *Culture, Medicine & Psychiatry, 43*, 404–424.

Archives consulted

Bishopsgate Institute, London: https://www.bishopsgate.org.uk/archives
Report of the Jamaica Royal Commission, 1866, Part II, Minutes of Evidence: p.23 charge of cruelty brought against Colonel Thomas Hobbs; pp.70—73, lines 3246—3365, Richard Clarke (a black) sworn and examined

British Library: https://www.bl.uk/collection-guides/india-office-records
Papers consulted from former *India Office Records [IOR]* regarding Faiz Muhammad Khan, later the Mir of Khairpur: R/1/1/2482 + 2845 + 2902 + 3116 + 4032; also R/2/453/63

The Gleaner: https://gleaner.newspaperarchive.com

Institute of Race Relations: www.irr.org.uk
Register of Racism & Resistance [RRR] 2014–date.

London Metropolitan Archives [LMA]: https://www.cityoflondon.gov.uk/things-to-do/history-and-heritage/london-metropolitan-archives
H12/CH/B/14/001 & 002 Case notes of female patients discharged from Colney Hatch Lunatic Asylum in 1915–16 (001), includes three-page folio for Alice Triggs; and in 1917–18 (002), includes two-page folio for Alice Triggs; WABG/114/035 Wandsworth Board of Guardians: examination of pauper lunatics, 1917, includes two-page folio for Alice Triggs

The National Archives (TNA): https://www.nationalarchives.gov.uk
CO 137/ 363, pp.251–298, 'The statement of Henrietta Dawson' (1861)
CO 137/ 350, folios 429–441, 'The testimony of Ann Platt' (1861)
CO 137/ 359, Public Hospital & Lunatic Asylum Commission, Evidence, Part 1 (1861), accounts of 'tanking', pp.49–56.

CO 137/382, folios 319, 328, 332, 338–344, 364–370, 378, Jamaica, correspondence (1864)

CO 137/ 388, folios 80–95, Jamaica, correspondence (1865)

CO 137/ 566/32 Report on the proceedings of the case of Alexander Bedward (1895)

CO 525/7 & 8, 'Case of Mr R.R. Racey' (1905)

FO 2/676 'Case of Mr R.R. Racey' (1896–1902)

MR 1/1013/3 'Sketch map of Ankole District by R.R. Racey Collector' (1901)

T 227/2460 'Repatriation of immigrant patients on medical grounds', includes 'West Indian patients in Broadmoor Hospital' (1960)

Survivors History Archive: www.studymore.org.uk

Created and curated by Andrew Roberts

Wellcome Library: https://wellcomecollection.org

SA/MAC/G.3/34: Box 42, pp.1–244 Case file of Alice Triggs from the Mental After Care Association

Name index

A

Achebe, C. 10
Ade-Serrano, Y. 213
African National Congress 208
Akala 4, 20
Akyeampong, E. 4, 14, 17, 97, 140–141
All African Women's Group 186
Allen, R.L. 96, 189
Allen, T. Dr 69–72, 92
Alleyne, A. 189
Althusser, L. 204
Altink, H. 41–42, 72
American Psychiatric Association 88
Amnesty International 185
Anderson, D. 78, 200
Andrews, J. 100
Andrews, K. 202
Angiolini Review 194
Anon 138
Anon 168–169
Arlidge, J. 99
Armstrong, T. 30, 32–33, 56, 57
Ashford General Hospital 164

B

Baden-Powell, Lord 141
Bailkin, J. 69, 123, 190, 201–202
Bakhtin, M. 62
Bancroft, E. Dr 43
Bardsley, A. 105
Barfoot, M. 12
Barham, P. 108, 133, 190, 191, 213
Barrington, E. 131
Bateson, G. 18
Baucom, I. 27, 30, 34
Baxter, A.S. 109–112

Beckert, S. 41
Bedward, A. 7, 29, 76, 78–82, 84, 85, 87–88
Bell, C. 26–27
Bellevue Lunatic Asylum 83, 85
Bellevue Mental Hospital 86, 211
Bennett, D. 165, 188
Bennett Inquiry 188
Bennett, J. Dr 188
Beresford, P. 11, 213
Berger, J. 190
Berrios, G.E. 23
Bethleham Hospital 167, 193
Beveridge, A. 12
Beveridge, W. 97, 100
Bhatia, M. 196
Bhui, K. 202, 203
Blair, E. 122
Black Health Workers & Patients Group 196
Black Mental Health (UK) 165
Blackwood, O. 8, 152, 165, 167–180, 188, 193
Blake, H. 80
Bland, L. 20
Bleby, H. Rev 74
Bogle, F. 52–54
Bogle, P. 79
Bogues, A. 73, 77
Bonnett, A. 4, 150
Booth, W. 97
Bott, E. 117
Bouras, N. 201, 203
Bourdieu, P. 169
Bourke, J. 201–202
Bowerbank, L.Q. Dr 44
BMA 197
Brand, D. 211

Briggs, L. 165

Brill, A.A. 124

Broadmoor Lunatic Asylum (Broadmoor Special Hospital) 3, 7, 10, 151–152, 167, 168, 169, 172, 173, 174, 175–177, 178

Bronte, E. 118

Brooks, D. 151

Brown, V. 28, 38, 41, 61

Bruce-Jones, E. 196

Bruce, L.M.J. 27

Buckley, C. 170, 175, 179

Bunting, M. 196

Burke, A. Dr. 152, 170, 175, 176–177, 178, 202

Burke, E. 95

Burnard, T. 27, 28, 30, 31, 33, 34, 37, 38–39, 40, 41, 60–61, 91

Burrell-Brown, K. 165

Bustamante, A. 86

Butler, J. 2, 187, 189, 196

Buxton, C. MP 73

C

Callaway, H. 123

Cameron, J.M. 68

Campbell, P. 11, 13

Campbell, R. 164

Campbell, T. 211

Canning, G. 65

Carby, H.V. 17, 20, 91, 92

Carey, M. 52–53

Cargill, J. Dr 80–81

Carlile, R. 35

Carlyle, T. 67, 68, 69, 73, 95

Cartwright, J. 35

Cartwright, S. 206

Casey, L., Baroness 184

Chadwick, K. 164

Chatterjee, P. 19, 66, 185

Chevannes, B. 83

Chown, E. 115–116

Clarke, R. 74–75

Clarkson, T. 34

Claybury Hospital 155–156

Cleall, E. 4, 97

Clouston, T. 12

Cobbett, W. 35–36, 95

Cochrane, K. 151

Coga, A. 15

Cokley, K. 213

Collier, C. 163

Collingwood, L. 30–31

Colney Hatch Asylum 99, 103, 105, 106, 109, 112, 118, 165

Comaroff, J. 95

Comaroff, J.L. 95

Commission on Race and Ethnic Disparities (CRED) 200–201

Connolly, J. 100

Conrad, J. 9–10, 155

Copland, I. 138

Cowan, V. 165

Cox, P. 105

Cox, T. MP 164

Crenshaw, K. 199

Croce, B. 18

Crown Prosecution Service (CPS) 186

Cruikshank, G. 36

Cumberbatch, D. 191, 193

Cummins, I. 169, 174, 175, 176–177

D

Daley, K. 4

Dalhousie, Lord 138

Davis, L. 199

Dawson, H. 20, 45–55, 62, 63, 193

Dawson, J. 46

Dayan, J. 5

Dean, N. 118

Delap, L. 102

Derrida, J. 73

Douglass, F. 57–58

Dowling, E. 196

Du Bois, W.E.B. 192, 205

Dubs, A. MP 164

Dunkley, D.A. 83, 84, 86, 87

E

Eddo-Lodge, R. 4, 5, 200

Edigin, E. 165

Edmonds, E.B. 83

Eley, G. 93, 101

Elgee, S. Dr 106–107, 108, 117

Elkins, C. 200

Elliott-Cooper, A. 196

Ellis, H. 96

Epstein, S. 15

Equiano, O. 32
Ernst, W. 138
Evans, C. 124
Eyre, E. 69, 71, 72, 73

F

Fabian, J. 11, 136
Fanon, F. 8, 21–22, 123, 173, 183, 189, 205,
        210, 211, 212
Faubert, M. 2, 30, 31, 32, 33
Fernando, S. 1, 20–21, 172, 175, 180, 202
Fischer-Tiné, H. 95
Fitzpatrick, J. Lt Col 140, 141, 142
Fleming, A. 52
Fletcher, M. 165
Floyd, G. 151, 153, 192, 196, 206
Forde, M. 77
Forrester, D. 7, 151, 153–166, 213
Foucault, M. 14, 16, 22, 27, 205
Foulkes, R.E. 76
Francis, E. 163, 165, 174, 202
Fraser, N. 196
French, E. 152, 180
Freud, S. 124, 142
Fricker, M. 12
Fryar, C.D. 43, 44, 54, 72
Furedi, F. 20

G

Garba, R. 213
Garson, J. 213
Garston, J. 13, 18–19
Garvey, M. 81, 84
Gibson, R.C. 38
Gillard, S. 207
Gillborn, D. 96, 189, 199
Gillett, G. 21, 135
Gilroy, P. 3, 41, 58–59, 205
Glasgow Royal Hospital 100
Godwin, W. 101–102
Goffman, E. 205
Goldberg, D.T. 15, 196
Goodfellow, M. 3
Goodley, D. 199
Gordon of Khartoum, General 141
Gordon, L. 210, 211, 213
Gosselin, A. 12, 18–19
Grant, J. 46
Grant, S. (Arike) 180

Granville, J.M. 97, 99–100
Green, E. 52
Gregson, W. 30, 31
Guillaumin, C. 39
Gutzmore, C. 163

H

Hall, C. 1, 59–60, 66
Hall, J. 52
Hall, S. 3, 151, 152, 166
Haller, J.S. 22
Hanley, R. 35, 36
Hansard, 73, 164
Hanwell Asylum 100
Harewood, D. 20, 174, 203
Harper, M. 213
Harris, E.J. 132
Harris, J. 95–96
Hartman, S. 3, 29, 58, 59–60, 93, 114, 200,
        207–208
Healy, D. 190
Hesse, B. 1–2
Heuman, G. 42, 43, 73
Heuring, D.H. 72
Hickling, F. 37–38
Hill, R.A. 83, 84, 85
Hilton, C. 56
Himmelfarb, G. 97, 98
Hinds, R. 83, 85
Hirsch, A. 4, 20
HM Government 222
Hobbs, A. 16
Hobbs, T. Col 73, 74 84
Hochschild, A. 2, 30, 32
Hoenisch, M. 84
Hokkanen, M. 134–135, 136
Holt, C. 165
Holt, T. 29, 67–68, 69, 75
Home, J. 12
hooks, b. xv, xvii
Houghton, B. 122–123
Howell, L.P. 7, 82, 29, 76, 82–88
Howell, M. 86
HM Prison Grendon 167
Hurran, E.T. 101
Hussein, E. 165
Hutton, C.A. 83–84, 87

I

Ikkos, G. 201, 203
Independent Office for Police Conduct (IOPC) 191–192, 194, 195
Ingold, T. 213
Inquest 186, 187–188, 191, 192, 193–194, 195
Institute of Race Relations (IRR) 186, 187
Ishiguro, K. 63
Ivey, R. 83, 85

J

Jackson, F.J. Sir 127, 129, 137
Jadhav, S. 196
James, C.L.R. 40
Jarman, M. 178
Jarmson, F. (nee Triggs) 103, 104, 107, 118
Jarratt, H. 52, 53, 54
Jarrett-Macauley, D. 211
Jeynes, T. 206
John, N. 179
Johnson, M. 76–78
Johnston, H.H Sir 125–128, 130
Johnston, J. 91–92, 93
Jones, M. 43, 44, 90, 97
Jones, M. 46–47, 52
Joseph, D. 8, 182, 202–203, 206

K

Kalathil, J. 202
Kant, I. 15, 19
Kapila, S. 139, 142
Keating, F. 165
Keats, J. 6
Ker, A. Judge 44
Khan, I. 184
Khan, F. M. (Faiz/Waliahad) 139–147
Kiernan, V. 1
Kincheloe, J. 17
King, C.B. 8, 182, 202, 203–207
King George V 84
Kingsley, C. 69, 95
Kingston Lunatic Asylum 6, 10, 43, 54, 56–58, 60, 61, 62, 69, 70, 72, 73, 98, 152
Kinouani, G. 213
Kitchener, Field-Marshall 141
Kolsky, E. 67
Kombe, T. 165
Kraepelin, E. 141, 142

Kristeva, J. 140
Kusters, W. 13, 14, 213

L

Lacan, J. 135
Lanigan, J. 80
Lansdowne, Lord 131
Laplanche, J. 213
Laqueur, T. 64
Larson, E.J. 96
Laurance, J. 11
Lawrence, C. 142
Lawrence, S. 151, 184, 187
Lee, H. 84, 85, 86
Lee, J. 32
Leith-Ross, S.H. 123
Levi, J. 152, 180
Levitt, P. 213
Lewis, G. 5
Lewis, A. 193–194
Lewis, O. 165, 193
Lewis, P. 185
Lewis, R. 82
Light, A. 102
Linstrum, E. 122, 123
Lipsedge, M. 17, 23
Littlewood, R. 5, 17, 23
Lloyd, N. 53
Locke, J. 15, 18
Lodge-Patch, C. Col. 144, 145
Long, E. 28
Lorimer, D. 15, 16, 23, 66
Low, D.A. 125, 126, 129
Lowe, L. 39, 61
Loyal, S. 169
Lugard, F. Sir 128
Luton & Dunstable Hospital 165

M

Macaulay, T.B. 66
MacLeod, E. 83
Macnicol, J. 99, 108
Mann, M. 188
Manning, W. 90
Mansfield, Lord, 32, 182, 184, 185, 186, 187
Manson, P. Sir 137
Maragh, G. (Gong Maragh/The Gong) 85
Markova, I.S. 23
Marley, R.N. 20

Marlow, C. 9–10
Marriott, D. 208
Marshall, A. 97
Marshall, R. 165
Marson, U. 210–211
Martin, M. 165, 169, 170, 174
Mbembe, A. 17, 26, 28, 29, 58
McCarthy, J. 208, 210
McCarthy, T. 66
McClintock, A. 66, 98
McCulloch, J. 1
McGrath, P. 152
McIntosh, S. 164
McKittrick, K. 26, 213
McWhorter, L. 66
Meade, R.C. 147
Mental After Care Association (MACA) 103, 104, 109, 111, 113, 115, 118
Mental Health Act Commission 171
Merivale, H. 73
Mignolo, W. 213
Miles, R. 39–40, 94
Mill, J.S. 66–67, 69, 95
Mills, C. 20
Mills, C.W. 1, 15
Milroy, G. Dr 90
Mojothi, M.Y. 165
Monaghan, K. 185
Moore, B. 76–78
Moyo, G. 165
Mubenga, J. 182, 184–187

N

Napsbury Asylum 108, 115
National Museum of Jamaica 74, 87
Nayak, A. 96
Nelson, A. Col 75
Nelson, C. 192, 196
Nettleford, R. 73
Ngomane, N.M. 213
Niaah, J. 83
NHS 188
Nobles, W.W. 213
Nuttall, E. 79
Nyong'o, T. 211

O

Obeah 41
O'Connell, A. 64–65, 66, 99

Ojieto, C. 179
Oliver, R. 125
Olusoga D. 20, 72, 75, 125, 150
Orwell, G. 122, 210
Oury, J. 172, 173
Owen, D.S. 4

P

Painter, N.I. 38
Pandey, G. 192
Pankhurst, C. 104–105
Parker, D. 20
Parola, A. 53
Paton, D. 43, 62, 76, 77
Patterson, O. 61
Perry, K.H. 150, 151
Pettican, A. 206
Philip, M.N. 34–35, 57
Pickens, T.A. 26
Pilgrim, D. 11
Portelli, A. 18
Porter, D. 96, 99
Porter, R. 16, 20
Post, K. 81
Poursanidou, D. 6
Powell, 165
Pratt, A. 2, 20, 54, 193
Price, C. 79, 81, 82–83, 85
Prince, R. 88
Prins, H. 8, 168, 178–179, 188
Prison Offers Association 152
Probyn, L. Sir 81
Pullen-Burry, B. 81
Punjab Mental Hospital 144

Q

Queen Mary's Hospital 164
Quick, E. 113–116

R

Rabelais, F. 62
Racey, R.R. 7, 10, 126–137
Rankine, C. 187
Razanajao, C.L. 21
Realpe, A. 206
Reay, D. 189
Reed, S. 194
Reid, E. Dr. 109, 112
Richards, G. 124

Rigg, M. 194, 195
Rigg, S. 165, 194
Ritchie, S. Q.C. 170
Robcis, C. 5, 21, 172, 173
Roberts, A. 150
Rollock, N. 8, 182, 189, 193, 194–195,
    198–199, 200, 203, 207
Rosaldo, R. 206
Rose, D. 213
Rose, W. 7, 13, 151, 153–166, 174, 193
Royal Edinburgh Asylum 12, 100
Royal College Psychiatrists 182, 200, 201
Rupprecht, A. 30, 33, 34
Russell, A. 211
Russo, J. 213

S

Saha, J. 123
Saint Alban Hospital 172–173
Sambrook, C. 185
Samuels, E. 145, 147
Sanghera, S. 3
Sashidharan, S. 1, 202
Sato, S. 200
Schoffeleers, J. M. 132, 136
Schuler, M. 77, 79
Schwarz, B. 17, 95, 151
Scott, J. 165
Scraton, P. 164
Seligman, C. 122
Semmel, B. 94–95
Seshagiri, U. 10
Sewell, H. 202
Sexton, J. 207–208, 211
Sey, I. 165
Shakespeare Wood, H.E. 78
Shapin, S. 14–15, 23
Share In Maudsley Black Action (SIMBA)
    xvi–xvii
Sharp, G. 2, 3, 30, 31–33, 34, 56, 185, 186
Sharpe, A. Sir 136
Sharpe, C. 35, 211
Shaw, G.B. 98
Sheller, M. 37, 92
Shepherd, J. 176
Shilliam, R. 95
Shohat, E. 66
Sillen, S. 5
Simpson, G.E. 88

Sinha, M. 139, 141
Smith, B. 206
Smith, L. 43, 44, 55, 72
Smith, R. 213
Song, M. 20
Spandler, H. 6, 11, 13
Spencer, R. 182, 186, 187
Stam, R. 66
Steedman, C. 102, 118
Steinhart, E. 126
Stern, P. 80, 81
Stern, V. 180
Stewart, D. 78, 79
Stubbs, R. 31
Stoler, A.L. 5, 14, 15, 16, 29, 66
Stubblefield, A. 92–93, 98
Suzuki, A. 100
Swartz, S. 44
Sylvester, R. 165
Szmukler, G. 118, 190

T

Tafari, R. 82, 84, 85
Tavan, G. 104
Taylor, D. 29
Taylor, H. Sir 29, 42, 68, 69, 73
Taylor, M. 65, 166, 185
Terrefe, S. 212
Thomas, A. 5
Thompson, K. 91
Thompson, V.E. 196
Thomson, M. 11, 99, 122, 124
Todd, S. 102
Tomasini, F. 11
Tosh, J. 141
Tosquelles, F. 22, 172–173
Tredgold, A. 107–108
Triggs, A.M. 103
Triggs, A.R. 93, 103–119, 165, 174
Triggs, J. 103
Triggs, J. 109
Turner, D. xvii
Turner, J.M.W. 31, 34, 162

U

UN Human Rights Council 194
Universal Negro Improvement Association
    84

V

Van Dijk, F.J. 84
Vaughan, M. 11, 132, 136, 137
Verley, Lord 78

W

Waldstreicher, D. 16
Walker, K. 86
Wallace, L. 206
Walmsley, J. 106, 117
Walvin, J. 2, 30, 33, 34, 35, 185
Watts, J. 165, 169, 170, 188
Webb, B. 95, 97, 98, 118
Webb, S. 95, 97
Webber, F. 186, 187
Webster, J. 30, 32–33
Webster, W.L. Dr. 141, 144
Webster, W. 151
Wedenoja, W. 78, 83
Weekes, J. 165
Weisz, G. 142
Wells, H.G. 97, 98
White, N. 165
Wilberforce-Bell, H. Lt. Col. 141, 142, 145
Wilderson, F. 8, 183, 197, 207–210, 211–212
Williams, E. 40
Wilson, G. 127, 128, 129
Winchester, S. 176
Winston Rose Action Campaign (WRAC) 163
Winter, S. 73
Wohl, A. 96
Wood, M. 36–37
Wrench, G. Dr. 141–145, 147
Wynter, S. 26

Y

Yates, K. 193
Yawney, C. 88
Yesufu, S. 164, 166
Young, A. 23
Younis, T. 189, 196

Subject index

A

abject, abjection 6, 59, 98, 102, 110, 183, 189
   Kristeva's concept of, 140
abolition 28–29
   as 'beneficent despotism' 67–69, 72–73
   British opposition to, 35–37, 65
   limited consequences of, 37, 41–43,
      58–60, 75
   working-class, 36
Africa/Africans
   psychiatrisation of, 97, 140–141
   'scramble for', 9, 125
Afro-Caribbean
   migrants in Britain 20, 150
   patients in Broadmoor 167, 170–171, 174,
      176–177
   population in Jamaica 43
Afro-Christianity 77
Afropessimism 8, 182–183, 207–213
Afropessimism (book) 208, 209, 210, 212
alienation/dis-alienation 21, 35, 129, 135,
      172–173
alienist(s) 14, 22–23, 69, 97, 100, 106, 144,
      165,
American Revolution 27, 37, 38
asylum(s), lunatic (*see also* mental hospital/
      institution; Kingston Lunatic
      Asylum; Broadmoor Special
      Hospital) 2, 10, 12, 22
   as means of social control 22, 29, 76, 82,
      85–86, 98–100, 117–118
   as racial project 22, 60, 81
Atlantic
   Black, 1, 41, 58, 101
   slave trade 27
   world 16

B

Bedwardism 79–80, 82–83
'big, black and dangerous' 165–166, 170,
      174–175, 186, 193
   Prins report 168
'biocertification' 145, 147
black and British 7–8, 166, 193
   right to be, 150–152, 167
black(ness) (*see also* whiteness)
   and class 189, 193, 199
   deaths in custody 164, 165–166, 179, 184,
      186–187, 188–189, 190–196
   disproportionate detention 190–191
   intersections with madness 3–6, 17, 20,
      21, 23, 26–28, 29, 69, 86 , 165–166,
      173, 190–192, 200, 210–211, 213
   lives (and deaths) 2, 3, 6, 189, 206,
      207–208, 211–212
   perceived inferiority of, 38, 43, 58, 67–69,
      73, 94–95, 189, 202–203
   as political identity *iii*, 82–83, 85, 150–151
   as racial category 16, 17
   women 199
bourgeois
   identity 16
   liberalism 16, 58, 66, 111
British
   identity,
      embattled, post-war 151
      racialised, 152, 184, 195, 198
   imperialism 95, 123, 124, 126, 151
      in India 138–139, 146–147
   superiority over other races 22
Broadmoor Special Hospital 151
   compared with Kingston Lunatic Asylum 10
   culture of, 169–172, 174–175

pastoral naming of SCU, 152, 178
patient experiences of, 168–169, 180
racism within, 175–178
staff attitudes to black patients 151–152,
    175–177, 180–181

C

'cannibal capitalism' 196
care (see also 'Zorg')
    'in the community' xvi
    as control/punishment 169, 171, 172, 175,
    of the 'feebleminded', 97, 106,
    hierarchies in access to, 195, 196, 203
    in Kingston Lunatic Asylum 57
    medical, in Jamaica 90
    mental health, 10, 29, 56n
Caribbean, the
    European colonisation of, 28, 37, 41,
    post-war migration to Britain 150
Christian/ity
    Afro-, 77
    missionaries in Africa 129, 135
class (see also poor, 'poor whites')
    'emancipated', of former slaves 42, 59
    gap between patient and professional
        175, 200
    intersections with madness 100, 189, 200
    intersections with race xv–xvi, 4, 17, 79,
        189, 200
    intersections with slavery 101
    poorer classes as 'a race apart' 15
    working-,
        and antipathy to black people 36
        Jamaican, re-education of 92, 98
        norms for women 107, 108
colonial/ism
    and Afro-Christianity 77
    criminality of, 130
    and 'fitness for self-government' 19, 28,
        39, 58, 61, 62, 64–65, 69, 72
    ideologies 7
    kickback to,
        from Rastafarians 82–88
        from Revivalists 76–82
    legacy of, 4, 19–20, 200
    and liberal imperialism 73
    links with psychiatry 4, 7, 21, 69, 76
    and 'lunatic state' 62
    'mad poor' as colonised peoples 20

    as 'occupation' 5
    'originary violence' of, 73
    'rule of colonial difference' 66–67
    social relations of, 29
concentrationism 22
coproduction 206–207
credibility
    hierarchies of, 15, 15n, 18–19
    of mad people/mental health service users
        6, 11–14, 19, 23, 58, 180
    predicaments 14–15
    and the racial code 200
    and 'rule of colonial difference' 19–20
critical race theory (CRT) 199

D

degeneracy
    and eugenics 92–93, 96–97
    in the family history of the Mir of
        Khairpur 140
    and the 'feebleminded' 93, 97, 98
    of the poor 65
    racial, and British national decline 7, 93,
        96, 100, 106
    and sexual diseases 105
    and threats to white superiority 98
dementia praecox 140, 141, 143, 144
'deserving'/'undeserving' 14, 28, 95
    of black people 187–188
disability 26, 145,
    as category of oppression 199
    and intersectionality 199–200
    and loss of personhood 178
    and race 26–27
domestic service 102, 105, 117
drapetomania 206

E

emancipation
    British attitudes towards, 35, 65
    failures of, 37, 41–42, 43, 58–60, 65, 67,
        72–73, 114–115, 207
empire
    degeneracy threats to, 92, 95–96
    Jamaica's role within, 27, 37, 60
    legacies of, 200–203
    as mirror of asylum world 12, 22,
    pathology of, 69, 123, 124, 190
Empire Windrush, SS 150

Enlightenment, the 13, 17, 18, 69, 100
'entanglements' (see also intersectionality)
    blackness and class 36, 59, 79, 92, 189, 200
    blackness and madness 1–4, 8, 17–18,
        21–22, 26–27, 38, 172–173, 189,
        190–192, 200, 205–206, 206n,
        210–212, 213
    domestic service and slavery 101
    and hierarchies of personhood 15, 32–33,
        100, 115, 178, 185, 186
    madness and class 93, 100–102, 105, 111,
        115, 117–119, 189
    mental patient and colonised subject
        21–22, 38, 71, 97, 122
    of 'moral imbecility' 105, 106–107, 165
equality
    for ex-slaves 67
    of mentally ill 19
    race, 36
    women's, 15, 102, 199
eugenics 3, 22, 96–99
Eurocentrism 17, 66
    of mental health sciences 29, 66
Europe/European
    assumed superiority of, 18, 23, 37–38
    bourgeois identity of, 16
    fears about racialisation of, 94
    and First World War 122–123
    and scramble for Africa 9
ex-slaves
    as 'idle residue' 68–69
    status of, 69, 72–73, 75

H
history/histories
    black, 3–4, 202
    colonial/colonised, 3, 37–38
    exclusion from, 18, 58, 202
    mad/of madness 3–4, 27
    of modernity 39, 58–59
    'outside', 3
    social, 15
        of psychiatry 201–202
    as trauma 57
hold
    'carpet karaoke' 185
    enduring influence of, 5, 207–208
    as grasp/neck-, 5, 155
    as site of erasure 5, 93, 118, 155

    of slaveship, 5, 57, 118, 212
human(s)/humanity
    boundaries/limits of, 14–16, 18, 39, 60,
        61, 62, 66, 107, 111, 200, 213
    as cargo/chattels 5, 32–33, 90
    exclusion of black, mad and poor people
        3, 4, 10, 19, 23, 28, 58, 64–65, 96,
        99, 166, 188, 255, 190, 193, 195,
        207–209, 211
    rights 166, 194
    whiteness as measure of, 1, 66
humanism 1, 3, 15
    bourgeois, 58
humanitarian sensibility 28, 34, 64, 99

I
imperialism/imperial (British)
    beliefs about racial hierarchies 10, 29, 66,
        92, 98, 150
    cultural, 94
    governance 61
    ideology 64–66, 95, 97
    liberal, 73
    and manliness 138, 141
    pathology of, 11, 61, 62, 122, 123
    'project' 10, 37, 108, 123
    racialised threats to, 95–96, 98
India
    constitutional reform of, 138–139
    feminisation of males in, 138
    government as 'benevolent despot' 66
    Office 123
    princely states 124
inquests
    into black deaths in custody/detention
        153, 163–164, 166, 185–186,
        193–194, 195
institutional
    culture of psychiatry 152,
    mental health care 152
    psychotherapy 172, 173
    racism 184
insurance law
    regarding African slaves as cargo 31–33
intersectionality 8, 192, 198–200

J
Jamaica(n)
    as a caste society 28

Morant Bay rebellion (1865) 73
opposition to abolition 56, 60–61
plantocracy in, 38, 56
Poor Law in, 90
post-abolition 41–43, 69
powerhouse of the British Empire 27
public health in, 90
racial liberalism in, 72–75
and Rastafarianism 82–88
repatriation to, 152
and the Revival movement 76–82, 78n
as a slave society 27–28, 37–39, 40–41
as tourist destination 91–92
workhouses, post-abolition 41–42

K
Kingston Lunatic Asylum, Jamaica 10, 43–44,
        56–57
    and Broadmoor 152
    inquiry into, 43–44, 69
    punitive regime of, 57–58
    reflecting 'madness' of post-abolition
            Jamaican society 58, 60–63, 73–74
    reform of, 69–72
    'tanking' in, 47–49, 51, 52, 53, 57, 177
knowledge
    'of madness' (Foucault) 14
    psychiatric, 4
    social, 4, 15

L
liberal/ism
    democracy 15, 18, 39, 42, 59, 60, 61
        limitations of, 64–66, 68, 73
    racial, 15, 23, 29
    and racism 8, 67–69, 189, 200
    and slavery 207–208
lunacy (see also mad/madness)
    management of, 29, 69
Lunacy Laws 81

M
Macpherson Report 185
madness (see also 'entanglements'; credibility;
        mental health)
    as absence of rationality/reason 11,
        22–23, 27, 32, 141–142, 143–144
    as 'alienation' 18–19, 20–23, 129, 130,
        135, 172–173, 212–213

and colonialism 20, 69–70, 82, 83, 85,
        122, 123–124, 129–131, 132–133,
        136, 137, 146–147
    as dysfunction/'deficiency' 13–14, 18, 19,
        98–99, 117–119, 145
    as 'feeblemindedness' 92, 98
    as 'moral imbecility' 106–109
    and race/blackness 26, 98–99, 165,
        190–192, 199–200, 204, 212–213
    'religious', 76, 79–82, 83, 85, 86, 87–88
    and Western modernity 16–18
masculinity/manliness/manhood
    British culture of, 59, 124, 141, 144
    colonial ideals of, 141
    psychoanalytic understandings of, 145
masturbation
    proclivity for among Indian men 139
Mbona cult 131–137
mental deficiency (see madness)
Mental Deficiency Act (1913) 7, 93, 96, 106,
        107–108, 117
mental health (see also madness;
        'entanglements'; care)
    and Afropessimism 211–212
    Caribbean, 37–38
    and psychiatry 200–202
    sciences and European hegemony 29, 66
    whiteness and, 3, 16–17, 23, 204, 205, 206
Mental Health Act 165, 191, 206
    Commission 171
    White Paper 206
mental health care
    'adversarial'/coercive, 169–171, 173–175,
        180, 190–191, 203
    black deaths in, 165–166, 191–195
    and race 8, 169–170, 171–172, 175–177,
        177–178, 180, 182, 188–189, 190,
        195–197, 199–200
    and seclusion 177
Middle Passage 1, 3, 5, 27, 30, 34, 56, 57
modernity/ies
    capitalist, 101
    colonialism and, 61–62, 66
    madness and Western, 16–18, 19, 37–38
    notions of human, 14–16, 33, 39
    psychiatry within, 57
    racialised/racist, 1–2, 26, 27, 29, 38, 207,
        213

slavery and, 40–41, 58–59, 60–61, 93
moral treatment 29, 69, 99–100
Morant Bay, Jamaica 92
    rebellion 37, 72, 73, 80
Myal, Myalism 77

N

New History of Capitalism 40–41
New Poor Law 18, 34 64, 99
n****r 9, 10, 53, 65, 155, 211
    'question' 67

O

occupation
    of the mind 45, 172–173
    of territory/space 5, 154–155, 172–173, 211
outrage/outrageous,
    madness as, 2, 49, 108
    over slavery 1, 2, 32
    over the *Zong* affair 34

P

person, personhood 15, 32–33, 100, 115,
        178, 185, 186
Pinnacle community 86–87
poor/paupers
    as contaminating 65
    mad, 7, 20, 92, 98, 99–100, 189
    'poor whites' 7, 92, 96, 98, 193
Poor Law
    infirmaries 98, 103n, 105
    lock wards 105
    system in Britain 43, 90, 98, 113–114
psychiatry
    as agent of state control 165, 172–173
    as alienating force 11, 18–19, 21
    Jamaican, 83n, 88
    as medical 'science' 14, 21, 23
    and race/blackness 1, 17, 175–177,
        182–183, 200–201, 213
    role in colonialism 4, 20, 22, 37, 38, 69
    social history of, 201–202
    as tool of political/social/moral
        governance 4, 76, 107–108, 124,
        139, 142, 190, 196n
    whiteness of, 23, 202, 204–206
psychology
    as basis for governance in Britain 69, 123,
        190

Black, 213
    racist philosophies of, 38, 122
psychoanalysis
    as cure for 'moral defects' 108
    insights into colonial oppression 122,
        124, 142–143
psychosis 12, 13
    colonialism as form of, 37–38
    and diminished credibility 12
    Rastafarianism as, 88

R

race (*see also* 'entanglements';
            intersectionality; madness;
            blackness; whiteness; psychiatry)
    and biodeterminism 145
    black, as inferior 36, 39, 66, 72
    British citizens as imperial, 95–96, 97,
        98, 102
        'feebleminded' as threat to, 98, 106
    within Broadmoor Special Hospital
        175–179
    as central to imperial project 66, 92, 150
    as developmental category 66
    erasure of, in official inquiries/research
        194–197, 205
    as ideological concept 15, 16, 39–40
    mixed-, 20
    and modernity 16, 26
    paupers as an inferior, 65, 96, 97
    positivism of, 14, 21, 145
    and reason 4, 58
    religion and, 76
    venereal diseases as race 'suicide' 105
    white as elite, 16
'race relations', critique of 39–40, 94
racial
    injustices in British penal/psychiatric
            systems (*see also* mental health care)
            166, 172, 173, 203, 204–205, 213
    segregation 22, 132, 137
    social relations 40
    terror 3, 34, 41, 58, 61
racial code, the 8, 198–199, 200
racism (*see also* intersectionality)
    in British society 15, 198–199
    hierarchies 4, 10, 15, 39
    psychosocial impacts of, 188–189,
        200–201, 202

Rastafarian, Rastafarianism 82–88
    and Leonard Howell 76, 82–88
    and psychiatry 83, 86–87, 88
    as political movement 85, 87, 88
    as social community 86–87
    stigmatising of, 85, 88
rationality/reason
    Age of, 16
    'Black', 26
    loss of, as social transgression/dysfunction
            13, 14, 17, 19
    as measure of civilisation/whiteness/sanity
            11, 13, 14, 19, 27, 71, 200, 213
    modern, 1, 11
    and negative capability 6
    and race 4, 16, 17, 34, 558 9, 60
    and racial terror 3, 58
    and unreason 16, 34
religious beliefs
    as 'race-making' 76
    representation as madness 80, 82, 84, 85,
            86, 87, 88
rescue homes 105
residuum 95, 97
Revivalist/ism 76, 77, 81, 83, 87
Royal College of Psychiatrists 201, 202
    critique of CRED report 201
    on race 182, 200–201

S

sanity (see also reason/rationality)
    as non-madness 13, 14
    segregation to safeguard, 132–133
    as whiteness 26
schizophrenia 140, 164, 176, 188, 189–190,
            202, 206
science(s)
    credibility of, 14–15, 15n, 22, 23
    eugenics as, 96–97
    mental health/mind, 29, 66, 124
    vs moral categorisation 108
    racial, 9, 75
    social, 23
scientific naturalism 183, 213,
Scientific Revolution 16
segregation
    of 'feebleminded' 106, 118
    of rich and poor 96, 98
self-government, capacity for,

of Africans 60
of black people 19, 87, 95
of ex-slaves, 68–69
of Irish Celts 69
of mad/working class people 19, 92, 95
of non-adults 97
of single, poor women 93, 95, 118
work-discipline test of, 68–69
servants/service/domestic servitude
    in colonial relationships 96
    equivalence of status with mental patient 93
    narrative voice in fiction 118
    and slavery, 67, 92, 93, 101–102
    women as, 93, 101
sexually transmitted diseases 104–105
'ship of fools' 27
slave(s),
    contested personhood of, 15, 32–33, 166
    plantation, 43, 58, 59, 65, 75, 90
    from property/chattels to subjects 5, 27,
            31–32, 39, 72–73, 101
    resistance of, 61
    scientific management systems for, 40
    torture of, 41, 57
    trade 27, 28, 30, 31, 34
slave societies 38–39
slavery (see also servants/service/domestic
            servitude; racial, terror)
    afterlife/aftermath of, 28, 37, 41–42, 43,
            60, 68–69, 200, 207–208
        as idealised existence 65, 67
    anti-slavery/abolition movement 1, 2, 34,
            56, 65
        opposition to, 65–66, 67
    and the British legal system 32, 64–65
    as foundation of social inequality 28, 39,
            43, 65–66, 207–208
    'rule of colonial difference' 66
    vs freedom 59
    as integral to modernity 41, 58–59
    and legacy in mental health care 203, 204
    and madness 57, 204, 206
    and modern capitalism 40–41, 101
    plantation, 58
    psychological trauma of, 33, 38, 60–61
    racialisation of, 16, 207
    as relational dynamic (in Afropessimism)
            209

Social Darwinism 99

spaces
　bounded human, 62, 198
　imperial, 61
　male and female treatment, 105
　storage, for human bodies 5
　white, 20

state
　anti-terrorism policy 196–197
　as arsehole/latrine 62
　custody, deaths in 166
　indifference to black people 187, 203
　indifference to mad people 189
　left and right hands of, 169
　lunatic, 62
　nation, 15
　-sanctioned violence 190–191, 194–195

subjects
　black/colonised people as inferior/non-,
　　5, 66, 68–69, 208–209
　ex-slaves as, 64–65, 66, 72–73, 79, 92
　hierarchies within, 39, 61
　'occupation' of, 154–155
　pauper lunatics as, 99
　racialised positions of mad people 4
　as victims of 'cannibal capitalism' 196

survivors of mental health system 13, 182

T

Tacky's Revolt 28, 41

trauma
　of psychiatric patients 37–38
　of slaves 37–38, 60–61
　as 'unfinished business' 57

U

Undercover Policing Inquiry 163

ungovernable (*see also* self-government)
　working class and ex-slaves as, 95

V

vagrancy laws 81–82

W

West India Interest 29, 65

white
　abolition, threat to status of, 84
　commonalities of assumptions among, 199
　fewer deaths in custody 195

men as masters/the norm 15, 17, 28, 204
people as superior 1, 17, 198
as 'the Police' 197
privilege 4, 203, 205
psychiatry/ists 8, 205–206
space(s) 20

whiteness (*see also* poor, 'poor whites';
　　reason/rationality; occupation;
　　black(ness))
　challenging, 86, 205
　and class 36, 189
　and colonial power 150
　'fitness' for self-government 19–20
　hegemonic power in psychiatry 23, 182,
　　201, 202, 204–206, 213
　ideological, 3, 16–17
　implicit, 205–206
　as the norm for health 66
　as occupying force 5
　and rationality/reason 1, 4, 17, 59, 200
　prevailing culture and social order of, 4, 17
　racial, 17–18, 93, 95, 98, 199
　and sanity 26, 29
　superiority of, 16, 60
　tainted, 92, 96, 98, 189

Winston Rose Action Campaign 163–166

Z

Zong, the
　court case 28, 32, 34–35
　insurance issue 31–33
　meaning of name/name-change 33, 58,
　　169
　parallels with care of mental patients
　　56–57, 58, 182, 184–187
　significance in anti-slavery campaign
　　32–33, 34–35, 56–57
　voyage of, 30–31

Zorg/Zorgue, the 30, 33, 57, 58, 169